TO THE CITY

TO THE CITY

Life and Death Along the
Ancient Walls of Istanbul

——◆❈◆——

Alexander Christie-Miller

**WILLIAM
COLLINS**

William Collins
An imprint of HarperCollins*Publishers*
1 London Bridge Street
London SE1 9GF

WilliamCollinsBooks.com

HarperCollins*Publishers*
Macken House,
39/40 Mayor Street Upper,
Dublin 1, D01 C9W8, Ireland

First published in Great Britain in 2024 by William Collins

1

Illustrations by Joe McLaren

A catalogue record for this book is available from the British Library

ISBN 978-0-00-841604-1 (Hardback)
ISBN 978-0-00-841605-8 (Trade Paperback)

Typeset in Adobe Garamond Pro by
Palimpsest Book Production Ltd, Falkirk, Stirlingshire

Printed and Bound in the UK using 100% Renewable Electricity
at CPI Group (UK) Ltd

This book contains FSC™ certified paper and other controlled sources
to ensure responsible forest management.

For more information visit: www.harpercollins.co.uk/green

To my parents, for their love, support and inspiration;
To Oya, for everything;
And to Batu, who helped me so much on this journey
but could not see its conclusion.

Contents

When I was a child, my father and I made the acquaintance of an old woman in an Arabian city. She often fell ill, and when the fever began she would recite the names of Istanbul's springs:

Çırcır, Karakulak, Şifa, Hünkâr, Taşdelen, Sırmakeş . . .

As these names squeezed through her taut, dry lips and her tongue that was heavy as molten lead, her lustreless eyes came to life . . .

Ahmet Hamdi Tanpınar, *Five Cities*

Strangely the long and countless drift of time
Brings all things forth from darkness into light,
Then covers them once more.

Sophocles, *Ajax*

Note on Turkish Spelling

Written Turkish with its array of accents can seem intimidating to those who are unaccustomed to it, but the language is not hard to pronounce. Unlike English, it is completely phonetic: every letter is pronounced the same way wherever it appears, and in general the stress in each word falls more or less equally on every syllable. In order to assist the reader I have included a short guide to the pronunciation of Turkish letters that do not appear in English, and those letters whose pronunciations are significantly different from their English counterparts. I have reproduced the phonetic guide from the first book I ever read about Turkey, Hugh and Nicole Pope's excellent *Turkey Unveiled*, which I found very useful at the time:

c as in '*j*anissary'
ç as in '*ch*urch'
g hard g: 'galatasaray'
ğ soft g: as in 'nei*gh*bour'
ı as in 'doz*en*'
i as in 'p*i*n'
j as in 'plea*s*ure'
o as in 'h*o*rde'

ö as in '*u*rge', e.g. 'döner kebab'
ş as in '*sh*oe', e.g. 'şiş kebab'
u as in 'p*u*t'
ü as in French 't*u*'

The capital versions of 'ı' and 'i' are 'I' and 'İ' respectively. One instance in which I have not followed modern Turkish spelling is in the name of the city 'Istanbul', where I have opted to use the version that the reader may be most familiar with, rather than the Turkish 'İstanbul'. In a rather more serious mangling of the language, I have also opted to pluralise Turkish words with the English suffix '-*s*' rather than the Turkish '-*ler/lar*'. Thus *kabadayı*, for example, is pluralised as *kabadayıs* rather than *kabadayılar*. This has been done for the non-Turkish speaking reader's ease of comprehension.

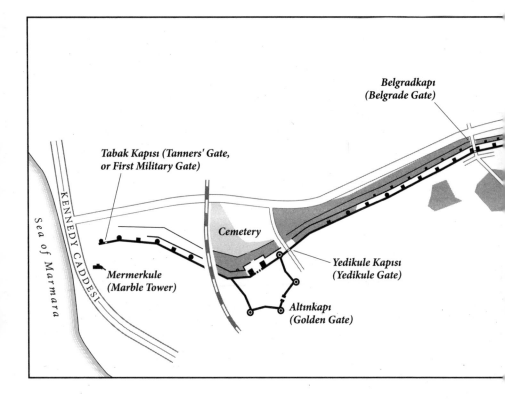

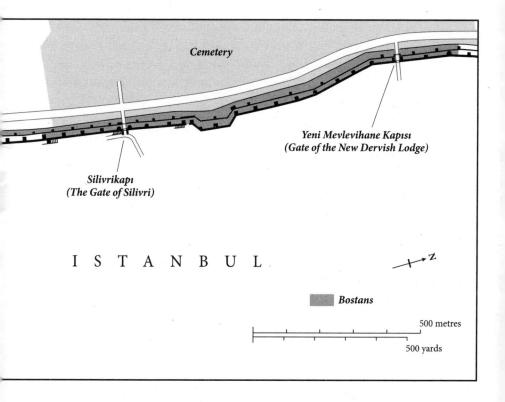

Cemetery

Yeni Mevlevihane Kapısı
(Gate of the New Dervish Lodge)

Silivrikapı
(The Gate of Silivri)

I S T A N B U L

N

Bostans

500 metres

500 yards

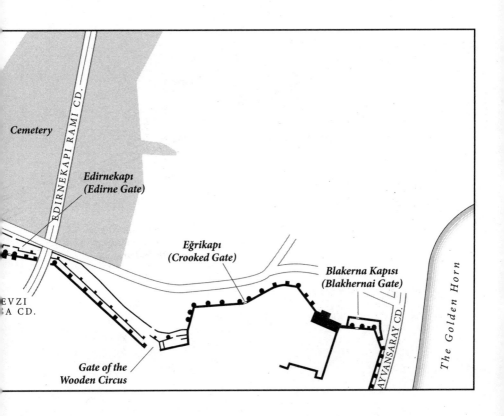

Cemetery

EDIRNEKAPI RAMI CD.

Edirnekapı
(Edirne Gate)

Eğrikapı
(Crooked Gate)

Blakerna Kapısı
(Blakhernai Gate)

EVZI
A CD.

AYVANSARAY CD.

The Golden Horn

Gate of the
Wooden Circus

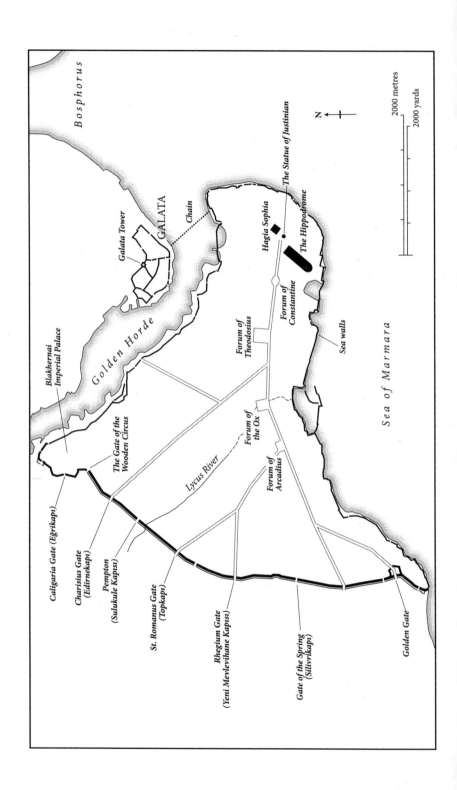

Bosphorus

Galata Tower

GALATA

Chain

Golden Horde

Blakhernai
Imperial Palace

The Gate of the
Wooden Circus

Caligaria Gate (Eğrikapı)

Charisius Gate
(Edirnekapı)

Pempton
(Sulukule Kapısı)

St. Romanus Gate
(Topkapı)

Rhegium Gate
(Yeni Mevlevihane Kapısı)

Gate of the Spring
(Silivrikapı)

Golden Gate

Lycus River

Forum of
Arcadius

Forum of
the Ox

Forum of
Theodosius

Forum of
Constantine

Hagia Sophia

The Statue of Justinian

The Hippodrome

Sea walls

Sea of Marmara

N

2000 metres
2000 yards

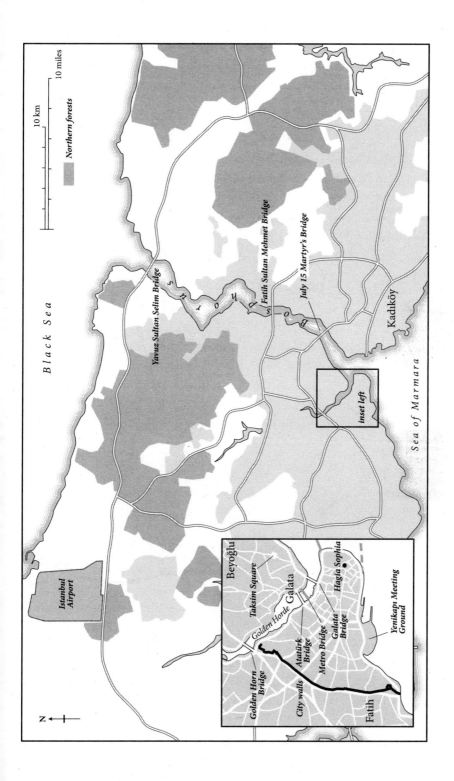

The Marble Tower

This is a book about the old Byzantine land walls of Istanbul and the people who have lived around them, their history, and their endurance through an era of relentless change. When I began writing it I had no strong thesis or idea but a feeling of a place and a handful of threads to pull on. It was ten years ago that I found the first of these threads in a neighbourhood called Tokludede, next to the Golden Horn at the walls' northern end. A tiny, tight-knit cluster of balconied timber houses in the old Istanbul style, Tokludede lay in a bulge in the fortifications, which curled around it like a cupped stone hand, protecting it from what lay without. Each home had its own back garden with fruit trees where the occupants kept chickens and grew vegetables. The outside world entered through a single road that doubled back on itself in a loop, as if realising it wasn't needed there.

Beyond the walls lay the Golden Horn Bridge, awesome in its utilitarian ugliness, a tangle of approach roads ascending a huge bank up to a twelve-lane span that roared high over the old harbour. Until the bridge was built in the 1970s, the area had been covered by centuries-old market gardens – *bostans* as they are known in Turkish – and many of the residents still recalled the diggers scraping away the fields when construction began, dumping soil and crops together in a great heap that the people sifted through so as not to waste what was left, a crop-of-crops from which no more seeds were sown.

Now Tokludede too was being scraped away, its wooden buildings demolished and its gardens erased, and new homes – in a pastiche of the originals and without gardens – were replacing them, along with a large hotel. Projects like this were happening all over Istanbul, pushed through under a rubric of 'urban renewal' and justified by the threat of the coming earthquake for which the city was woefully unprepared. Their animating principle, however, was more often the profit margin of the various stakeholders involved, which never included the people living there. Building codes and existing communities were treated as impediments to be overcome. Getting rid of the current inhabitants as cheaply as possible was a matter to which developers and the local authorities devoted considerable energy. Home owners were enticed or coerced into leaving, their homes taken from them in exchange for a sum far below market value. Often they were shepherded into tower blocks on the fringe of the city, supposedly more valuable than their old homes, and left with loans to pay off to the developer.

As a neighbourhood emptied out, the municipality would start to dig up the roads and cut off the water, then the electricity, and then the street lights – even the sewage system – until the place was all but dead and only the desperate or uniquely obstinate remained. That was who I had come to see: an elderly couple named İsmet and Mahinur Hezer.

When I visited they were the only people still living in Tokludede. The neighbourhood had been screened off with high metal sheeting and was patrolled by security guards, so İsmet met me at the small gap he used to get in and out. He showed me the home he and Mahinur had lived in for more than forty years and where they had raised their children; it had a low sunken doorway, a ground floor of masonry and a projecting first floor of blackened timber. It was the last of the old houses remaining; around it rose the concrete shells of their replacements.

I had heard that a few months earlier İsmet, overcome by the pressure and threats of eviction, had attempted suicide; he had tried to kill himself by drinking a bottle of agricultural pesticide, but one of his sons had discovered him and called an ambulance. He'd penned a suicide note addressed to a public prosecutor, in which he blamed his death on everyone from the developer behind the project to the district mayor and the Istanbul metropolitan mayor, right up to the man who was then prime minister: Recep Tayyip Erdoğan.

The couple led me to a tiny orchard that survived amid the construction work where we sat and drank tea. It was a hot summer's afternoon and the walls behind us offered welcome shade; the workers had downed tools for the time being and it was quiet. İsmet showed me the suicide note, scrawled in a spidery hand on a small page of lined paper, and he also had his hospital report and the latest threatening letter from the municipality. Whatever depths of depression he had sunk to, his fighting spirit seemed to have revived.

'It was real poison I drank,' he told me with peculiar eagerness. 'You can't even stand its smell, but I swallowed it all without water or anything . . . I wanted to die. It would have helped my family, because after I'd gone people would have woken up and seen what was happening. They wouldn't touch my house any more and they would give everyone their rights.'

'Ha!' his wife scoffed quietly. 'That would never have happened.'

İsmet and Mahinur had both moved to Istanbul from the

distant province of Bayburt in the north-east of Turkey. İsmet had arrived in the 1960s as a boy on the post train, drawn to the city like so many others by the industrial boom that was underway. The pair reminisced about the neighbourhood in its heyday. Beyond us the ancient walls rose up, casting their shade over the orchard. I thought there was a kind of attentiveness about them, an air of reverent sadness, as if they were bearing witness to something. I was aware of their history in a general way: that they were built many centuries ago by the Byzantines and protected the imperial capital for a millennium before failing. Long defunct and utterly neglected, it seemed remarkable that they survived. At one point in our conversation İsmet drew my attention to a plum tree that stood near us in the orchard, its boughs weighed down with overripe fruit, and he lamented that no one was left to harvest them. As we talked the plums fell to the ground with soft slaps, like faltering footsteps.

That was the moment: the quietness of the emptied-out neighbourhood, the sagging branches of fruit, the walls behind imposing their silent presence. I thought of the span of history contained in those stones, how they seemed so utterly divorced from the realities and pressures of the people who now lived beneath them, but also obscurely connected to them in a way that touched the soul of this city. I wondered if I could articulate that connection.

———

And so it was that in the summer of 2015 I began exploring the land walls and the communities that lived along them. The walls ran for four miles, enclosing the western, landward side of Istanbul's historic peninsula, and on the first of those walks I began at their southern terminus, where the Marble Tower overlooked the Sea of Marmara. At that time Istanbul had been stewing in a heatwave, and over the course of a few days the dust, smog and humidity had built up as if in unison with the tension rising in the country. The evening before I was on my way home when a cold wind swept in, bringing cloud as black as smoke. As I reached my apartment the first fat raindrops heralded the coming downpour, and by morning the humidity had gone, the sky had been rinsed clean and the city was bathed in a new light, sharper yet kinder, as if its debts were forgiven, its sins forgotten.

The Marble Tower was tall and square, built in the dying years of the Byzantine Empire from the cannibalised columns of older structures, and stood on an expanse of grass separated from the walls themselves by a busy coastal highway. In the days when most travellers had reached Istanbul by sea, it had announced their arrival to the city. A nineteenth-century litho-graph showed it jutting out from the shoreline, its tapering base rooted like a tree trunk at the conjunction of the rocks and the waves. That coastline has long since been filled in and the lowest section of the tower buried so that it seemed as if it had been swept inland. I too would see it on my arrival whenever I took the coastal highway from the airport, but Istanbul had multiplied in size so many times that it no longer marked the city's outer boundary but the beginning of its centre.

The tower had a lonely and neglected feeling. Streaks of soot from tramps' fires ran up its flanks and broken beer bottles littered the grass around it. One morning I climbed a section of wall that still adhered to it and looked down into a collapsed cistern full of rubbish: used nappies, half-eaten bread, shattered plates, polystyrene packaging, a broken plastic stool, empty Coke bottles, old leather shoes, bin-liners bulging with rubbish, a woman's handbag caked in dirt.

Thirty metres away the shoreline was marked by a concrete promenade. Gulls wheeled by on stiff wings, blazing like emblems in the sunshine, and when I looked out over the water, I could make out the rust on the hulls of the tankers and container ships waiting to pass through the Bosphorus. They were always there, those ships, dozens of them scattered motionless across the horizon, prows poking in different directions. I had noticed them the very first time I'd come to the city, and they were the sight I most associated with arriving in Istanbul. They struck me with a sense of awe and unease, as if they hinted at some sickness, as if the Bosphorus was a blocked artery at the heart of the world.

I headed north along the walls, walking until the lunchtime heat once more became oppressive. A few impressions stuck with me from that day: the triumphal Golden Gate rising from a courtyard of weeds, inaccessible behind the iron-shod doors of its outer portal; families of Syrians picnicking on the lawns; a dishevelled-looking man gazing over the city from high up on the ledge of a ruined tower, glorious and lonely as a stylite; the bostans, tilled with the precision of a Zen garden and exhaling a sweet humidity in the growing warmth of the day.

That was the first of many wanderings along the walls. The neighbourhoods I explored comprised a patchwork of Turkey's various religions and ethnicities, with centuries-old communities rubbing up alongside newcomers fleeing turmoil from across the region. Their lives seemed to offer a window onto our era of crisis. There were Syrian refugees, Kurds displaced by the fighting in the south-east, and communities torn apart by profit-grabbing developers. I came to see the walls as a symbol of resistance to all these forces of upheaval; they seemed less an architectural feature of the city than a geological one that time had yet to erode, protruding from the past like an outcrop of rock anchoring an eroding headland, the remnants of an older world clinging in their lee.

Istanbul has pulled people in for centuries. Once it was Constantinople, capital of the eastern Roman Empire, which morphed into the Orthodox, Greek-speaking polity we posthumously call Byzantium; later it was the capital of the Ottoman Empire. At their peaks both of these states controlled vast territories straddling parts of Europe, Africa and the Middle East, and at their heart lay 'The City'. Many of the world's great metropolises have been referred to in this way – as if there were no other in the world, but Constantinople may have been unique in that this colloquial name overwhelmed its formal one. 'Istanbul', which first emerged in the eleventh century AD, derives from the medieval Greek *stin polin*: 'in/at/to the city'. It has been suggested, perhaps fancifully, that this prepositional form arose due to foreigners arriving there having heard it referred to in this way by Greeks. Whatever the reason, Istanbul has always been a place that sucks humanity into itself. At several points in its medieval and early modern history it was the world's largest city with a million inhabitants; at other times, hollowed out by plagues, fires, earthquakes, stagnation, and civil strife, its population dwindled to no more than 50,000. But it has always risen again, always pulled in more people.

Turks like to ask about *memleket*: homeland or hometown. It does not mean where you currently live, or even necessarily where you were born, but where your family is *originally* from – as vexed a question as that may be. People ask it in the same reflexive way the English talk about weather, and they expect a clear answer. It's one of the first things in any casual conversation: *nerelisiniz?* – 'Where are you from?' No one ever says Istanbul; it isn't an acceptable answer, and even people whose families have inhabited the city for a century will dig back far enough to save themselves the hassle of the follow-up: 'But where were you from *before* that?' Because in Istanbul, everyone is from somewhere else. Even among the tiny proportion of inhabitants who *have* been rooted in the city for generations, many are from ethnic or religious minorities now considered foreign by many of their own countrymen.

In 1923 the modern Turkish Republic rose from the ashes of the Ottoman Empire following the decades-long upheaval of the Balkan Wars, the First World War, and a brutal conflict with Greece during which the people of the region were bloodily sifted along ethnic and religious lines and deposited into nation states. Though it largely escaped the fighting, Istanbul was at the centre of this prolonged trauma and the destination for many of its refugees. A few decades later, Turkey's industrialisation and the mechanisation of agriculture pushed millions more people, like İsmet and Mahinur, to the city. More recent arrivals include Kurds fleeing unrest and oppression in the south-east, as well as hundreds of thousands of Africans, Central Asians, Iraqis, Iranians, Afghans and Syrians fleeing war, poverty and societal collapse. Its population, less than one million in 1925, now stands at as many as twenty million. Istanbul is a city in which almost everyone is an immigrant, everyone an outsider. And even those who find an unalloyed sense of belonging may eventually feel like strangers, because it is always changing, often in sudden and disorientating ways.

I moved there at the start of 2010, and worked for six years as a freelance journalist, principally as the Turkey correspondent for *The Times*. When I arrived my ignorance was profound – I'd never set foot in Turkey before, nor did I know any Turkish people, and my knowledge of the country was gleaned from feverish reading and a few conversations with other journalists.

The picture I was given was of a nation on the up with a booming economy, a vibrant civil society, and a reformist government that was grappling with dark episodes in the country's past. In order to understand what was happening in Turkey, went the prevailing narrative, you had to ditch positive received notions about secularism: the Islamist-rooted government of then Prime Minister Erdoğan was expanding the breathing space for civil society, and the old secularist establishment was the chief impediment to it. Erdoğan seemed to be serious about EU membership; he'd launched a peace process to try to end the country's three decades-old Kurdish insurgency, and a series of trials were subduing an interfering military that had carried out four coups over the previous fifty years.

At that time Turkey sustained the hopeful view of many policymakers in Western capitals that the lure of liberal democracy was as irresistible and natural as the pull of gravity. In the wake of the US invasions of Iraq and Afghanistan, which were partly premised on this idea, Erdoğan and his government were held up as a model of what a Muslim democracy looked like. They had disavowed their Islamist roots and preferred to compare themselves to Germany's Christian Democrats. Erdoğan had left the economy and central bank safely in the hands of experienced technocrats whose curriculum vitae were burnished in the brokerages of London and New York. Turkey had emerged quickly from the 2008 financial crisis and its GDP was posting double-digit growth.

Within a short time after my arrival this optimistic narrative had been blown away, and over the following years I would witness the achievements for which Erdoğan was lauded in his early years unravel in their entirety. Bolstered by a set of constitutional reforms that handed the government greater control over the judiciary and a resounding election win the following year, he began to step up his domination of the media and adopt a more hectoring tone, talking openly about his plans to remould society. In 2013, mass protests erupted against his incipient authoritarianism and were violently suppressed. Soon afterwards a power struggle broke out between his party and an Islamic movement with which he had once been allied, leading to tens of thousands of people being arrested or purged from the state apparatus; the row involved an airing of dirty laundry that laid bare breathtaking government corruption.

Simultaneously, a revolution had erupted in neighbouring Syria in 2011, morphing into the civil war whose effects steadily seeped across the 560-mile shared border between the two countries. The Syrian conflict was unreal in its hellishness but impossible to ignore in its proximity. In Turkey, some two hundred people died and hundreds more were injured in a campaign of suicide bombings by the so-called 'Islamic State', and refugees began to arrive in the thousands, then in the millions. An initial outpouring of goodwill soured into xenophobia and hatred. Catalysed by events in Syria, Turkey's own long-simmering Kurdish conflict reignited following the collapse of peace talks. Towns and cities in the south-east were reduced to rubble in urban fighting. Hundreds died; tens of thousands more were displaced.

Amid this pervasive sense of crisis the charisma of Erdoğan became the rock on which an angry brand of authoritarian populism arose. He seemed to stand astride the nation: scolding and inspiring his people, promising deliverance for Turkey and defeat for its enemies at home and abroad, his voice booming from radios and TV sets in convenience stores and neighbourhood teahouses across the country. For some his rule represented hope, empowerment or the promise of national pride and prosperity; some saw corruption, fear and oppression; others saw no better option. Turkey's free press was crumbling, critical journalists were being thrown in prison or forced to flee abroad; ordinary citizens were dragged from their beds in the early hours of the morning for mocking him online. Turkey's state institutions, after decades of fitful progress towards democracy, were being co-opted and corrupted.

Just as insidious were the transformations occurring in the urban landscape and environment around me. Places like Tokludede were being emptied out and razed to make way for luxury developments, their former inhabitants pushed to the fringes of the city. Beyond the outlying districts, forests and hills were being carved apart to make way for new highways, and to the north of the city, an undulating landscape of woods and lakes was being scraped flat to create the runways of the world's largest airport. The function of these projects was often less to meet a public need than to fuel a construction sector which acted as life support for the now-ailing economy and to lubricate a system of patronage and graft that demanded the parcelling out of public contracts to Erdoğan's business allies.

As a journalist I reported on all this. After a while I had grasped enough of Turkey's politics and society to affect the tone of authority expected of a foreign correspondent. And yet I found that as my knowledge grew, my confidence diminished. As the atmosphere in the country became more oppressive and my relationship with it more intimate, I started to feel compromised by anger and fear. I felt angry at seeing friends and colleagues kicked out of the country or imprisoned, at the contracting red lines that governed what you could and couldn't write. And having married into a Turkish family, I felt vulnerable to the penalties for transgressing them.

I had colleagues during those years whose skill, bravery and dedication I admired enormously, but I wanted to write about Turkey in a different way. The needs of the news cycle meant that I when I wrote about ordinary people, it was usually to illustrate some point, and because their personal stories tallied with what I understood to be the issues of the day. I wanted to try something different, to explore and relate people's lives

– constrained by the geography of the land walls – in an organic way, and to see what understandings this would lead to.

———

The book you are reading tells the stories of those people, which between them tell a version of the tumultuous past decade and a half of recent Turkish history. Told alongside them is a far older tale: that of the siege and capture of Constantinople in 1453 by Mehmet II, the Conqueror – 'Fatih' – as he is known in Turkey. It is an event that reverberates into the present as the apocalypse of one nation and pinnacle of triumph for another. It is also a talisman of modern Turkish identity, and continually evoked by Erdoğan, who has cast himself as a kind of modern Mehmet in his quest to return Turkey to its Ottoman roots both in culture and in international ambition.

The first half of the book focuses on the years prior to the summer of 2016, when a failed coup attempt took place which greatly heightened the atmosphere of oppression in the country and precipitated my and my family's freely made decision to leave. The second half of the book covers the period following that, when I returned to speak further to the people I had met and chart their lives through the tumultuous events that followed, culminating with a global pandemic, a worsening economic crisis, and in early 2023, the massive earthquake that struck southern Turkey and Syria, leaving tens of thousands of dead and displacing millions more. Following these events it was widely predicted that Erdoğan could be in serious trouble, but in May 2023 he narrowly won re-election following a campaign in which the country's disparate opposition parties rallied behind a unity candidate. Some of the voices of the people in this book may help shed light on some of the reasons behind his enduring hold on power: both those who continue to support him, sometimes grudgingly, and those who suffer under his increasingly oppressive rule. In many instances I have changed their names, for their own security or privacy.

Through all their stories I have sought to draw a portrait of Istanbul: a city where the past looms like a shrouded mountaintop, the future bears down like an avalanche, and the present – vast, chaotic, vital – stands undaunted by either of them.

I. DREAMS

They were never content with what they had, nor allowed
others to be. They never considered what was present of
any value, as they always went after the things they did not
have, and they considered what they had not yet attained
but had in mind, as if they already had it.

Mehmet II on his ancestors, as rendered by Kritovoulos

I sometimes think that the price of liberty is not
so much eternal vigilance as eternal dirt.

George Orwell, *The Road to Wigan Pier*

I

The Tanners' Gate

The smell of dog shit, thick and cloying despite the salt breeze blowing in from the sea, announced my arrival at the animal shelter. It seemed of a piece with the open sky and the cawing of gulls, the sparkle of freshly hosed asphalt and the glint and clang of food bowls washed in the morning sun. It was the smell of a day's work to be done. Beyond the shelter stood the broken towers of the walls, their heads laureated with tufts of grass, fig and ailanthus. A community of sparrows lodged in the masonry, sharing the slop fed twice-daily to the dogs; on sunny days their shadows shot clear and sharp across the yards. Near the top of one tower an inscription in Greek proclaimed that 'Romanus, Great Emperor of all the Romans, the Most Great, erected this tower new from the foundations'. It was like a message seeping in from another world, and I felt the same, as if I had slipped out of the city into some other place entirely.

Istanbul was full of tricks like these: old and new pressed together so closely as to create dizzying shifts in perspective;

ancient monuments shorn of all context like keyholes into a distant past and clutches of wooden Ottoman houses marooned amid tower blocks and highways. Driving to the animal shelter from where I was living near the Black Sea, I would glimpse the megacity unfold along the orbital highway: vistas so abrupt and expansive that they struck with the force of revelation. The road soared over valleys on concrete viaducts named after Ottoman pashas, and below I saw toylike mosques, malls, apartment buildings, and solitary human figures labouring up steep streets, unwitting as ants under a child's magnifying glass. From this vantage point, the city was a frightening thing, inhuman, a congregation of grey towers stretching to the farthest hills, assembling for some great purpose of their own knowing.

When the road crossed over the Golden Horn I would come to the old land walls. Long engulfed, they were looped with highways and pierced here and there by the wide avenues thrust into the heart of the old walled city. Then I'd park on the narrow lane that led to the animal shelter, get out of the car and be struck by that smell, by the elements, by the improbable sense of space, and the animals all around – the dogs and the gulls and the sparrows – and it would seem as if the city had disappeared. You could breathe here, and what you breathed in was the smell of dog shit.

I had discovered the animal shelter while walking along the walls and had decided to begin volunteering there, and much as I tried to find another starting point, I kept being drawn back to the dogs, and to the noise and the smell of animals. It is generally reckoned that *Canis lupus familiaris* emerged as a subspecies of the grey wolf between 16,000 and 18,000 years ago, when humans had all but filled the globe and were driving the megafauna of the Pleistocene to extinction. They arrived at our side on the eve of that obscure but pivotal moment in human prehistory that we call the 'dawn of civilisation', when our ancestors began carving the first stone temples and sowing the first crops.

It was the first species that we know of, plant or animal, to form a domestic bond with humankind. No one is sure how it happened, or why. The most obvious explanation – that humans took wolf pups, raised them, and selectively bred them – doesn't address the issue of timing. Humans and wolves had inhabited an overlapping ecological niche for thousands of years, and while there is some evidence that we did occasionally keep tame wolves, a sustained lineage of dogs never previously emerged. Scientists have suggested a link to an ecological crisis unfolding at around the same time. In Europe – the dog's likely birthplace – the main human prey species, such as the mammoth and the woolly rhinoceros, were being hunted to extinction. Humans were forced to change their habits, developing new hunting technologies to catch smaller, more nimble but plentiful prey, and this may have led to a growth in population and the development of larger and more permanent settlements. In time our more sedentary lifestyle would give rise to agriculture and architecture, but our abundance also created a new niche into which moved the first dogs: not wolf-pups reared by humans, but scavenging wolves who overcame their fear of man and moved into this new human environment in order to live off our waste.

We were a good match: both opportunistic pack hunters living in tight-knit, family based units for whom vocal and facial signals were the key elements of communication. In time social and genetic drift isolated dogs from their wilder cousins. They developed shorter snouts and higher foreheads, the result of thyroidal changes linked to reduced aggression and increased stress tolerance. Like the first settled humans, they became smaller in response to a poorer diet. Over time we began to bury their dead with our own.

The companionship of animals, the critic and essayist John Berger has written, differs from human companionship 'because it is a companionship offered to the loneliness of man as a species'. The dog emerged at a time when this loneliness had begun to deepen, as a more sedentary lifestyle created a boundary between human and natural environments. It is hard to say if or when our ancestors began to envision themselves as separate from the animal world, but the emergence of the dog exposed that boundary as a myth. In the new habitats that arose around us, it entered both as a pioneer and as the herald of the growing disequilibrium between us and our surroundings. It has stuck more closely to humanity than any other creature: our victim and accomplice, still at our side even as the walls between our human and natural worlds are finally collapsing.

A little beyond the shelter stood a modest but finely built gate with a rounded arch of white marble, its only distinctive feature a device on the outer keystone showing a wreath in which the Greek characters 'XP' were superimposed: the first two letters of the name of Christ and an emblem of the late Roman Empire. It was referred to in some sources, a little too grandly, as the 'Gate of Christ', but had once been the First Military Gate, of which there were five in the land walls that were spaced between the public gates and reserved purely for military use. The most fitting name was that given to it in Ottoman times: Tabak Kapı, the 'Tanners' Gate', due to the large number of leather tanneries that operated in the nearby neighbourhood of Kazlıçeşme. The tanneries dated to the time of Mehmet the Conqueror, who, a few years after capturing the city, relegated the leather trade and other malodorous industries to this then-isolated spot.

'The overwhelming reek prevents people of quality from taking up their abode here,' the Ottoman traveller Evliya Çelebi wrote of the area in the seventeenth century, 'but the residents are so used to the stench, that should they happen to meet any musk-perfumed dandy, the scent quite upsets them.' Leather tanning was a notoriously foul business. Raw hides were left putrefying for several months so flesh and fat could be flensed off with ease; after that, the skins would be treated in urine to soften the remaining hairs and allow for their removal; finally, the dried hides were soaked and kneaded in watered-down animal dung, which contained enzymes that softened them. Despite the advent of chemical tanning processes in the twentieth century, it remained a smelly business, and it was only in 1993 that the tanneries finally departed Kazlıçeşme when the leather industry was exiled once more, this time to the industrial zone of Tuzla across the Bosphorus on the city's Anatolian side. In Ottoman times, however, the excrement used to soften leather had traditionally come from the city's many dogs. According to Çelebi the collection of dog faeces was undertaken by criminals who the tanners pressed into service in exchange for sheltering them from the authorities; later it was the work of impoverished or homeless children. Istanbul's street dog population was so large that their waste was exported across the Atlantic, and during the nineteenth century barrels of it were shipped to Philadelphia for use in the production of kidskin leather.

From as early as the sixteenth century, European visitors to Istanbul had puzzled over the extraordinary solicitude that the people of Istanbul displayed towards street animals. The city's dogs and cats had their own drinking troughs, special wooden huts were built for them on the street, and there were even vendors who sold scraps of meat for people to feed them. Religious foundations were dedicated to their upkeep, to which wealthy people left bequests in their wills. The animals were a kind of 'public property', wrote the Flemish diplomat Ogier Ghiselin de Busbecq, who came to the city twice in the 1550s as the envoy of Ferdinand I of Austria. '[I]f there is a bitch with puppies in the neighbourhood, they go to her and make a heap of bones and scraps of porridge and bread, and regard such actions as entirely pious.'

Busbecq visited Istanbul during the reign of Sultan Suleiman I – 'the Magnificent' – when the Ottoman Empire was at its zenith, a superpower that seemed poised to sweep away the feudal states of Christian Europe. On his second embassy, he was detained in the city for several years under a kind of cordial house arrest due to disputes outstanding between the two rulers, and recorded his impressions in four vivid and humorous letters written in Latin.

He could not help but regard many aspects of Ottoman society as superior to his own, ranging from political organisation to sartorial habits. He marvelled at the principle of meritocracy that held sway in Suleiman's court: 'They do not consider that good qualities can be conferred by birth or handed down by inheritance, but regard them partly as the gift of heaven and partly as the product of good training and constant zeal . . . This is why the Turks succeed in everything they attempt and are a dominating race and daily extend the bounds of their rule.' Observing a parade of the elite Janissary corps, he was struck by the discipline and cleanliness of what was at that time the only professional army marching in Europe; and faced with the elegance of the Ottomans' robes, which flowed down to their ankles and seemed to add to their stature, he reflected uncomfortably on his own Frankish attire, 'so short and tight that it discloses the forms of the body, which would be better hidden'.

However the Turkish tenderness towards animals, which seemed to serve no obvious purpose, baffled him. Their sensitivities were especially acute when it came to birds. Busbecq tells the story of a Venetian friend of his who 'was something of a joker' and liked to trap birds. He caught a nightjar, and – impressed at how large its mouth was – tied it to his door with its wings spread and its beak propped open with a stick. After some Turks passing by saw it was still alive, they were so furious at this cruelty that they dragged him before a judge, who was about to sentence him to be thrashed before the *bailo* – the Venetian official in the city responsible for dispensing justice to citizens of Venice – managed to rescue him from the furore.

Western visitors of Busbecq's time often described the Ottomans' treatment of animals with a tone of tolerant bemusement or even admiration. 'I have often seen them practice such as to us would seem very ridiculous,' wrote the seventeenth-century French traveller Jean de Thévenot. 'I have seen several men in good garb, stop in a street, stand round a Bitch that had newly puppied, and all go and gather stones to make a little wall about her, lest some heedless person might tread upon her . . .' Describing the religious foundations that cared for street animals, he considered it 'very pleasant to see every day Men loaded with meat, go and call the Dogs and Cats of the Foundation, and being surrounded with them, distribute it among them by commons.'

Some writers sought to explain these customs on utilitarian grounds: as well as providing the ordure used for tanning leather, the dogs cleaned the streets of waste, and guarded their neighbourhoods from strangers. Others looked to the tenets of Islam, since this tenderness towards animals seemed to be specific to the city's Muslims. The modern historian Ekrem Işın has offered an explanation that perhaps strikes closest to the heart of the matter, based on the spiritual scheme governing domestic and urban space in the Ottoman world. For Istanbul's Muslims, the geography of daily life was divided into sacred and profane spaces, with the home, the mosque, and the bazaar forming the designated grounds in which personal, business and spiritual affairs were conducted. To stray beyond these was sin; streets were profane – women did not walk them and respectable people did not loiter there. Western visitors often remarked on how, in contrast to the mainly European and Christian-populated districts of Pera and Galata, Muslim neighbourhoods seemed lifeless and inert, except for the dogs. According to Işın, these were supported and tolerated precisely because Muslim society made no claims on the streets in which they lived. The dogs and the cats, along with the guilds of beggars which were also a prominent feature of the city, were unclean but legitimate denizens and custodians of the streets. As such, they were beneficiaries of what Işın calls the 'institutionalised compassion' of Islam, in which donations to the poor and helpless were a religious duty, and the wasting of uneaten food a sin.

For whatever reason, the Muslims of Istanbul viewed the animals with which they shared their city as falling within the aegis of human toleration and compassion, while the Europeans did not; and it is hard to say which, if either, position was the more natural one. There is something disarming about the response given to Guillaume Antoine Olivier at the start of the nineteenth century, who was among several writers to express astonishment at the huge flocks of pigeons and sparrows that would regularly feast unmolested on barges of fruit and grain lying at harbour. When a Turk was asked why they tolerated this, he received the disarmingly simple reply: 'Must not these innocent creatures find their subsistence?'

The Yedikule Animal Shelter was run by a woman named Meral. She liked to call it 'the Door that Opens to Love', but she didn't show me much when she caught me eating a ready meal that was meant for employees only. It was my first day volunteering: I hadn't known. I'd been helping another volunteer who was cleaning out the cats. It was lunchtime and she'd shown me into the empty cafeteria. I hadn't thought to bring my own lunch so she offered me a ready meal, putting it in the microwave along with one for herself, and I unwittingly accepted. We sat eating them together: soggy *köfte* meatballs, over-boiled greens, grey mash like cardboard. I felt aggrieved to be eating something so awful in a country blessed with good food; I wasn't even hungry, but I felt I had to finish it because she was sitting right across from me at the small table. Then Meral came in and saw us.

She was in her fifties with dyed red hair and kohl-lined, piercing eyes that seemed to bore into you. She was angry to find us in the cafeteria, and angrier still to see us eating the ready meals. She directed her rage mainly at the other volunteer, an older woman, who cringed and arched her eyebrows and murmured quiet apologies. I sat there embarrassed and terrified and said I was sorry. I guess she didn't tell me off because I was new, and a foreigner, and she knew I was planning to write something about the shelter, but to be shielded by this privilege only increased my shame. 'Well, clean up and get out!' she said finally. We hurriedly disposed of the empty trays. 'Out, out!' she barked as we trooped ahead of her in humiliated silence.

That was Meral. The animal shelter was her creation and fiefdom, and she was its engine; the place ran on her energy, obsessiveness and judiciously applied terror. It was a big operation. There were about three thousand dogs, a hundred cats, twenty-five employees, as well as volunteers and a constant stream of visitors. The animals all needed feeding and cleaning out several times a day. Food donations had to be processed. There were school trips, and visits from prospective owners, each of whom Meral personally interviewed to gauge their seriousness and suitability; sometimes she'd even inspect their homes before agreeing to an adoption. The local municipality provided the buildings, utilities, and employees' salaries, but on top of this the running costs of the shelter had to be met through charity. The gift shop sold T-shirts, diaries, calendars, and nicknacks: when I first came there a couple of volunteers were busy folding and decorating invitations for a dog-themed wedding.

Meral told me how she had set up the shelter twenty years earlier. One day she was driving to her job as an architect at the local municipality when she got stuck in traffic and decided to take a different route that led her beneath the walls. She saw an old man there feeding bread to a pack of dogs.

'I had two voices inside me,' she recalled. 'One voice was saying, "Just carry on, you're going to be late for work", and the other said, "Wait, stay and ask what this is all about." I listened to the second voice.'

Every day she started bringing food for the dogs and helping the man distribute it, and soon they increased – twenty to thirty, thirty to forty. After a while she took over entirely, and soon, by canine word of mouth, all the dogs of the area were there. In the neighbourhood it became known as 'Meral's Place', and when people found an injured animal or a pet that someone had dumped, they would bring them to her. After two months there were two hundred dogs. The area had been a municipal tip for old buses and construction material, and she used her connections with the municipality to have it cleared out and some prefab buildings installed. A few years later, the government passed a law requiring every municipality to have an animal shelter, and hers became one of a network across Turkey.

She ran the shelter according to a radical principle which was probably unique among the country's municipal-run shelters: that no animal would be destroyed – every creature should live, no matter how sick, no matter how old. Street dogs that had been brought in injured were released back to the street after regaining their health. She would often take them herself, seeking out the locals who had fed and watered them in order to make them aware the animal had returned and remind them of their responsibilities to it. Sometimes a dog would be brought to the shelter because it had bitten a human, and the municipality was obliged to quarantine it for rabies. Even these, if given the all-clear, would eventually be released back to where they came from. Those that remained were either dumped pets, or else too sick, old or vulnerable to be released.

As a result of this, the dogs in the shelter were mostly a parade of the sick, the crippled and the elderly. Some that were considered unthreatening lived loose at the entrance of the shelter. A couple of them had makeshift two-wheeled carriages to bear their crushed hindquarters, and one had mastered the knack of walking on his forelegs: positioning himself on the edge of a curb then launching his weight forward and tottering along like a chicken, shattered hind limbs dangling like limp tail feathers. He would watch vigilantly for mealtimes in order to position himself in advance at one of the round aluminium food troughs, wrapping his legs about it and snarling at any others who came near.

New arrivals poured in daily like casualties from the front lines of an ongoing war: dogs struck by cars, dogs burned with cigarettes or cut with razor blades, or dumped on the streets to be found wandering confused and terrified. I saw a cocker spaniel that had just been hit by a car. Its back legs and hips were ruined and caked in its own excrement. The vets had sewn it up as best they could but it was still incontinent. It sat among the tables out the front, trembling and almost catatonic with shock. There was a bowl of food next to it, which it sniffed at distractedly but wouldn't eat. I sat stroking it and holding its head. The softness of its coat suggested a loving home and I wondered if its owners had dumped it or if they were out there looking for it now? No one ever came to collect it, and over the course of the months I volunteered at the shelter, I watched it slowly heal. As it overcame the trauma of its injuries its coat became dusty and coarse and it blended in with the rest of the pack.

There was one dog in particular which stuck with me. Tied up just inside the main enclosure, she had been brought in about two years earlier after being doused with paint thinner and set on fire by a group of addicts. When she first arrived burns covered nearly a third of her body; the wounds had festered so badly that the flesh stank and was riddled with maggots. Meral showed me a photo. Everyone had said she should be put to sleep. Even the vet felt ill when he saw her. Moreover, she was a pitbull, a breed that under Turkish law could not be released or adopted – a pariah ordained for extinction.

It was high summer and flies swarmed on her wounds. Meral bought a flyswatter and a tent from a camping store, and sat inside it with her, swatting all the flies until every last one was dead. She consulted a burns specialist who taught her and her staff the proper way to treat her. Every day she used special pads to dress the wounds and slowly the dog began to recover. They named her Alev, which means 'Flame', and one year after her arrival they held a birthday party to commemorate her 'rebirth'.

By the time I came to the shelter Alev's scars had contracted into whorls of shiny pink scar tissue that ran down her flank and thighs. As I approached her she radiated excitement, wagging her whole body, rearing up on her chain and cycling her legs in the air. I was a little afraid of her – of what she had suffered, of what she was – but she licked my hands as I stroked her head. Placing my palm on her shoulder, I felt the strength of her bunched muscles rippling beneath her scarred hide.

When I had first come to Istanbul it had been the animals that got me through the early weeks. After arriving in a strange city where I had yet to find much work, had no friends, and where I did not speak the language, I began to fear I had made a mistake. It didn't help that I brought with me an insular mode of living, a rigid attachment to habit, and an allergy to community. After finding a restaurant I liked, I'd go there more or less exclusively for the next year or so, ordering the same food and barely exchanging a word with the waiters or other clients. I sublet a ground-floor apartment on a steep hillside in Beyoğlu, a bohemian neighbourhood popular with Westerners. The flat was run-down and unheated, and although I thought it was romantic when I first saw it, it was freezing in the winter and stifling and airless in the summer. The only windows were those onto the balcony and even leaving them open at night failed to produce a draught, although it meant I'd often wake up with cats on my bed.

I soon realised I was living in a neighbourhood of animals and animal lovers: dogs, cats, pigeons and neat little doves with delicate brick-coloured breasts, *Streptopelia senegalensis*, the 'laughing dove', which took its name, I fancied, from the hoarse chuckle of its wingbeats reverberating off the narrow walls between apartment blocks. The cats hung around butchers and restaurants, sitting on the thresholds, waiting for their daily feed. Some lay peacefully asleep on the seats of parked motorcycles, or on cars, stretched out in the nook between the bonnet and windscreen. They sat on the seats in restaurants alongside the diners. There was never any question of shooing them away. A big group would congregate outside my neighbour's window, and occasionally I would see her cast her withered arm into the street with food for them.

These animals were what connected me to the neighbourhood: the dramas of their lives became the stuff of my own. A big sand-coloured dog took up residence on my doorstep, and in the afternoons a young girl would sit hunched next to him in her school uniform, stroking his head with a kind of mechanical diligence. He would sit there with the tolerant indifference with which dogs tend to treat children. 'What's his name?' I asked her once. Turning, smiling up at me, she exclaimed with warmth: 'Pasha!'

I think Pasha had been turned out of a nearby flat, perhaps because the weather was warming up, because every time I opened the main door, he would try to poke his nose in, wagging his tail at me as if he'd just lost his keys and it was all terribly embarrassing. Someone put food out for him each evening. As time went on he began to look more dejected. Sometimes when I was going out he would follow me before getting sidetracked by a scent. He had a more cheerful friend who kept him company, and who appeared perfectly reconciled to his life on the street. Once I bought him dog biscuits from a local pet shop. 'Kedi köpek?' (cat or dog?) asked the man as I entered the shop. 'Köpek,' I replied, putting the dog biscuits on the counter, adding: 'ama köpeğim değil' (but not my dog). 'Street dog!' he pronounced knowingly, as if there were nothing more natural in the world than to buy treats for a stray dog.

Later I would discover that in some neighbourhoods people not only fed and cared for street animals, but even clubbed together to pay their medical costs. Particular dogs or cats became beloved characters in their communities. The rise of social media only seemed to enhance their fame, to the extent that in one

Istanbul neighbourhood a statue was built in homage to a local cat that had been photographed in a particularly winning pose. Individual stories of abuse or mistreatment often garnered national media attention.

I knew the names of my local street dogs before I knew the names of my neighbours and shopkeepers. The nearby street corner was ruled by Chico and Herkül, a shy, elderly Alsatian and a large marmalade-coloured mongrel. They surveyed comings and goings on the street with professional seriousness, occasionally chasing young men who struck them as suspicious. I made a point of greeting them every time I saw them and occasionally gave them bones, but I was never more than a blip on their radar. There were various people they followed about town and occasionally I would see them far from their haunts with one of their favoured friends, and felt deeply envious. Up the hill there was a more unruly pack looked after by a gypsy family, including an enormous Great Dane. Two of the dogs had puppies, one of which grew up on the street and became so wild it led the others into harassing passers-by at night, until eventually the municipality took them away.

The lives of the dogs seemed more real to me than those of my human neighbours. One day, when I was still living in that first apartment, I came home from the office I had rented with another journalist to a smell of something dead in the foyer of my building. I assumed a cat had died in the basement, and left home thinking no more about it. Later that evening my landlord called to warn me that when I came home there would be police and TV cameras outside. My next-door neighbour, the woman who had fed the cats, had been found murdered in her apartment. Her remains lay undiscovered for at least a week, until the smell finally caused her neighbours to investigate.

It was unnerving to think of this unfolding only a few metres from where I was lying in bed, perhaps, or eating dinner. I felt a kind of guilt, as well, that I couldn't even picture the woman's face, and that all she had ever been to me was a hand feeding cats out of a window. A few years later I decided to look into her story and I managed to find a local estate agent who had been born in Beyoğlu and lived there all his life, and had known her well. Her name was Neşe, and the estate agent had once been a neighbour and managed several properties she owned. Neşe had made her money as a prostitute (the man's elderly mother had whispered the word as she told me, covering her mouth with her hand), and later as a pimp. She worked in the 1980s and 1990s, when the neighbourhood was a seedy, dangerous place full of *gazinos* – nightclubs with live singing acts where hookers often worked.

The estate agent wanted to remain anonymous as he didn't want to be associated with her by name ('I want a clean and proper life,' he said), but he confessed to admiring Neşe. 'Everybody knew her, and everybody knew what she was doing but they pretended they didn't. Of course, we treated her like a lady because in those days it was like a small family here.'

She had always been immaculately turned out, and when she was shopping, everyone addressed her respectfully, like 'an Istanbul *hanımefendi*', he said, 'a real lady'. As she grew older, she dedicated her life mainly to caring for her elderly parents. Occasionally he had heard her speaking on the phone in *lubunca*, a special argot used by Istanbul's sex workers since the nineteenth century. She had an aggressive streak that would emerge if she was threatened: 'When someone spoke rudely to her then you would see her real face. She would start swearing and hurling insults and the guy would regret he'd crossed her.'

She had drunk heavily for as long as he'd known her, but had always lived alone and never shared her life with a partner. But she did have a drinking companion, a quiet man, older than her, perhaps in his mid to late seventies, a former journalist who'd covered politics in Ankara. He was adamant that the man was not her boyfriend. 'He was doing all the shopping for her, and they would drink together and she was telling her stories to him. They knew each other from long before, he knew all about her lifestyle, and she could feel relaxed with him. He was like a puppy next to her.'

The estate agent said he had spent time with the two of them and that they would argue when they were drunk. Neşe would get angry and hurl abuse at the man, calling him a parasite. He didn't know how the murder had happened but thought he must have cracked during one of these arguments. He'd battered her with a blunt object, killing her, and then gone down to the subway market in nearby Karaköy, where he bought a small electric saw that he used to cut up her body. He stowed her remains in the kitchen fridge in an apparent effort to conceal his crime, but didn't clean up the blood and gore properly, and so after a few hot September days the smell seeped out of the apartment. He didn't try to run away – perhaps he didn't have the energy or the will to evade his crime – and was picked up at his usual haunt in a local teahouse only a couple of hundred metres from where her body was discovered, convicted of her murder after a swift trial, and died in prison a few months later.

The messiest job was cleaning out the kennels first thing in the morning. I had come to gather up the sheets of newspaper put down the night before. As soon as I entered all the dogs would jump up at me in delight, smearing the shit from their paws all over my trousers. I gathered it into piles with a brush but still had to pick it up to bag it, and then I'd feel the cold squelch of it through the thin surgical gloves I was wearing, which would always end up breaking. Afterwards, there was so much shit on my trousers I couldn't get my phone out of my pocket without getting it on my hand.

My companion in this task was a small wiry man with a heavy moustache and eyes that twinkled beneath the rounded peak of a baseball cap. When I asked him his name he told me Dede, 'Grandpa', which is what everyone else seemed to call him. He was the one who did all the dirty jobs. When the dogs fought, he would jump in and deftly separate them. He shared his cigarettes with me and we fetched each other tea. When I asked him about himself he told me with pride about his children: he had a son who was an officer in the army – posted to 'the terror region', he said, meaning the Kurdish provinces – and two daughters who were both teachers. In a couple of years he and his wife would move to his home village on the Mediterranean coast, where he had ten horses. He was looking forward to that.

Dede had come to Istanbul when he was about nine years old. His father had just died, and so his family were forced to send him to the city to become an apprentice and learn a trade. He went to school during the day and at night he served at a clothing workshop. He started out cutting fabric then gradually learned the different aspects of the trade. He worked there for about twenty years until the master of the workshop died and left him the business.

They were good years, he said. He created designs that he sold to the country's top luxury brands, big names like Beymen and Vakko. He had personally designed dresses and coats that would be worn by the country's top fashion models, basing his ideas on pictures he found in fashion catalogues which friends sent him from France or England.

'Paris, generally,' he said. 'I'd look at the catalogues and if there was something I liked, I would make something inspired by what I saw and then I'd take it to Vakko or whoever, and offer it to their production department, and ask if they were interested, and if there's a piece they liked, they'd say, "Yes, we want two thousand of these, or five thousand of these", and we'd go back and produce them.'

Then about four years ago he had suffered a stroke and had to stop working. It affected the left side of his body, his arm and leg, and also his face. For a while he couldn't speak at all, and it also damaged his memory. It wasn't just the skilful nature of the work that was now beyond him, but he found to his frustration that he couldn't recall the detailed knowledge he'd built up. 'You need to know about every different kind of fabric,' he said, 'you need to know how it will distort the first time you wash it or dry clean it, and account for that when you cut it. You need to follow all the new technology as well.'

Not long after his stroke he happened to come and visit the shelter with a friend who was working there, and fell in love with it. 'This place was really good for me because of the open air and animals and so on. It helped me a lot in terms of dealing with the problems related to the stroke . . . After I came here, I couldn't leave. I can't be away from here. The animals have become like my children, they're like my passion and if I go away even for a couple of days I have to come back.'

The stereotype regarding Turkish attitudes to street animals had inverted since Ottoman times; it was now generally reckoned that street dogs and cats are the concern of the so-called 'secular' and more affluent parts of Turkish society. But the people volunteering at the shelter seemed to come from all levels of society, both socially and politically. There were young, liberal animal rights' activists, but many others too. There was Ümit, a rangy young man with a shaven head and a fresh tattoo of a howling wolf on his neck, an ultra-nationalist symbol. There was a young woman wearing a hijab who helped out for a few days because she wanted to adopt a cat (Meral would often ask prospective owners to come in and volunteer to prove they were serious). There was the elegantly dressed young woman who could have been a model from one of Dede's Parisian fashion catalogues, who dropped in to check on a sick cat she'd left the previous week. I remember one couple who brought their young son just to look around and see the animals: the father was decked out in a long black coat, a turtleneck, and Ray-Bans, with a fastidiously trimmed beard that made it hard to tell if he was pious, a hipster, or a pious hipster. He seemed even more excited than his young son, and he whirled around in circles, arms flung out, giggling as he ran among them.

Almost every day some school and university group would drop in for a tour. There was the 'Marmara University Animal Lovers' Society', and others whose visits seemed only tenuously connected to their studies, such as a group of finance students who came to learn about the running of the shelter but clearly just wanted to pet the dogs. There were endless classes of schoolchildren of all age ranges, including a class of headscarved girls from a religious high school. Sometimes Meral or Arzu, the manager, would ask me to guide them round. I was amazed by how unafraid they all were. The dogs were often sick, or dirty, or disfigured, but the braver children would thrust their chins out and close their eyes in delight as they leapt up to lick their faces; their more squeamish friends shrieked and giggled and danced around just out of reach, while the boys from the back of the class struck bored poses and speculated in authoritative tones on which ones were the best fighting dogs. One girl who was too scared to go into the inner kennels stayed outside, where she found a small puppy and sat stroking it. I watched one group who gathered in delight around a beautiful soft-furred husky that was tied up out the front. The dog was blind – its eyes were a milky blue and bulged alarmingly – but it never opened them, laying there as if asleep while the kids stroked it.

The diversity and joy of the animal shelter offered a stark contrast to the fear and mistrust I felt beyond it. The shelter represented a kind of alliance between the warring factions of Turkish society. Among all the volunteers and employees I spoke to, almost everyone said the same thing: that spending time at the shelter felt like an escape – from the city, from their daily lives – and that the animals gave them a feeling of relief. One day I sat chatting with a retired university teacher called Sankur; she was frail and nervous like a bird, with a burnt-out air about her. She said she'd been coming to volunteer once a week since she stopped working two years ago. She guided school groups, but mainly just sat with the dogs.

'I don't seem to do a lot of things, but I still get very tired,' she said. 'I don't know . . . I have back problems. I get a lot out of this though, because I love the animals. I have two cats at home. I had a dog as a child, but now we can't afford one. I feel rewarded by helping them, the way they look at me – like they love me.'

After a while I realised that Meral's authoritarianism was underpinned by forbearance towards the people that came here; she understood that they were more than just bodies lending a hand, that they too needed something. When I put this to her – that this was a refuge for people as well as animals – she just laughed, and said, 'We should start charging entry.'

2

The Buried Gate

There was not one wall but two that ran parallel: the high inner wall and the low outer wall, and even a third and fourth if you included the scarps that once held up the banks of the moat, which still survived in a few places. From the inner wall to the moat's outer scarp was a distance of more than two hundred feet, so that the fortifications were not so much a line through the city as a zone within in it, with the liminal, unsettled sense which that implies: frontier zone, restricted zone, war zone. The run-down neighbourhoods that lay along their course kept their backs firmly to them, and other than the areas given over to market gardens or cemeteries, they were a no-man's-land. Friends would warn me against going there; they were not like the city's other landmarks, cushioned in its touristic heart amid the crowds and watchful eyes of shopkeepers and police. There were stories of muggings, attacks, even murders.

Once within this zone you were hidden from the outside world. The place seemed empty, but was filled with signs of occupancy: empty beer cans and wine bottles, dirty mattresses arranged around the remains of cooking fires that sometimes still smouldered. Paths trodden down by unknown feet led off in all directions, threading up drifts of collapsed masonry into the tops of towers or down into the damp chambers beneath them. As I explored, I felt like a thief in a still-warm home whose occupant might return at any moment. Sometimes I'd hear voices around a corner and pause, deciding whether to turn back or head on. When I did see people – usually men alone or in pairs, occasionally a man and a woman – I'd slow my step and gauge them from a distance. They'd look back at me with the same wariness. When I emerged back into the world it was with a rush of exhilaration, like coming up for air.

It was while exploring in this wall zone that I found the cannonballs. They were lying near the exposed and broken lintel of an old gate; it had once been designated for military use but was long abandoned and had only been uncovered by some recent excavation. The site was unguarded and there was no sign of any current work being done. Nearby, two large orbs of stone lay nestled into the soil like a clutch of fossilised eggs. They too had been recently unearthed, but looking around, I saw fragments of others, broken and moss-covered, strewn among the rubble. The size of them astonished me: each was more than two feet across, barely large enough for me to encompass with my arms.

Later I read about the life of those stone orbs, the processes and elements that created them and the artillery piece that fired them. In a masterful account of its construction, the historian Roger Crowley has listed the various materials that were involved: 'cannonballs from the Black Sea, saltpetre from Belgrade, sulphur from Van, tin from overseas trade, scrap bronze from the church bells of the Balkans'. The eight metre-long cannon that fired them was cast upright like an obelisk, muzzle to the earth, inside a great pit. The mould consisted of a solid inner core to create the hollow of the barrel and a larger outer casing surrounding it like a scabbard. This was bound about with iron hoops before wet sand, stone, wood and earth were packed tightly around it to hold in the thirty tonnes of molten bronze that would be poured into the top. Afterwards the whole thing was left to slowly cool. Later it was dug out and hauled from the ground by teams of oxen, like the idol of a vanished people; its moulds were cracked away, and the final object deposited into the light.

In January 1453 it was tested at Edirne, then the capital of the Ottoman Empire, about 150 miles from Constantinople. This moment was described by the Greek historian Doukas, who was present or nearby at the time. The people of Edirne were warned in advance 'that the impending blast and crash would be like thunder from the heavens' so that 'the sudden shock would not leave some speechless or cause pregnant women to abort'. He described a 'piercing air-rending sound' that could be heard for miles around and a great pall of smoke as the first of the huge stone balls was hurled a mile through the air before burying itself nearly six feet in the earth. So prodigious was this weapon that contemporary chroniclers struggled for terms to describe it. They called it a 'device', a 'terrible machine', an 'implement' of 'unbelievable and inconceivable nature'. 'Such a thing the ancients, whether kings or generals, neither had nor knew about,' wrote one. 'Had they possessed it, nothing could have withstood them at all.'

No one had ever created an artillery piece on this scale. No one had been able to, or indeed wanted to. Cannons were expensive to make, hard to move, and though the technology itself had existed for a century they were still considered newfangled and unreliable. The logistics involved in the creation of even small artillery pieces were beyond the reach of most nations, and this particular project involved a drawing together of material and manpower that only the most powerful states of the time could hope to attempt. It was a moonshot in medieval warfare, a leap forward in the long battle between the wall and the gun, preservation and destruction, one safeguarding what exists, the other tearing it down to make way for something new.

The man who ordered its creation was the young Ottoman Sultan Mehmet II. Mehmet had been obsessed with conquering Constantinople since childhood. The city had occupied a coveted place in Islam since the faith's inception; the Prophet himself was said to have foretold its capture. In the seventh-century AD, armies of the Caliphate twice besieged it unsuccessfully. By Mehmet's time, the territories of the Eastern Roman Empire (or the Byzantine Empire, as it would posthumously be known) had been reduced to a handful of scattered territories and islands, with the old imperial capital little more than an impoverished city state entirely surrounded by Ottoman territory.

The Ottomans had emerged around the turn of the fourteenth century, one of several Turkish tribes in Anatolia, a land which had largely been wrested away from the Byzantines in a process of slow conquest driven by the westward migration of Turkic peoples. Osman, the founder of the dynasty, was a figure largely shrouded in myth. He was said to have had a dream in which it was revealed he would found an empire, but his descendants did most of the conquering. By Mehmet's time, the Ottomans controlled most of Anatolia and the Balkans, and were the most powerful and efficient state in the region.

Despite the weakness of the Byzantines, capturing Constantinople was a formidable challenge. Lying on a peninsula, the city was roughly triangular in shape and its three sides were each highly defensible. To the south, a long section of sea walls overlooked the Sea of Marmara, where strong currents made amphibious assault difficult. To the north-east, another section of wall looked onto the harbour of the Golden Horn. This could be sealed off with a chain and easily defended by a fleet. It was by taking the harbour and breaching the sea walls that the Fourth Crusade had captured the city in 1204 (the only previous time it had been taken by force), largely thanks to the maritime might of Venice, an advantage the Ottomans still lacked. It was the western, landward side of the city that was most naturally vulnerable, but this was defended by the great line of fortifications built in the fifth century AD by the emperor Theodosius II. On at least twenty occasions attackers had pitched their tents before them – Avars, Slavs, Persians, Arabs, Bulgarians, Russians and Turks. During their millennium of existence they had never failed.

These walls were every bit as remarkable as the cannon Mehmet had made to bring them down. They comprised a triple layer of defence: inner wall, outer wall, and moat. Approaching them, attackers would first encounter the moat, eighteen metres wide and at least seven metres deep in some places, depending on the topography. The inner supporting scarp of the moat was crenellated and acted as a third defensive wall. Beyond this was the outer wall, eight metres high and two metres thick, and beyond this the larger inner wall, between twelve and fifteen metres high and about five metres thick. Ninety-six towers jutted out from its four-mile length, with a similar number staggered in front of them along the outer wall. This design meant that any aggressors who succeeded in penetrating the outer wall would find themselves in a kill box, fired on from above on every side by the inner wall and the towers. At the time of its construction and for centuries afterwards, it was virtually impenetrable to the military

technology of the day. Throughout the city's history the maintenance of the walls remained a key civic duty that often
involved the assistance of the general population, and repairs
continued until the end, so far as the city's rulers were able to
finance them. Even when maintenance began to lapse in the
Byzantines' final decades, they remained a formidable barrier.

On that winter's day in Edirne, the young man who would
conquer them watched as his great cannon was fired for the first
time. He was twenty years old, pale-skinned with large, dark
eyes beneath arched eyebrows and a narrow chinless mouth that
fell away under a hawk-like nose. We can picture him like this
from the single compelling portrait that exists from around that
time, a medallion of unknown date and authorship that shows
a slender youth in profile with a beard looping from chin to ear
and a turban tipped forward to reveal the rear of his scalp shaved
up to the crown at the back of his head. It suggests a more
tentative, owlish person than the corpulent and watchful old
man of later portraits with his heavy-lidded eyes set imperiously
to the middle distance. I imagine him on that winter's day in
Edirne as gaunt and brittle-seeming, tense with untested ambition as he approached the fulcrum of his existence.

We shouldn't make too much of his youth. In those times
the heirs of the Ottoman sultans were prepared for the business
of ruling almost from birth. Mehmet had been appointed a
provincial governor at age five, became sultan at twelve on his
father's abdication; was deemed unready and forced to step aside
a year later; fathered his first son at fifteen, went to war at
sixteen, and then at nineteen became sultan once more on his
father's death. He had two older brothers, but they both died
when he was still young; in any case there was no law of seniority

and each was raised as if he would become sultan, the idea being that when the time came, natural ability and divine favour would ordain the successor. It was a system that made for bloody interregnums and exceptional rulers.

His father, Murat, was one of these. He had taken over the empire at a time of peril; his grandfather – Bayezit I, 'The Thunderbolt', one of the great conquering sultans – had died in captivity following a crushing defeat at the hands of Tamerlane in 1402, resulting in the fragmentation of the nascent empire and a prolonged period of internal strife. Murat II emerged as sultan in 1421, and dedicated his thirty-year reign to consolidating and stabilising the empire. Among his chief reforms was the expansion of the elite Janissary corps made up of converted Muslim soldiery. Murat was a seeker of peace who was none-theless formidable in war, and who sought, where possible, to find peaceful accommodations and alliances with his various neighbours. But he still inflicted several devastating defeats on his rivals in conflicts that he had not looked for. At Varna in 1444, he routed and destroyed a Crusader force led by the young Ladislaus, King of Poland and Hungary, who was killed on the battlefield. Four years later, at Kosovo, he triumphed against another Hungarian-led crusader force sent to avenge the defeat at Varna in a bloody three-day battle that permanently broke the power of the Hungarian state and opened the way for Ottoman expansion into eastern Europe.

Murat had attempted to capture Constantinople at the very start of his reign in 1422. The Byzantines had stoked the Ottoman internecine struggle that preceded his accession by promoting a pretender – it was one of the few cards the Byzantines could play against their more powerful adversary. Murat wanted to quash any possible remaining rival. But the walls defied him as they had defied all others, and he was forced to abandon the siege in order to address a rebellion in Anatolia. As it was, the city of the Romans remained impotent but unmolested for the rest of his reign, a vassal state in all but name, paying an annual tribute to the sultan and contributing soldiers to his campaigns. Murat and his advisors perceived no threat from it, could bully it at will, and saw little need to change the status quo. Moreover, long centuries of coexistence meant there were friendly links between the two courts, dynastic marriages and familial links, all of which made the need for action less pressing.

Mehmet's eldest brother Ahmet had died when he was five, and his remaining brother, Alaeddin Ali – his father's favourite – was murdered six years later along with his two infant sons in mysterious circumstances. At this point Murat began to take a keener interest in his surviving heir, and summoned him to court. He didn't like what he saw. Mehmet was an arrogant and uncouth boy whom the efforts of an army of tutors and advisors had failed to tame or instruct. Appalled, he summoned a renowned mullah to take over his son's education. Murat is said to have handed him a switch and given him express permission to beat him. When Mehmet laughed at this severe new tutor, he was thrashed so harshly that he thereafter became an avid and precocious student. Under this regime he memorised the Quran, became fluent in Greek, Arabic, Latin, Persian, and Hebrew, well-read in Islamic and Greek literature, and achieved a good command of philosophy and the sciences. It is a story that would typify his character: he was headstrong but not unmalleable, arrogant but could accept and learn from defeat.

Murat was keen to begin delegating leadership to his son under the supervision of his chief vizier, Halil Pasha, and left him as regent of Rumelia – the empire's European province – while he went off to meet the ill-fated crusade of Ladislaus. Mehmet chafed against Halil's tutelage and fell under the influence of an Iranian preacher he permitted to spread heretical ideas around the capital. Eventually Mehmet was forced to surrender the cleric to an angry mob who burned him alive. Shortly afterwards the Janissaries rebelled, demanding a pay rise and burning several quarters of the city before Mehmet granted them one.

In spite of this inauspicious start, a few months later Murat abdicated outright in favour of his son, retiring to Manisa and again trusting Halil to keep an eye on things. It is unknown why he did this: he is sometimes said to have been weary and grief-stricken at the death of Alaeddin Ali, his favourite, and desired to end his days in spiritual retreat. Whatever the reason, Halil begged him to reassume control after only a few months, after he became alarmed at a plan Mehmet was hatching to attack Constantinople. Murat returned and reassumed power, a transition that Ottoman historiography has tended to smooth over, but the fact that we know he paused on his way to Edirne to record a will implies there may have been some risk involved.

Among these details (the mysterious murder of Alaeddin Ali, Murat's abdication and return, Mehmet's botched efforts at command) are the broken pieces of a story that will probably never be told. It may relate to a power struggle playing out at the Ottoman court at the time, in which a clutch of aristocratic families who had hitherto held sway were being pushed aside by a newer caste of advisors known as the *devşirme*, former Christians and slaves who had converted to Islam and were loyal only to the sultan. The converts were generally more hawkish and radical, the old aristocracy more moderate and invested in the status quo. Murat had raised up the *devşirme* as a counter-weight to the old elite, but had sought to balance the two. Halil, Murat's senior and most trusted advisor, came from one of these noble families, but the coterie of advisors who coalesced around Mehmet were *devşirme*, of a zealous frame of mind, echoing and encouraging the boy's dreams of conquest.

When Murat died peacefully in 1451, his death was celebrated in Europe, where the memory of his humiliation of the Crusaders was still keen, and where most observers were ignorant of the dynamics of the Ottoman court. Mehmet was widely thought to be weak and ineffectual on the basis of his first tenure as sultan, and Christian Europe believed it would have little to fear from him. But those closer to hand knew differently. Doukas, one of the most bitterly anti-Turkish Greek chroniclers, was uncharacteristically generous in his assessment of Murat: 'Murat's wrath was not intemperate,' he commented. 'He did not set out in hot pursuit of the fleeing enemy. Moreover, he did not thirst after the complete destruction of the fallen nation, but as soon as the vanquished sued for peace, he eagerly accepted their terms.'

Meanwhile, George Sphrantzes, an advisor to the Byzantine Emperor Constantine XI, was filled with dread when he heard the news of Mehmet's accession. He was well aware of the new sultan's obsession with Constantinople. 'Overcome by grief,' he recalled in his memoirs, 'as if being told of the death of those nearest to me, I stood speechless.'

The young man who took the helm following Murat's death was very different from the child who had failed so humiliatingly a few years before. The setbacks of his youth had made him ruthless, pragmatic and secretive. He hid his intentions behind a mask of cold reserve; his former impetuousness had been honed into an obsessive focus and a belief in his own destiny that exceeded even what one might expect from the heir to an empire. From the first moments of his rule he moved with patience and surgical intent. His only male sibling – his father's infant son Ahmet, just eight months old – was drowned in his bath as his mother came to make her obeisance. Murat's other widow, an Orthodox Christian princess whose father was the despot of

Serbia and a powerful vassal, was sent back to her homeland with every honour; she would prove an important ally. Mehmet kept Halil in place, while appointing Halil's close comrade, Ishak Pasha, as governor of Anatolia – an honoured position, but one that would take him away from the court and leave both isolated – and replaced him with the *devşirme* Zaganos Pasha. To the various visiting ambassadors who came to reforge treaties made with his father he seemed pleasant and amenable, reaffirming the old agreements, sometimes on even more generous terms than before, thus maintaining a sense of complacency among his potential enemies. To the ambassadors from Constantinople, he swore on the Quran to respect the integrity of their territory, and even offered to pay an annual sum of 3,000 aspers for the upkeep of Orhan, a pretender to the Ottoman throne who was exiled in the city, on the condition that he continue to be detained there. Thus he ensured that there was peace and quiet on his borders as he set about enacting his plans.

In the winter of 1451 he called together a thousand skilled masons and a larger number of labourers to assemble at a spot he had chosen on the European shore of the Bosphorus where the straits were at their narrowest opposite the existing Ottoman fortress of Anadoluhisarı. There they began the construction of a huge new castle, to the consternation of the Byzantines, on whose territory it stood. It became known among the Turks as *Boğaz Kesen* – the 'Throat Cutter' – and its purpose was to control traffic through the Bosphorus and cut the city off as part of an attempt to capture it. Mehmet personally supervised its design and construction. That was one of his qualities: an ability to immerse himself in technical details and close planning without losing sight of the bigger strategic picture. His tuition had instilled in him a fascination with engineering and technical innovation and a passionate belief in the possibilities of the practical sciences. He seems to have been a polymath, his interest extending also to history, the arts and literature. In the winter before the siege, he was said to have spent his time reading about the feats of Alexander the Great and Julius Caesar, conquerors whom he hoped to emulate and exceed. When the fortress was finally complete, a battery of guns were placed in it and the newly installed garrison was ordered to enforce a toll on all passing traffic. After a couple of ships successfully ran the gauntlet, a Venetian galley was blasted out of the water. Its surviving crew were beheaded and the captain impaled and publicly displayed as a warning to others.

It was only after these preparations that Mehmet spoke openly of his imminent plans. Kritovoulos, a contemporary Greek chronicler who wrote an approving history of his life, penned a rendition of the speech he supposedly gave to his court and soldiers, making the case for war. It is impossible to say what basis, if any, it had in reality – he apparently followed the example of Thucydides by giving the speeches he thought his protagonists should have given – but it is nuanced and persuasive in laying out a case for action. Mehmet highlighted the city's miserable and depopulated state, its weakness and lack of outside aid; he warned of the danger of leaving it unmolested in case it should fall into the hands of a more powerful adversary, such as the maritime city states of Italy; he mentioned the Byzantines' centuries-long history of antagonism with the Ottomans, and pronounced that his people could never consider themselves safe as long as the city lay like a dagger at their throat.

Hidden in the lines of this speech, as rendered by Kritovoulos, there seems to be a pointed refutation of Murat's relative pacifism. He condemned the kind of inaction that left one responding to crises rather than pre-empting them, and extolled the conquering zeal of his earlier ancestors, like his great-grandfather Bayezit, who had expanded the Ottoman realm to its current extent. 'They were never content with what they had, nor allowed others to be. They never considered what was present of any value, as they always went after the things they did not have, and they considered what they had not yet attained but had in mind, as if they already had it.'

His court had little choice but to accept his plan, even though some such as Halil held deep reservations. The old chief vizier, whom his father had hoped would temper and guide him, but who Mehmet felt had thwarted him, was widely known to oppose an assault on Constantinople. His motivations are described in several of the contemporary sources as being corrupt (he was rumoured to be in the pay of the Byzantine court), but they may also have been honestly held. He had a keen appreciation of the instability underlying the House of Osman and the ease with which it could slip back into the kind of civil conflict that had almost destroyed it in the past. After all, what threat was the city to them, already a vassal in all but name? For a young sultan who had yet to firmly win the trust of his court and soldiers, was the prize of it worth the risk of failure and humiliation?

But like the great cannon he had ordered into being, there was something portentous about the young Mehmet: a will to break and remake the world. He had poured his molten ambition into a single mould, pinning everything on its success or failure.

'Go and tell the emperor that the present ruler is not like his predecessors,' he is reported to have said to an anxious envoy from Constantinople, who came to protest at his preparations for the siege. 'The things which they were unable to do, he can achieve at once and with ease, and those things which they did not wish to do, he both desires and is determined to accomplish.'

3

The Gate of Saints

İsmet Hezer lay on a narrow bed in the back room of the apartment, a tube running to a colostomy bag by his bedside. When I'd last seen him, he had been a forbidding old man with a skullcap, beard and the kind of granite visage which the action of time had not so much aged as polished to its essential hardness. But now his scalp was bare, his chin messily stubbled, his skin hugging the sunken orbs of his eyes; he looked like a day-old chick blown from its nest in a storm. He and his wife Mahinur were vague about the nature of his illness, but they suggested it was a result of his suicide attempt. The warm fug of the apartment smelled of sickness, and although he seemed eager to talk, I felt bad for having come.

Their old home had finally been demolished and they were now living on the ground floor of a 1970s apartment block directly next to Tokludede. The neighbourhood was still surrounded by metal sheeting that hid the buildings inside and the only visible edifice was the new hotel, a long building that wrapped around the side of the neighbourhood facing towards the city, rendering the new luxury development even more separate than the old neighbourhood had been; it was loosely in the style of the traditional buildings it had replaced except for a huge neoclassical arch that incongruously framed the entrance. The development had been delayed due to a court case lodged by Istanbul's Chamber of Architects, which vigorously resisted these kinds of projects, and which claimed that the hotel contravened laws governing the preservation of historic areas.

Even among the atmospheric neighbourhoods of Fatih (as the old walled city was named, in homage to the Conqueror), Tokludede had been a special place. Sitting within the broader district of Ayvansaray, it took its name from one Toklu İbrahim Dede, a soldier in the army of Sultan Mehmet II who had settled in the area following the capture of the city. After the Conquest, Mehmet had ordered his prominent soldiers and members of his court to take in hand different patches of his new capital and to beautify and restore them, constructing schools, markets and mosques, and it is likely that this is how Toklu İbrahim Dede became connected with the area. The neighbourhood's chief pride lay through an adjacent low gate, once known as the Blakhernai Gate – after the late Byzantine palace that once stood on the spot. This gate opened to a small courtyard where there were a number of graves of grey marble planted with roses and surrounded by green-painted iron palings. They were said to belong to Muslim saints martyred during the first Arab siege of Constantinople in AD 674, among them companions of the Prophet himself. These illustrious historical connections made the area desirable real estate, and were almost certainly one of the reasons why it was chosen for urban renewal.

When I first saw İsmet and Mahinur in their new apartment I assumed they must have lost their battle, but this was not the case. Their old home was gone, but the developers had eventually allowed them to build its replacement themselves and retain the ownership.

'It's a victory,' İsmet croaked from his sickbed. 'They bought everyone else's house, but they couldn't buy mine. I've become like an eagle here.'

They were still under great pressure though. They had run out of money to finish the new house and the local municipality was threatening to expropriate it if they didn't meet certain construction deadlines. They'd already spent all their savings on the structure and foundations. Mahinur showed me the new house, which looked almost identical to the old. The local planning inspectors had rigidly enforced the regulations on earthquake-proofing and the reconstruction of historic buildings, but İsmet complained that the standards had not been applied so rigorously to the other buildings, and that corners had been cut to maximise profit.

'I'll tell you something,' he said. 'These people think they are Muslims, but they can't even compare with the non-Muslims. There is no morality. Their religion is money.'

İsmet told me about his life and the neighbourhood. When he'd come to Tokludede city years earlier, the Golden Horn and its docklands were the pumping heart of industry in Istanbul, and the whole area was full of factories and workshops. He remembered travelling alone from Bayburt on the post train to join his older brother who was already there, and described arriving at the Haydarpaşa train station, the imposing terminus of the Baghdad–Hejaz railway that sat on the Bosphorus' Anatolian shore; it had wide steps leading down to the ferry stops on the water, where you'd board a boat to cross to the European shore.

'When we saw the sea we said, "Now we're in Istanbul."' It was an experience shared by hundreds of thousands of Anatolian migrants and immortalised in films and books: the empty-pocketed migrant arriving for the first time at the broad marble steps of the great train station and stepping down to gaze at the silhouettes of the mosques and towers that stretched out across the far side of the Bosphorus; a moment of wonder and possibility before the city claimed them and they plunged into its dark streets to whatever life awaited them.

İsmet got a job at Tekel, the state alcohol company, first working in their factory, and then driving a truck delivering alcohol and cigarettes around, and remained in that job for the rest of his working life. Mahinur had also come from Bayburt; the match was organised by their families back home. When I asked him how Tokludede had changed in the time since they'd first lived there, İsmet recalled the city's old Christian and Jewish inhabitants, some of whom had still lived in the neighbourhood and surrounding areas when he'd first arrived, but were already in the process of departing. In 1955, a couple of years before he'd come to Tokludede, a devastating pogrom had been launched against the city's Greeks in which more than 3,000 shops, churches and homes were attacked, and more than a dozen people killed. Over the following thousands of Greeks emigrated from Istanbul.

'I wish they would come back,' he said. 'We were neighbours with Armenians and Greeks. They were beautiful people. The people who came here loved them. If they poured a glass of tea for themselves, they would pour one for a neighbour too . . . People scared them away to get their hands on their property.'

As we talked further he seemed to become confused between this old exodus and the recent redevelopment project. 'They were forced to leave,' he told me. 'Even recently, they left by force. We stayed in Ayvansaray but it's not Ayvansaray any more. Back then it was Ayvansaray . . . Constructions, buildings, inhabitants, the living . . . Those who lived there knew it as

Ayvansaray. Now it's not Istanbul and it's not Ayvansaray. It was when they were living here.'

İsmet was tired, and when I asked who else I should speak to about the neighbourhood and its past, he told me to go and see someone named 'Redhead' Salih. 'He's a very good kid,' he murmured. He said I would find him at the local teahouse.

———

Later I would wonder if there was a kind of truth behind İsmet's confusion and that the pogrom of the Greeks and the redevelopment of Tokludede were indeed connected, or part of a continuous process: the death of the community and a model of communal urban life that stretched back far into the past and which was now in the last stages of falling away. It was something people would refer to repeatedly during my visits to the walls: they felt their communities were dying, that their neighbours were becoming strangers, and that the support and closeness they had once known was withering away. It was strange, because to me it had seemed to be something that was relatively strong in Turkey. I felt safer in most Turkish streets than in their equivalents in the UK. Crime data suggested that this was indeed the case: Istanbul had lower levels of street violence and muggings than most major American and European cities. I had wondered if it was to do with the fear instilled by a stronger and more punitive police presence, but it also seemed to me that there was a feeling of community extending into the streets that was absent back home.

I once met a Middle Eastern history professor who had grown up in Ayvansaray and spent a number of years teaching at the London School of Economics. He had a similar impression. 'The difference for me living in Britain was that fifteen- or sixteen-year-olds here, if I see them misbehaving I have the right to slap their face and send them home, for their own good,' he said. 'But in Britain I looked in the kids' eyes and for the first time saw that they could kill me . . . Once in London, in Crystal Palace near where I lived, I was leaving a train station. It was rush hour, thousands of people coming out of the train, and I saw a boy grabbing a girl, threatening to throw her onto the rails. Everyone was passing by as if nothing was happening. I went up to him and said, "Stop." He let her go and the girl ran away. I went out and there were twenty more of them outside. I don't know how they let me go . . . Here, that kid might answer back at me, swear at me, whatever, but in Britain they would look into my eyes, stab me, and walk away. That's what I felt. I felt less safe.'

There were the vigilant eyes of the shopkeepers standing in their doorways, the street vendors and the neighbourhood dogs, but it was more intangible than this. The street was not no-man's-land. You could see it in the way people walked, in the way they addressed each other in public, in the attitudes of the teenagers – a kind of relaxed informality, an at-homeness that came with a community asserting ownership of its streets.

That was changing though. Many people cited the effect of social media, of lives lived online rather than face to face; but also there was a trend in which spaces that were once communal were becoming commodified and privatised – small parks concreted over to become cafés or car parks, and the atomisation of communities that were low-rise housing into towering apartment blocks.

In Turkish, the word for neighbourhood – *mahalle* – carried greater heft than its English counterpart. For several centuries prior to the establishment of the Turkish Republic, the *mahalle* was the basic administrative and social unit of society. Neighbourhoods were self-sufficient in most matters. They took care of their own security, their own street-cleaning, fire-fighting and education, which would take place at the *medrese* of the neighbourhood mosque or other place of worship. The neighbourhood was represented to the state by its local imam, rabbi or priest, and later on by its *muhtar* or elected headman. In Ottoman times, entire lives could pass almost entirely within its confines, from birth to schooling to the arrangement of marriage and funeral rites.

'In those times,' wrote the historian Şerif Mardin, 'the *mahalle* was more than an administrative unit with somewhat arbitrarily drawn boundaries; it was a compact *gemeinschaft* with its boundaries protected by its own toughs and faithful dogs, and a setting within which much of the normal life of an average Ottoman citizen was shaped.' *Gemeinschaft* – the German sociological term he used – denotes a community in which bonds are personal and defined by physical proximity, with members united by emotional closeness and moral obligation; it is set in contrast to *gesellschaft* – society – in which the bonds between members are impersonal or indirect and where people are bound by ideas and institutions, their participation guided less by mutual obligation than by economic, political and personal self-interest.

It was therefore predictable that the *mahalle* would be a target for the project of nation-building and societal reform undertaken by the Young Turks and then pursued more radically in the Republican era by their ideological successor and Turkey's modern founder, Mustafa Kemal Atatürk. The *mahalle* was the very substance of the antiquated social fabric he wished to tear apart to allow Turkey to join the family of 'advanced nations'; its grip, he believed, was smothering progress and shackling the minds of the country's citizens. This was the deeper struggle that lay behind the question of street dogs, whose territories were usually contiguous with the *mahalle*'s borders and who were an intimate part of its life, and the contempt which the reformists felt for the dogs was an expression of that which they felt for the *mahalle* itself. Pulling people out of the *gemein-schaft* of the neighbourhood and into the *gesellschaft* of the nation was one of the implicit aims of Atatürk's social reforms. It was a goal furthered by the closure of the *medreses*, the emancipation of women, the reordering and centralisation of education, and the physical urban planning of Istanbul and other major cities through the construction of parks and prom-enades that allowed for free and mixed social gathering of a kind that was impossible in the old neighbourhoods. The ideal of the 'modern' city encapsulated in the new capital Ankara, a *tabula rasa* elevated from little more than a small town and built to a Western model, inspired Turkey's leaders to view Istanbul's entire urban fabric as in need of replacement. At one point its own mayor even opined that the entirety of the city, with the exception of its monuments, should be demolished and rebuilt.

The all-encompassing nature of the *mahalle* in Ottoman times was swept away by this storm of modernisation, but something of the closeness of neighbourhood life survived. Indeed, other policies of the early Republic tended to preserve its survival. While encouraging the integration and broadening of city life, Atatürk pursued an opposite approach in rural areas, where village life was eulogised and migration to the cities all but prohibited. This pursuit of 'peasantism', in which the rural population was seen as the nationalist rootstock of the country and the core of its future stability, was ultimately unsustainable. After the Second World War, aid from the United States led to a mechanisation of Turkish agriculture, which in turn made poverty and unemployment in the villages unbearable; over the following decades hundreds of thousands of rural Turks, like İsmet and Mahinur, made their way to the cities. In this way whole communities were transferred to an urban setting, replicating the intensely close social relations which still prevailed in rural life. İsmet and the regulars at the Ayvansaray Sports Club, most of whose ancestors had moved from rural regions of Anatolia within the span of a single lifetime, had brought with them a new infusion of life to neighbourhood culture.

To be part of a neighbourhood was to be enmeshed in a network of support and obligation that was familial in its closeness. To some it signified the safety net of community and the upholding of moral values; to others, it was an oppressive, coercive force breathing down your neck, watching your every move, enforcing conformity. When the historian Mardin had written about the *mahalle*, he had coined a phrase – 'neighbourhood pressure' – which the more secular part of society adopted and ran with as a way of expressing the sense of encroaching conservatism under Erdoğan and the AK Party. At that time, it was hard to point to specific laws or formal actions that the Islamist-rooted movement was taking to narrow the secular space, but there was a sense of a growing moral pressure to conform to conservative values that was occurring both in the media and on the national stage, but also on the neighbourhood level. It was ironic, therefore, that Erdoğan's AK Party would become the catalyst for economic forces that were destroying neighbourhood life.

The Ayvansaray Sports Club, where İsmet had sent me to find 'Redhead' Salih, looked much like any other of the tens of thousands of teahouses that ran the length and breadth of Turkey: a place where the men of a neighbourhood would gather to gossip and argue, a little node of community life. On the walls inside – along with the mandatory no-smoking signs, portraits of Atatürk and verses from the Quran – were photographs of the long-defunct neighbourhood football team from which the café took its name. The former footballers were now old men seated in groups near the door playing *okey* – a popular game using numbered tiles with rules similar to rummy. In the wet winter months the place smelled of tea, rain and sweat, and echoed with the plasticky clack of the *okey* tiles. The café's glass frontage looked onto a meagre park, beyond which the wind whipped the grey waters of the Golden Horn. Once this area had been a hub of industry and the waterfront thronged with factories, docks and workshops, but that time was long gone. Now there was just the bare park with its geometric walkways and skinny saplings; the kind of place people hurry through on their way elsewhere. The thing that made the Ayvansaray Sports Club extraordinary was that the community it served no longer existed in any physical sense. Tokludede was gone, and some of the old men who sauntered in each morning, greeting their former neighbours as if they had just stepped a few metres from their front doors, had travelled an hour or more across the city to be there.

I sometimes thought it was tea that held Turkey together. There were grander adhesives, like God and Nation, but theirs was not an all-compassing embrace nor always a welcome one. Tea bound at the molecular level, lubricating business deals and easing transactions with officialdom, soothing the grief-stricken and loosening the tongues of shy suitors. A study in the mid-2000s found that its citizens brewed an average of seven pounds of tea leaves per capita each year, far ahead of their closest rivals in the UK and Republic of Ireland.

The story of Turkey's teahouses is intertwined with that of the neighbourhood. They were originally coffee houses and began their life in the sixteenth century with the introduction of coffee to the Ottoman Empire. Banal and innocent though it may now seem, coffee caused significant disruption and controversy on its introduction to Ottoman society. Its burgeoning popularity brought a change to the pattern of daily life for ordinary citizens of Istanbul, especially Muslim men. For them, the coffee houses that sprang up across the city offered a new venue for gathering and socialising beyond the home, the mosque and the market, and in a manner that was free from any religious or temporal authority. It was greeted with alarm by the authorities, who regarded it as a foreign toxin in the body politic. Banned by *fatwa* in 1543, contraband shipments were dumped in the Golden Horn. But over time coffee houses persisted and thrived despite the state's intermittent attempts to suppress them. In Istanbul they evolved into two separate and seemingly opposite varieties. There were the *semai* coffee houses in which coffee was a gateway drug to music, revelry and indulgence. These were often associated with traditional firemen's guilds or with members of the Janissary corps – which by the eighteenth century had degenerated from a professional fighting force into a semi-criminal cartel whose members had largely abandoned the barracks and inserted themselves into urban life. The patrons of *semai* coffee houses drank booze, consumed opium, and procured prostitutes along with their coffee, while travelling singers performed ballads. They gained a reputation as dens of political as well as moral subversion.

The other kind was the *mahalle* coffee house. These generally opened up near a mosque and were places which men repaired to either side of prayers. Local notables could be sought out there: the imam or the *muhtar*. They were places where disputes were aired and resolved, and came to serve as a 'virtual neighbourhood parliament' in the phrase of historian Ekrem Işın. In reality, the separation between these two could be quite fluid – a coffee house could be part *semai* and part *mahalle*, like the local pub in Britain: a source of social cohesion or disruption depending on your perspective or the time of day. With the liberalisation of alcohol consumption in the twentieth century, the Dionysian elements of the *semai* coffee houses fell away as the seedier custom they attracted graduated to bars and clubs, and what remained were the *mahalle* coffee houses, Apollonian pillars of neighbourhood life and order.

And how did tea come to be drunk in them? Turkey remained a coffee nation until the mid-twentieth century, when a sweeping act of top-down economic planning ended its dominance. The government of Prime Minister Adnan Menderes was looking for ways to boost the country's poorer regions, which included the wet and mountainous eastern Black Sea coast. Studies had pointed to it as a promising place for tea cultivation, so Menderes threw the state's full weight behind the plan, creating a state monopoly tea industry from scratch: subsidising plantings, building the factories, training the workers, and buying the crop. He also created the market: hefty tariffs were slapped on imported coffee, and almost overnight Turkey became a nation of tea-drinkers, and an economic boost was delivered to a hitherto impoverished part of the country. Cheap and ubiquitous, the tea of the Black Sea coast became a source of pride: a drink of the people, grown by the people, for the people, each act of consumption completing a virtuous circle through which the nation strengthened itself. Tea united neighbourhood and nation – *gemeinschaft* and *gesellschaft* – which is perhaps why it occupied a special place in Turkish society and also why, when you stripped a place like Tokludede down to its bones, the teahouse endured.

————

I found 'Redhead' Salih there, as İsmet had said I would. He was sat among a group of younger men towards the back of the café. He was middle-aged; his hair a short sweep of copper, like brushed wire, with a lean, chiselled face and light blue eyes. He looked like a gunslinger in a Western: the man the bad guys haven't factored in, gazing calmly from his porch as they ride into town. He was an electrician.

Like İsmet, Salih had fought hard against the developers but his had been a very different battle. He'd shared the ownership of his house with several members of his family, while he himself had moved away from Tokludede a few years earlier. He had realised it would be impossible to keep their property, so instead he had secured the support of his various relatives and took the developers to court in order to squeeze as much money from them as possible. Things had gone well. The developers' offer at the outset had been 165,000 Turkish lira, but after various rulings, this had been upped by degrees to nearly ten times that. However, he still believed they were undervaluing his house and kept appealing and demanding more.

'I'll make them regret what they've done,' he told me. 'If it's urban renewal, you do it with the people in it. If you take it all and give it to someone else, it's not urban renewal any more.'

Salih had heard nothing about the plan until a group of well-heeled outsiders descended on the neighbourhood to warn of what was coming. They were from the Istanbul Chamber of Architects, which often led the way in opposing such projects, and they aroused the immediate suspicion of most people in the neighbourhood. He described his first meeting with them in the café, which went disastrously.

'I asked them why they wanted to protect my rights? How did they find me? How did I know they hadn't already cut some deal with the other side?' Salih recalled. When the head of Istanbul's chamber of architects encouraged him to take a seat on an association representing neighbourhoods affected by urban transformation, he refused because, 'It was probably set up by outsiders like you.' He called her a 'snob' and she threw a glass of water in his face, he recalled with amusement. That seemed to have won his respect, because he did eventually join some meetings and protests.

Tokludede was among dozens of neighbourhoods either undergoing or threatened with demolition. What lay in store for Tokludede could be seen in nearby Sulukule, a little further along the walls, which had been home to a Roma community since Byzantine times; or in Tarlabaşı across the Golden Horn, where a community of Kurds, Roma, immigrant groups, and transgender sex workers were being cleared out to make way for a lucrative development. In Sulukule, despite international media attention and an energetic campaign by locals and urban rights activists, a project was forced through that resulted in the inhabitants being turfed out and the bulk of the neighbourhood being levelled and replaced with a gated complex of 'luxury villas' that stood empty for years, before eventually being bought up by wealthy Syrians fleeing the civil war in their country. The Roma who had lived there were relocated to apartments in a newly built neighbourhood of tower blocks on the city's outskirts. Faced with isolation and few work prospects, almost all had filtered back to the area near their former homes, where they continued living, now in more difficult circumstances than before.

The projects that garnered most attention were those targeting areas inhabited by marginalised ethnic minorities, such as Kurds, Roma or members of the Alevi religious sect. Rights organisations and activists suspected such places were chosen deliberately, either out of antipathy or a desire to disrupt and further marginalise these groups; or perhaps just because they were seen as easy victims.

However, Tokludede was different. Its residents were not part of any ethnic, political or religious minority. In fact, they represented a section of Turkish society that was as mainstream and ordinary as you could get: they were, to be reductive, the urban Sunni Muslim lower-middle class. Some were pious, some were not, but a majority were fervent supporters of Erdoğan and the AK Party. Initially, I assumed this was why staunch hold-outs like İsmet Hezer were rare, but there was more to it than that. Even among those like Salih, who was outraged at what he regarded as state-backed theft, there was a sense of resignation at what had happened. In the telling of the teahouse regulars the demolition of Tokludede was the final act in a longer story of decline that had begun years or even decades earlier – with the driving out of the non-Muslim minorities, with the abolition of the industries that once lined the Golden Horn, with the closure of the local football club. To them, the development project was not so much the death of Tokludede as the sweeping away of its corpse.

For Salih, Tokludede had died with the *külhanbeys*. He told me about them while regaling me with stories of the neighbourhood's past as we spent a day wandering around the environs of Tokludede and visiting the places where he'd spent time as a kid. We couldn't go into the neighbourhood itself – it was still sealed off and zealously guarded by private security.

'That could never happen if the *külhanbeys* were here,' he'd fumed. 'It was our neighbourhood and we could go in whenever we wanted.' I'd never heard the word before – I would learn that it was a somewhat old-fashioned term for the young men more widely known as a *kabadayı* – neighbourhood youths who trod the line between vigilantes and racketeers. Their heyday had been in the nineteenth century, when they'd been Robin Hood figures whose exploits had been a part of the city's folklore. These days, the term was generally used to refer to a basic street thug. In Salih's youth, however, they were far more than that.

He told me about the *külhanbeys* of his youth – young men in their late teens and early twenties – with an almost childish excitement. In many Turkish neighbourhoods everyone seemed to have a nickname prefix they universally went by – Salih was 'Redhead' Salih, İsmet was 'Bayburt' İsmet. Perhaps it was a cultural survival from the time before the adoption of surnames, which only happened in Turkey in the 1930s. Tokludede's *külhanbeys* were 'Crazy' Aşur, 'Cobra' Osman, 'Panther' Turan, 'Boxer' Selahattin, and another Selahattin, who didn't seem to have a nickname, and wasn't much of a fighter, 'but had the same heart as the others', according to Salih.

To him and his friends, they were role models and champions of natural justice, dispensing moral advice to the younger boys, and teaching them the way of the *külhanbeys*. 'If you're in the right, you have to stand up for yourself, and then even if you get beaten up, it doesn't matter,' Salih remembered Aşur telling him. 'If you don't stand up for yourself, then when I hear about it, I'll beat you up myself.'

He recalled a winter when he was twelve years old and he and a friend had visited a local *hamam* when an older man came along and turfed them out of the spot they had paid for. When they protested, the man hit them and chased them away; so they went out and found 'Crazy' Aşur and told him what had happened. Aşur marched into the *hamam*, pausing only to replace his muddy shoes with a pair of sandals, found the culprit and dragged him naked into the street, where he beat him in the snow.

Another time, Salih recounted, the Tokludede *külhanbeys* went to drink at Sarayburnu, at the tip of the old city's peninsula, where a row of cafés served *rakı* and beer. 'A BMW pulled up, and this spoilt rich guy got out and started a fight with them . . . Because he was rich, the waiters came and joined in on his side. There were like thirty or thirty-five people and three of them – Aşur, Turan, and Osman – beat them all up, while Selahattin just leaned against the car, watching them, smoking a cigarette, and afterwards he was like: "OK, are you done? Let's go."' This had all filtered back to him as gossip, Salih hastened to add: 'These guys would never tell the kids about their fights, because they didn't want us to be violent, they wanted us to study.'

The *külhanbeys* were one of the things that Salih believed held the neighbourhood together. Another was football. When Salih was growing up, the local Ayvansaray football club, which covered Tokludede and the surrounding neighbourhoods, was a big deal. Every week, ten or twelve buses of local residents would go off to watch matches against other amateur Istanbul sides. The sports club also had an athletics team and for a while a volleyball team. Salih had been in the youth team.

'Football kept us together,' he said. 'I was studying in the high school, and there were a few other kids also going to school, but the rest were working . . . Despite all the academic stuff and the jealousies, at some point we were kids of the same neighbourhood; they couldn't go to school, but we were respectful to each other. They worked, we studied and come the weekend, we had the matches. Everybody was united . . . We needed something to hold us together, some kind of cement, and football was the cement. It stopped us from separating due to cultural, educational, or economic reasons.'

The cost of running the football club and the other neighbourhood teams was met by donations from the community: principally from the money flowing into the neighbourhood through the factories and industry on the Golden Horn. Local businesses donated to the club and kept it going – especially the *kalafatyeri*, a factory that produced wooden yachts and which had existed since Ottoman times.

The roots of the area's industrial history stretched back to the nineteenth century, when a state-of-the-art textile factory had been built at Eyüp to produce the fez, a newly designed piece of headgear that would be worn by the reformed army of Sultan Mahmut II. As demand for the fez grew, the so-called *feshane* was expanded and by the 1890s had an annual production capacity of half a million metres of fabric. Other factories had sprung up around it, mainly providing clothing and equipment for the military, and on their heels came other workshops, along with power stations, abattoirs and docklands. By the Republican era the Golden Horn had become the de facto industrial hub of the city, and a role that was further embraced in a master plan devised by Henri Prost, the French city planner who was commissioned by Atatürk to redesign Istanbul in the late 1930s.

From the 1940s onwards, union activity began to proliferate and by the 1970s, there was an alphabet soup of different organisations representing workers in the area. Conditions had improved, but Turkey's status as a front-line Cold War state and US ally made the unions the focus of intense political and state pressure, and the different organisations aligned along those which had been co-opted or infiltrated by rightists or the state and those which remained genuinely left wing.

'Everybody worked,' said Salih. 'We had unions. No one was afraid of life. This was the true centre of Istanbul: all the services came here first, both the economic power and the tradesmen. It was the single biggest population that took care of Turkey in terms of production and tax. This was Turkey's backbone.'

Nonetheless, in Salih's recollection, the intimacy and fundamental bonds of *mahalle* life endured. 'At that time there wasn't much to do in this neighbourhood and there were only two entrances, and no cars at all, and we were all out on the streets all the time, because there was no danger,' he recalled. 'Women would sit and drink tea together and the men would all go to the teahouse and the children would even play at night. Whenever we got hungry, we'd go to the closest house, four or five of us, and they'd feed us. It wasn't like you had to go to your own house . . . We were like one big family, as if everyone was related to everyone else. In that culture, the *külhanbey* is like the defender of the neighbourhood. For example, if a man who was an outsider passed two times through the neighbourhood, on the third time he'd be stopped.'

The archetype of the *külhanbey* and the *kabadayı* originated from the rich urban subculture of nineteenth-century Istanbul, where they referred to two distinct types. The *kabadayı* was the Robin Hood-type figure Salih evoked, blurring the line between protector and oppressor. The exploits of famous *kabadayıs*, their feuds and romances, were the grist of the city's rumour mill and sometimes filled the pages of its newspapers. A good *kabadayı* was self-confident, courageous, and a formidable fighter who adhered to a code of honour bound up with that of the neighbourhood he protected. He should be able to resolve a dispute quickly using a minimum of violence, and to knock an opponent senseless using a single open-handed blow – an *Osmanlı tokadı*, or 'Ottoman slap' – but could resort to knives if things got more serious. Like the *semai* coffeehouses, which they often ran, they had roots in Janissary culture and the firemen's guilds, and usually had a foot in the city's criminal underworld, running protection rackets or brothels.

'In the power vacuum between the administration and the neighbourhood residents, they informally served certain administrative functions, which the local people appreciated because they did it in a more honest way than the authoritarian and repressive formal officials,' write Yücel Yeşilgöz and Frank Bovenkerk in a study of nineteenth-century *kabadayıs*. Like the *mahalle* culture, of which they formed a part, they were at their strongest when the state was weak and communities looked within for sources of authority, either to replace or defy a corrupt and distant central power.

———

The urban subcultures of nineteenth-century Istanbul were long gone by the time of Salih's childhood, even if some of their names and associations survived. But the era in which he grew up, the late 1970s, was another time when the state's grip on society was again slipping. Through the course of the decade, Turkey entered a spiral of intensifying political violence between right-wing and left-wing factions fuelled by the climate of the Cold War. Turkey's state, military and security apparatus, supported and sometimes leaned on by its patron and NATO ally the United States, was intensely fearful of communist influence and used all means to suppress it, including extrajudicial killings and the employment of right-wing paramilitary groups. The sense of lawlessness and instability was heightened by large-scale unemployment, rampant inflation and a succession of ineffectual and fleeting coalition governments. Ultranationalists clashed on the streets with a kaleidoscope of socialist, communist and anarchist groups in campaigns of assassination and murder. Political allegiances were signified by clothes, hairstyles, even moustaches: the scruffy bush of the leftists and the long handlebars of the rightists. Neighbourhoods, streets and universities became segregated according to who held sway, and walking along the wrong street could mean death.

The violence eventually took on an intensity more often associated with ethnic conflicts. More than five thousand people were killed in assassinations, street battles, massacres, bombings and bank robberies, and at its crescendo in 1980, twenty people were being killed a day. Tokludede and the broader Ayvansaray district, whose working population was heavily unionised, leaned to the left. Among those killed were Salih's father's boss, drowned in the Golden Horn by a rightist group. Even schoolchildren became radicalised. Salih remembered gendarmerie soldiers being posted in classrooms at his high school, which was dominated by leftist organisations. He once wore a shirt with a picture of a white horse on the back, not realising it bore a similarity to the emblem of a centre-right party, and a rumour began that he was a fascist. To quell suspicion, he memorised a leftist poem and recited it out loud in his literature class. After that the leftists tried to recruit him; to put them off, he told them he was already a member of a party.

This period of violence would end with an event that would reshape the lives of everybody in Turkey and its future generations. On 12 September 1980, the military stepped in to end the chaos gripping the country by seizing control in a coup d'état. It was the third time in two decades they had done so, but the scope of this intervention dwarfed previous coups. Parliament, the government, and all political parties and labour unions were disbanded and their leaders arrested. Martial law and curfews were imposed throughout the nation; all newspapers were closed for 300 days. The violence stopped overnight (it was widely believed that the military itself had played a role in orchestrating some of the bloodletting to justify its intervention) and an uneasy calm settled over the country. In the ensuing weeks and months around 650,000 people would be detained for at least ninety days; around 250,000 criminal convictions were handed out. Five hundred death sentences were passed, of which forty-nine were enacted. Most of those detained suffered some form of torture in custody, with more than two hundred people beaten to death and tens of thousands more left with lasting physical and psychological wounds. Many thousands fled to Europe, with ten thousand of these refugees eventually stripped of Turkish citizenship.

The 1980 military coup and the unrest preceding it marked the nation like a fire passing through a forest. Everyone would bear the scars of that time; everyone I spoke to who lived through it was affected. Some, like Salih, shared their experiences of navigating the violence of the late 1970s; others told of the months they spent in prison leading up to or after the coup, or of friends and relatives broken by torture or forced to flee into exile. But it was the decisions later enacted by the generals that would make it so consequential.

Flushed with power and a sense of paternal duty, the ruling junta attempted to enact a programme of social engineering to create a more 'healthy' nation. Part of this involved stepping up the existing suppression of Kurdish identity. Article 66 of the new constitution imposed by the junta declared that: 'Everyone bound to the Turkish state by the bond of citizenship is a Turk.' The clear aim of this clause was to enshrine the erasure of the Kurds, who made up around a fifth of Turkey's population. The heightened oppression that ensued would fuel the insurgency of the separatist Kurdistan Workers' Party, blighting the country for decades, and costing tens of thousands of lives.

The generals also pursued what they called the 'Turkish–Islamic Synthesis': the idea of promoting the Sunni Muslim identity as a way of uniting the country, weakening the left, and fostering moral virtues as a counter to what they saw as their people's more anarchic tendencies. As a result of this, compulsory religious education was increased, new theology departments set up at universities and the budget of the Diyanet – Turkey's Ministry for Religious Affairs – greatly boosted to finance the building of thousands of new mosques. Ironically, given that the generals remained staunchly committed to Atatürk's secularist principles, these reforms would open up crucial breathing space for political Islam.

The other far-reaching consequence that led indirectly from

the coup followed the formation of a new centre-right government under the charismatic prime minister Turgut Özal. After the generals stepped back following elections in 1983, Özal enacted with their tacit backing a raft of radical free market reforms that transformed the Turkish economy. The command economy of previous years was abandoned and the country embarked on a new era – enthusiastically embraced by many – of free enterprise inspired by the neo-liberal creed of Reagan and Thatcher. An end was called to many state monopoly industries and protectionist measures were scrapped, opening the way for the emergence of a new class of businessmen from the cities of Anatolia. The reforms generated wealth and innovation, but they also drove up inequality, and in particular urban poverty.

———

Tokludede was one of the places that would be profoundly affected by this process. The political rise of Özal's centre-right Motherland Party was replicated in municipal elections in 1984, which brought a new administration to Istanbul led by one of its founders, a former electrical engineer with no previous political experience named Bedrettin Dalan. Urban redevelopment and infrastructure projects had long been regarded as a kind of yardstick for political ambition and success: it was part of the Republican culture of government going back to the urban and social re-engineering plans promoted by Atatürk and his followers. Such projects almost always seemed to be defeated by the lack of a lastingly stable political environment to push them through, by a divisively ideological focus, by corruption and cronyism, or by the sprawling complexity of Istanbul itself.

However, the government had just passed a series of laws expanding the power of municipalities, and armed with this mandate, Dalan set about putting his stamp on Istanbul. Dalan opted to set his sights on the Golden Horn and the industries around it on which neighbourhoods like Tokludede relied. This booming industrial zone had brought economic life and prosperity, but also ecological ruin. So much pollution was being released into the harbour that its waters had become a fetid, lifeless soup, a mark of shame on the face of the city that was evident to the thousands of tourists and residents who daily flocked across the Galata Bridge that linked the old city with the European districts. Dalan, who was known for his blue eyes, famously vowed to make the waters of the Golden Horn the same colour as them. He sought to reimagine it lined not with factories and docks, but with promenades, cafés, and beaches. Using beefed-up municipal powers and a disregard for due process, he shut down the industries there and moved them to more remote regions, such as Tuzla, and across the Sea of Marmara to the Gulf of İzmit, where they would continue out of most people's sight on a far greater scale. The cleanliness of the water was restored – at least in the Golden Horn – but the disappearance of the industry meant that areas like Ayvansaray sunk into poverty. Skilled workers left, homeowners moved away and rented out their properties. The second part of Dalan's plan, in which the Golden Horn would become a hub of tourism and leisure, had still not materialised nearly thirty years later.

According to Salih that spelled the end for the football club, which eventually folded. 'It ended for completely economic reasons,' he said. 'If we look into it, we can say it is the move [of the industry] to Tuzla. There was no *kalafatyeri* any more, which used to support it economically, and then no one stayed either.'

As for the *külhanbey* culture in Tokludede, that too came to an end with the young men Salih had known. The defining event came with the death of 'Crazy' Aşur, who was hit by a car and killed while walking on the street. It appeared to be an accident but people in the neighbourhood were suspicious. He had recently started doing driving work for the Mafia in nearby Eyüp, and Salih had heard that he'd had some disagreement arising from this. When the man who hit him was arrested, the other *külhanbeys* went and shouted outside the police station, demanding that he be handed over to them, but of course the police refused. After that the others went their separate ways. 'Cobra' Osman made a career out of acting in the films of the action movie star Cüneyt Arkın, before setting up his own karate school to train people in martial arts. 'Panther' Turan wanted to settle down and get married and ended up leaving the neighbourhood. Selahattin emigrated to Switzerland. After that there were no more *külhanbeys*.

As I spent more time at the teahouse, its very ordinariness began to strike me as significant. It was like a bellwether, the kind of place foreign reporters sweep into ahead of elections to take the 'pulse of the nation', and after observing it over time I began to draw sweeping insights from its most trivial features. There were the contradictory signs at the entrance, one reading 'Welcome', and the other warning that 'non-members may not enter', which to me seemed to encapsulate the duelling attitudes of warmth and wariness characteristic of small communities in Turkey. The ground floor with its pictures of Atatürk and the Quran – nationalism and Islam – the twin pillars of modern Turkish identity, seemed to me to be the public face of the nation; the first floor, where I'd often conduct interviews away from the noise below, was the id to the ground floor's superego, a place of hidden urges where the smoking ban was flouted and Atatürk and the Quran had been swapped for a couple of mildly saucy posters: a close-up of a woman's bared leg, toe poised on the wave-line of a beach, and another in a set of keyboard tights, draped chameleon-like across a piano. The only people up there were a group of sullen students from a nearby university, slouched in armchairs by the window, silently glued to their phones.

Once when I was talking to Salih up there, Serdar – a friend of his – sidled over with a black plastic bag which he furtively opened to reveal a bottle of Johnnie Walker. Serdar was a middle-aged man with a wide jaw, thick square glasses, with a stoic, downtrodden air about him. He lived in the teahouse – literally: his bedsit was on top of it and could only be entered through the first floor. He invited us up, where we sat drinking the whisky at a little table by his wide window that looked out over the Golden Horn. A rainbow, perfectly framed, stretched over Galata on the opposite shore. The pair opined on one of their favourite themes: the hypocrisy of the neighbourhood's many residents who had found God after lives spent drinking, smoking, and in one case running an off-licence.

Salih and Serdar both hated Erdoğan and the atmosphere of what they regarded as faux piety in the country. They believed people were cleaving to religion because they saw how the wind was blowing and thought they might accrue some advantage from it. They were in a minority though. Many of the older men had been members of the main opposition Republican People's Party, former unionised workers and leftists who had now transformed into ardent supporters of Erdoğan's government.

Another of the neighbourhood men, Mustafa, had been pious since he was young. A genial bear of a man with a neatly trimmed beard, who excused himself for prayers at the appointed times. He came from a well-off local family and was a small-time property developer. Like İsmet, he had won the right to build his own replacement home in the neighbourhood, but through connections rather than stubbornness. He believed the development was transforming what had been a poor neighbourhood into something better with amenities that would benefit the wider district of Ayvansaray. He and Salih and Serdar disagreed on almost everything. In fact, the only point which the three of them seemed to agree on was the question of the Kurds, where any sign of accommodation to Kurdish cultural or political demands horrified them. One time when I visited the teahouse, a controversy was simmering over a visit to Ankara by the leader of Iraqi Kurdistan, during which the autonomous region's flag was flown as he appeared with Erdoğan. The men of the teahouse were scandalised that this flag should be flown in their country. It was the only time I ever heard Mustafa question Erdoğan's judgement. 'I used to think he was independent,' he said, 'but perhaps he is just being used by the Americans.'

Such moments of doubt were rare, however. Erdoğan's success, he believed, was rooted in his competent tenure as mayor of Istanbul. The kind of Islam he had championed, he said, was in line with people's values. 'It's a moderate interpretation of Islam, not like in Pakistan or Afghanistan. And people are happy with this. People were at first afraid that Erdoğan would introduce a radical interpretation of Islam, but it was seen that he didn't do that. People can still drink alcohol.'

Downstairs, the TV was usually set to a loyal channel – though perhaps this didn't say much in itself because by that time most of the channels were loyal. The voice of President Erdoğan frequently issued from it in a rolling boom, muted but instantly recognisable, addressing some rally for one of the elections that seemed so numerous in those years as to blend into one endless frenetic campaign.

His popularity in the café also had something to do with the fact Erdoğan had practically grown up in the area. Among the collage of football photos was one of him posing with a group of the club members back when he was mayor of Istanbul in the 1990s. He had grown up on the other side of the Golden

Horn in a community called Kasımpaşa, similar to Tokludede, and many of the old men sitting at the *okey* tables had known him before his political days, either as an opponent or teammate on the football pitch. As a teenager and young man, Erdoğan had played semi-professional football for a string of local clubs. His family had moved to the city from the Black Sea region in the 1930s; his father had been a boat captain on one of the skiffs that plied the Golden Horn.

One of the old men, Yusuf, showed me a black and white photo on his phone of Camıaltıspor, the amateur side in which they'd played together as teenagers. Erdoğan was in the back row, a lanky kid half a head taller than the rest with a wavy side parting. He was almost unrecognisable apart from a certain jut of the lower lip that lent him the air of defiance that he still retained. Yusuf said he was a good striker, but there was nothing to suggest he would go on to do great things. If there was anything remarkable about him, he recalled, it was his piety. He was the only member of the team who left during training to pray at the appointed times.

The known facts of Erdoğan's youth are scant given the wealth of books written about him, the most recent of which are a crop of fawning hagiographies that obscure as much as they reveal: 'holy scriptures' in the words of Mustafa Hoş, a journalist who wrote his own book about Erdoğan. 'These books of compliments are either approved by Erdoğan or the circle close to him,' Hoş wrote. 'But in spite of this the stories and rumours keep changing, because as Erdoğan rises higher, more and more of his human frailties are erased.'

The books nonetheless agree on a few details. Young Tayyip Erdoğan grew up in relative poverty with a strict and pious father. 'On the weekends,' according to one of the earlier and more even-handed accounts, 'little Tayyip used to walk to Eminönü from Kasımpaşa and sell candies and water he bought

around the football field in his childhood neighbourhood . . .
After that, he bought stale *simit*s, which normally would cost
10 kuruş, for 2.5 kuruş and brought them home, and his mother
used to steam them to make them softer. He then sold them
for 5 kuruş the next day.' During the week he attended a boarding
school in Fatih, just above the hill from Ayvansaray, a religious
vocational school known as an *imam hatip*, a clear sign of his
family's religious conservatism.

He became involved in Islamist politics as a teenager, attending
the National Turkish Students' Union, the youth group for
Turkey's main Islamist party, and juggled his education, football
and politics well into his twenties. He also worked at IETT, the
Istanbul public transportation company. He had a talent for
public speaking and reciting poetry, and was taken in hand by
Necmettin Erbakan, the leader of Turkey's Islamist movement,
who would go on to become the country's first Islamist prime
minister in 1996. Before the 1980 coup, Erdoğan served on the
board of the Istanbul youth arm for Erbakan's National Salvation
Party until it was banned following the coup. Later he would
rise up the structure of its successor party before eventually being
chosen as its candidate for Istanbul mayor in 1994. He won the
election against a wide field of other candidates with just over
25 per cent of the vote, stunning much of the country, and
heralding the rise of political Islam. Istanbul would prove to be
his springboard to national politics.

———

One time when I was up in Serdar's apartment I learned something which put a new perspective on the Tokludede development.
He had come from Friday prayers a couple of hours earlier,
where he had visited the grave of a nephew who had died eight
months earlier in a car crash north of the city near the Black

Sea. He'd been twenty-eight years old. Now Serdar was slumped in a chair, drunk; I wondered whether he'd been in that state during prayers or had attained it since.

'August, September, October, November, December, January, February, March . . .' He recited the months that had since elapsed since this tragedy like the words of a litany, muttering disjointedly about grief and faith. 'You just can't, you know, you can't explain it to anyone . . . I am consoling myself – is it an excuse? No . . . My sister is writing prayers. Her belief is so strong, stronger than I am.'

Salih talked over him, explaining what had happened: 'The car was parked on the hard shoulder, up by the third bridge, on the road to Şile. The truck struck him from behind; his neck was broken and he had a brain haemorrhage. They couldn't keep him alive for one day.'

It was only now, though, talking about Serdar's nephew, that I learned something which put a different complexion on the Tokludede project. It turned out that the man behind it was Serdar's brother-in-law, the dead boy's father. His name was Ertan Şener, head of SNR Holding, a business empire that included two shipyards, a fleet of tankers, and various other enterprises in tourism and construction. They were a local family; Ertan's father, Niyazi, had run a restaurant in Ayvansaray before going into shipping, and Ertan himself had married Serdar's sister, a Tokludede girl. In the past he'd occasionally come into the teahouse and play cards. Ertan owned the building, and had provided the premises rent-free as a gesture of goodwill after the old place was knocked down as part of the project, which also explained how Serdar ended up living there. So Tokludede, it turned out, had been consumed by one of its own. Ertan Şener had been one of the names İsmet had singled out in his suicide note.

'He's a commoner,' said Salih. 'He lost his ring finger – a

machine broke when he was at sea. He knows about that kind of stuff, he worked on the ships since he was young.' The Şeners' empire had grown out of the Golden Horn, where they'd started out with a few small boats transporting oil, which they had built up into a fleet. Now they were politically connected and close to the government, although Şener was a private man and didn't like being seen with the politicians in public. I repeatedly tried to contact Ertan Şener to interview him via his personal assistant, but received no response. I also emailed him about İsmet's claim that the developers working on the project cut corners in terms of construction codes, but again received no response.

Initially no one had known the Şeners were behind the redevelopment. When Salih found out it was the Şeners who were behind the whole thing, however, he went to Ertan and asked him frankly what he should do. 'I wasn't sour, like, "You're taking my property away", I was more like, "What do you recommend?" . . . We discussed it face to face and he himself told me not to sell until the very last moment. So I went down every road, knocked on every door.' Although he railed against the injustice of the whole process, Salih was also oddly sanguine about it. He wondered whether Ertan had come up with the idea himself, or whether he'd been brought in by the government because his local connections would smooth the process. His anger was directed more at Ertan's underlings – the foreman of the building site, and so on – who acted 'more kingly than the king', as the saying went. The Şeners were among the winners of the economic liberalisation put in train after the 1980 coup, and now here they were years later, coming back to devour their community, or clean it up, or bury its corpse, depending on how you looked at it.

Salih believed that the redevelopment project had been inevitable. 'I always say that if he didn't buy it somebody else would have done. It would be accomplished one way or another.' He mentioned Çalık, another big conglomerate with close government ties. 'I don't know anything about Çalık, if I came across them, clashed with them. If Ertan did not buy it, Çalık would, Ülker would, and if someone has to buy it, better it's my friend.'

When Ertan's son died, Salih had called by the company offices to offer his condolences. 'Inwardly I prayed that Ertan would not be there. I didn't want to have to say it to his face. I have sons too. When you imagine it, it's a pain beyond comprehension.' The tragedy wiped away whatever anger he had felt for him: 'When there is real pain or real struggle we know how to become one heart, one fist.'

4

The Cannon Gate

More than anywhere else along the walls, the gate of Topkapı retained a sense of arrival, of lying at the threshold of a great city. In fact it was just one synapse in Istanbul's sprawling public transport network, but the other gates were either blocked up, redundant, or had narrow roads pressed through them that were clogged with vehicles, whereas at Topkapı a wide cobbled footpath passed through the walls connecting a tram stop outside to an open-air bus station within, and throughout the day there was lively foot traffic between the two. Like a deep sea vent, this constant flow of people attracted its own ecosystem. A row of harried-looking vendors sold tobacco, lighters and knock-off watches from folding wooden stands, ready to be snapped up at a moment's notice if the municipal police appeared. Rubbish collectors hauling huge trolleys behind them picked through the bins, and the wide grass verge in front of the outer wall was a favoured outdoor drinking spot where groups of men sat alone, in pairs, or sometimes in rowdy groups whenever the weather permitted. On the breastwork of the former moat stood a gnarled terebinth tree, its trunk charred where someone had lit a fire against it, still doggedly alive; sometimes a Turkish flag fluttered in its branches. Amid the flow of people it seemed more solid than the walls, black and emphatic, cast in iron.

In Byzantine times Topkapı had been called the Gate of St Romanus, after a nearby church, but its later name – the 'Cannon Gate' – came from the time of the siege. It was here that Mehmet set up his great bombard. The gate's location on the valley sloping down to the nearby Lycus river gave the attackers a height advantage, and it was widely known as the weakest point on the walls. Both Mehmet and the Byzantine commanders realised that this was the place where the siege would be won or lost, and both pitched their headquarters opposite it.

I went there in all seasons; on winter days when commuters painted a path of muddy slush through the snow and old men picked their way crow-like in heavy coats; in the damp heat of summer, when lanky Kurdish or Afghan boys slouched from the handles of their rubbish carts and the sweating vendors splashed water across their pates; in the spring and autumn – Istanbul's long goldilocks seasons – when the drinkers gathered in roaring packs, bottles of *rakı* sparkling in ice buckets cut from plastic water flagons. There were a couple of liquor stores nearby, and in the warmer months these sent out 'waiters' to take orders. The ground all about was carpeted with bottle caps, cigarette butts, and the husks of sunflower seeds. In the corner of one tower was a stinking patch of mud where everyone went to piss.

Once I noticed a burly man with a microphone and camera crew interviewing people among the crowds near the tram stop. He had a neatly trimmed beard and wore a puffa jacket, large aviator sunglasses, and a kind of Central Asian wool and leather hat. I recognised him vaguely as a YouTube personality, a provocateur and entertainer who made video content for an Islamist TV station. He had formerly been a correspondent for the Islamist Akit TV, part of a media group known for its toxic brew of conspiracy theories, racism and zealotry. Its newspaper counterpart had once run a crossword puzzle with a photo of Hitler in it, the solution to which was the phrase 'We long for you'. As Turkey's media environment withered under sustained government assault, the voice of this formerly marginal media group filled the growing void. It was like an attack dog for Erdoğan's government, broadly upholding the direction of travel but impatient at its master's pace.

Once it had been the pious who had felt pressured and marginalised in public, but now the man in the Central Asian cap, Bülent Yapraklıoğlu, was turning the tables. In his videos he liked to troll and bully those on the other side of the barricades: leftists, feminists, secularists and so on. One of his favourite locations was Istiklal – the long pedestrian thoroughfare on the other side of the Golden Horn – where in the evenings he could count on finding some liberal types whose tongues had been loosened by a drink or two. The encounters – edited and uploaded online – made for uncomfortable viewing, especially when bystanders assembled behind them with glowering looks: the moral majority bearing down in judgement on whatever suspect opinions Yapraklıoğlu had goaded from his target. Sometimes these bystanders weighed in on his side: 'A journalist girl, who says the state is a murderer, is cut down to size by a patriot' crowed one caption; 'When a "deist" comes face to face with a Muslim' read another. At that time Turkey's Islamists were particularly vexed by 'deists', the growing number of mainly young people who described themselves as believers in only a vague and general sense.

When I later trawled his videos, it turned out that Topkapı was another favourite haunt of his, but here he sought out milder fare, testing people on their knowledge of religious matters and posing moral questions. On this particular day he was asking people to name the miraculous birds that had rescued the Ka'aba from an invading army. Occasionally the sound of his shrill laugh reached us. Some of the people he spoke to knew the answer, others made a show of racking their brains and then apologised that they'd forgotten; most simply shrugged him off with baffled indifference and continued on their way. Eventually he found a young African man – he might have been Somalian – who not only knew the name of the birds – *ababil* – but could recite the relevant sura of the Quran from memory. He continued reciting for about fifteen minutes without pause, his fine wavering tenor rising and falling with the wind and reaching the men drinking by the moat.

It was possible, in moments like this, to imagine Turkey as a country in a kind of harmonious tension, a place where one man could sing the Quran while another sipped his beer, and both could go about their lives in freedom within the security of a greater social compact. It was a possibility hinted at by the kind of cohesion I had seen among the men of Tokludede; it was also a vision of the country's future that many of Erdoğan's supporters had encouraged in the early days – mainly the self-styled liberals and who saw his rule as a process of normalisation after the country's restrictive past. They might point at the men drinking, sometimes in their dozens, and hold it up as an example of tolerance, of something that would not even be permitted in many Western countries.

Public space had always been a battlefield in Turkey; the language of architecture, the positioning of mosques and stadiums, the razing of neighbourhoods – all these were aimed at imposing a particular structure on society. Yapraklıoğlu's aim was not so much normalisation as a turning of the tables, a reconquest of the public space in which the secularists had once breathed freely and the pious had not.

———

I met a young man named Kader at the AK Party's local headquarters, a surprisingly shabby fourth-floor office that smelled of cigarette smoke and looked out onto the broad thoroughfare of Vatan Caddesi – 'Homeland Avenue' – the long thoroughfare punched through the walls near Topkapı which was dominated by the sprawling police headquarters building. Kader was twenty-four years old, burly with a thick beard and woolly jumper with the sleeves pulled up to his elbows; he looked like the captain of a fishing boat. He had an easy-going, instantly likeable manner, and spoke with an openness that was rare among AK Party apparatchiks. He had grown up in a village in Kahramanmaraş, a province of dried peppers and cotton fields tucked in the armpit of Anatolia. His first name, Kader, meant 'destiny', and was given to him in memory of a cousin. This other Kader, who was from the same village, had graduated from high school and qualified to enter university, an impressive achievement for a village child at that time. He and his friends had decided to go swimming at a nearby dam to celebrate his success, but instead of going to their usual spot they chose a different place. Kader was first in; he dived headlong into the water and never resurfaced.

'It was mud,' Kader told me. 'It took them three months to find his body.'

He mentioned it almost casually, but I couldn't shake the image afterwards: the feted boy aloft one moment, suffocating the next, the instant exchange of air for earth, flight for interment. It struck me as a lurid illustration of life in an Anatolian village: either you escape or are sucked in to remain forever among the poplars and the wide sky, its beauty and openness as deceptive as the mirror of a silted lake.

Kader had grown up in the same village, the third of six children; his father was a tailor and the family kept a herd of goats. But he had left and moved to Topkapı, where he was now the deputy head of the AK Party's youth arm in Fatih. The story of how he had arrived there began with another macabre misfortune: when he was young his mother was crushed by a poplar tree cut down by the village carpenter, breaking her back. His father was tending the livestock and by the time he was alerted she had already been taken to the local hospital, bumping along in a motorcycle sidecar, draped in a blanket. Kader remembered arriving there with his father just in time to see her being stretchered out the front door and transferred to another hospital. He remembered seeing blood dripping from the stretcher. Soon afterwards she was transferred again to a state hospital in Ankara, and there she would remain for years, bed-bound and paralysed.

He was six at the time, and his mother's accident upended his childhood. His father moved to Ankara to be near her, leaving the family in the care of Kader's eldest sister, ten years his senior, and his blind grandmother. Even at that age, he felt that his parents' absence imposed a burden on himself, the eldest son. It made him studious and hard-working, and from a young age he began taking jobs out of school hours to supplement the family income.

'I worked in a job every summer since I was in fifth grade, once the school goes on holiday. I did every job you can think of: butchering, making spices, working in a cotton factory, ice-cream making.'

Eventually, after six years had passed, his mother was discharged and his parents returned home. She remained almost completely paralysed. At the age of fifteen Kader performed well in his high school exams; the grades he achieved would allow him to get into a better school than any of those in his local area, and so his parents decided to send him to Istanbul to live with his older sister, who was now married there. That's how he arrived at Topkapı.

His mother's accident left Kader with a lingering sense of outrage, from the sight of that blood dripping from the stretcher (why had she still been bleeding?) to her long absence. But he was especially horrified at the state she had come home in: she was suffering from bedsores that were festering, having been left untreated, and sometime later they discovered a long knitting needle embedded in her shoulder. They realised it was from the blanket that a neighbour had thrown over her when she was put on the motorbike in the immediate aftermath of the accident. In all her years in hospital it had never been discovered.

'Nobody noticed it,' said Kader. 'Think about how terrible the situation has to be to allow that? She went through MRI scans, lung and spinal cord X-rays . . . No one saw it.'

Turkey's health system at the time was a mess: an underfunded patchwork developed through haphazard and often conflicting reforms of successive governments. Its backbone was a series of social insurance programmes covering civil servants and various private and public industries paid for by employers and employees jointly but administered by the government, which could – and often did – plunder these insurance funds for other purposes. There were various elite hospitals for the small segment of society that could afford private insurance, and a 'green card' system through which the poorest could access free healthcare – but not free medication, except through a prohibitively bureaucratic process. Between these extremes were large numbers of people who had no kind of health coverage at all, and on the eve of Erdoğan's rise to power more than a quarter of all healthcare costs were met by the patients. Kader's family was on the green card system, which meant a free bed for his mother in a state hospital, but even then some elements of her treatment needed to be paid for.

When the AK Party came to power a few years after Kader's mother's accident, one of their first priorities was healthcare reform. The system was in crisis, and by fixing it they could please a number of their constituencies at a time. The government enjoyed a hefty parliamentary majority, but it was largely as a result of a quirk of the electoral system, and their true power was fragile: they had only won 34 per cent of the vote and much of the electorate remained sceptical of them. In those early years strong Western backing was crucial to Erdoğan in countering his domestic foes, and he cleaved closely to his stated aim of EU membership as well as sticking to a programme of economic reform mandated by the IMF during a bailout following the economic crisis a couple of years earlier. Many in the West – obsessed with Islamic radicalism in the wake of the 9/11 attacks – saw in Erdoğan's politics a synthesis of moderate Islam and democracy that they hoped would serve as a template for other Muslim countries. Time would give its judgement on the various elements of this so-called 'Turkish Model', but the area in which the AK Party's embrace of it would prove most zealous and lasting was its commitment to full-throated privatisation and marketisation, the so-called neo-liberal system that was ascendant in the West.

Turkey had been moving down this path since the 1980 coup, but the AK Party turbocharged it. Radically expanding a programme of privatisation offered them both the chance to please and impress the Western politicians and economists whose positive perception were an important crutch for Erdoğan at that time, and also to reward its domestic financial backers by selling off state assets and expanding its own supportive economic elite.

Healthcare reform was low-hanging fruit which offered the government the chance to please the millions of people who were being failed by the existing system, and to the delight of their Western supporters, they largely followed a neo-liberal blueprint developed by the World Bank. It took relatively little investment and a few practical reforms to improve upon the dire situation they inherited. The plethora of existing insurance schemes were streamlined and put under the direct control of the Ministry of Health. Compulsory universal health insurance was introduced, to which every citizen had to contribute, with the poorest exempt. The state matched this to the sum of a quarter of the monthly contributions, and small out-of-pocket payments were paid for hospital visits and medications, which were justified as a way of preventing needless visits; people with defined medical conditions or serious illnesses were exempt from these fees. Meanwhile, new hospitals constructed in alliance with the private sector on a build-operate-transfer model sprung up at an extraordinary pace. Between 2002 and 2015, around four hundred new hospitals were opened, three quarters of which were private. Public satisfaction with the health system increased from 40 per cent in 2001 to nearly 75 per cent a decade later. The editor-in-chief of the *Lancet* praised Erdoğan's government for overseeing a 'remarkable revolution in health'.

———

Now a high school student in Istanbul, Kader found life in the neighbourhood of Topkapı lonely and bewildering. For the first year, his sister banned him from leaving home apart from to go to school. 'The walls were a place where drugs were rampant,' he recalled. 'They were open and deserted so you could do anything . . . My family were saying, this would happen, that would happen. I wasn't hearing good things.' The apartment

building where he lived felt isolating. He didn't know his neighbours or other children in the area, and he missed the warmth
of his village in Kahramanmaraş. 'When I came here, the people
who lived in the same apartment building didn't even say hello.
I found this the hardest. You have to call someone and ask if
they are free before you pay a visit. There's nothing like this in
Kahramanmaraş. You go to someone's house the moment you
feel like it. The household is always prepared for guests. Someone
can pop in for a plate of food anytime.'

At some point he became aware that there was a first-class
hospital only a few minutes' walk from his home; connected to
Istanbul University, Çapa Hospital was one of the top-flight
institutions that Erdoğan's reforms had opened up to people like
Kader's mother. He and his sister suggested that she come to
Istanbul and seek treatment there.

'When my mother visited the hospital they took her to the
short-stay unit for one month and there was an 8 per cent
progress in her condition. She started to feel her legs and that
was after six years in Ankara with nothing happening. When
we touched the soles of her feet she responded.' His parents,
amazed by this progress, moved to Istanbul a year later to
continue his mother's treatment and took an apartment in the
same building as Kader's sister. Because she was registered as
disabled, the local AK Party-controlled municipality began
sending the family regular food packages.

'Butter, sugar, chickpeas, pasta – that sort of thing,' said Kader.
'She didn't apply for it but they kept sending it.' They also sent
her, free of charge, something she had never had before: a
wheelchair. When his sister had a baby, they sent free nappies.
The solidarity provided by Erdoğan's party reminded Kader of
the village community network whose absence he felt so keenly
in Istanbul. 'People are inclined to choose things that speak to
them in these kinds of organisations. If I didn't find anything

that spoke to me I wouldn't be here. There is more solidarity and charity towards the public and the nation [in the AK Party] – I've seen it. It's another version of our solidarity in the village.'

After he turned eighteen and reached voting age, he decided to cast his vote for the party at the next general election. But he had a problem: he had recently moved back to Kahramanmaraş to attend university but was still registered as living in Istanbul. In Turkish election law there was no postal voting and you had to physically cast your ballot in the district you were registered in. He didn't have enough for the ticket fare back to Istanbul. He called the local AK Party headquarters in Fatih and asked what to do.

'I said I was a student in Kahramanmaraş and had no money. They said give us a minute. I said OK and they directed me to someone called İlyas. He said, "Go to the Kahramanmaraş bus station, we've bought you a round-trip ticket." Then he said, "Call me back from this number once you are done," and hung up. I was shocked, I was thinking he didn't even know me. He just said come. First I thought it was a joke. I hesitated. I went to the bus station and the ticket was there.'

The value of the return ticket was more than 160 Turkish lira, equivalent to around £60 at the time; it was a fifteen-hour, 650-mile journey each way, and Kader took it just to vote. While in Istanbul, he called the AKP office to thank this İlyas, who had got him the tickets, but couldn't get through, so he decided to drop in at the headquarters in person.

'I said I was looking for someone called İlyas. They directed me to him and that's how I met him. I said, "You did this for me and I would like to return the favour" . . . I said I wanted to be a volunteer and make things happen. It was a duty of loyalty for me.'

That was the 2011 general election. Four years earlier, Erdoğan had already won a second term more convincingly than the first, with just over 46 per cent of the vote, a hard feat to exceed. However, they did it, winning a fraction under 50 per cent against a field of three significant opposition parties and a number of smaller ones. For Kader, there was an added resonance to the victory. The defeated opposition leader, who had recently been elected as head of the People's Republican Party – a mild, greying, bespectacled former bureaucrat called Kemal Kılıçdaroğlu – had headed up one of the largest public healthcare providers during the pre-Erdoğan era: it was the organisation which oversaw the hospital in Ankara where his mother had languished for all those years.

———

Sometimes when I was visiting the walls and found myself at a loose end, especially on grey days when the weather was oppressive, I would go to a large domed building that sat in a park across the highway opposite the Topkapı Gate. It was the 'Panorama 1453' museum, the centrepiece of which was a 360-degree mural and diorama representing the siege. After a series of rooms covering its history and context, you ascended some stairs into the dome and found yourself standing beneath a painted sky. There was something magical and restful about the quality of the light there – like the glowing of billboards at dusk – which was at odds with the violent scenes depicted on the mural itself. To one side were the walls, the same ones that stood outside, now draped with tattered Byzantine flags and vignettes of battle unfolding along them: here, a group of Turkish soldiers was scaling a ladder as defenders poured burning oil on them; there was the celebrated Hasan – the Janissary who was said to have been the first to plant the Ottoman standard on the battlements before he was cut down; over there were great breaches blown out by the cannons, with soldiers skirmishing over the rubble of the masonry. In the foreground was Mehmet himself, poised on horseback surveying the scene. On the floor of the dome were replicas of the great cannons, along with huge polystyrene cannon-balls waiting to be loaded into them. There was usually a steady stream of visitors, mostly Turkish or Arab tourists. Of course the irony struck me that here they were looking at fake cannonballs and painted walls when the real things were lying only a couple of hundred metres away, crumbling and moss-covered and visited by almost no one. What lay behind this indifference – or some-times even hostility – to the past? What was this preference for ersatz history over the real thing?

One of the defining features not just of the Erdoğan era but of the modern Turkish Republic had been a rejection of a complex and often painful heritage in favour of a simpler, ideol-ogised version of it. Every nation performs this kind of myth-making, but rarely with the kind of destructive, amnesiac eagerness I had seen in Turkey. Turkish history was certainly complex and painful. At the extreme end was the trauma and shame of the Armenian Genocide, an act of mass slaughter which helped lay the groundwork for a culturally and confes-sionally unified Turkish state. The mass population exchange with Greece a few years later, in which millions more people were forced to move between the two countries, served the same purpose. These were communities which had co-existed, if not always in harmony then at least in mutual tolerance, for gener-ations as part of the multi-ethnic polity of the Ottoman Empire.

Since that time, the monuments of these now-vanished peoples had often been the target of neglect and sometimes outright destruction. Sometimes they were seen as simply foreign and therefore not worth maintaining unless there was some overriding tourism potential, in other instances there was a sometimes literal fear that if evidence of these people was not erased they might return and reclaim what had been theirs; these old monuments were a tacit reminder that Turkey had not always been there, that it had nearly not been born at all. This existential national fear, which could be likened to that of Israel, was rooted in the Treaty of Sèvres that the allied European powers tried to impose on the defeated Ottomans after the First World War, which would have handed control of parts of Anatolia to other nations with foreign zones of influence over remaining Turkish territory. It was only Atatürk's War of Independence that forced its abandonment.

This hostility to a multi-cultural, multi-confessional past was partly rooted in this abiding fear of dismemberment. However, in the early Republican era, it was not just the non-Muslim past that was swept away but the Ottoman past too. Atatürk and his followers condemned the later sultans as feckless and effete, having neglected the Turkish nation and people in favour of a cosmopolitanism that had almost seen them destroyed. Istanbul was the essence both of the old empire and its institutions and of this despised cosmopolitanism, which was one reason why Atatürk moved the national capital to the backwater town of Ankara, deep in Anatolia. A new Turkic version of history was produced that was often comical in its tenuousness, and the Ottoman past was minimised and downplayed.

The conquest of the city, however, was an event of such unambiguous achievement that it was integrated into this new history rather than ignored, and was even listed in an early Republican textbook as the founding date of the nation. But it was only on the fifth centenary of the Conquest in 1953 that it began to edge towards the centre of Turkey's popular historical consciousness. The centenary fell soon after the country's first multi-party elections, when the harshest and most unpopular elements of the Kemalist regime were being softened; celebrating it allowed for the synthesis of the Republican version of history with older Ottoman heritage which many Turks had never really wanted to reject. From that time onwards annual celebrations became more and more prominent.

In Erdoğan's Turkey, the Ottoman past would be fully rehabilitated and glorified as part of a new national narrative that sought to reconnect Turkey to its Islamic heritage, and even more so to its imperial heritage. It was both a way of justifying a more assertive foreign policy, and restoring a sense of national confidence that never recovered since the collapse of the empire. When I looked at the faces of the Turkish soldiers in the 1453 panorama they struck me as strangely modern; there was none of the hairiness or dirtiness with which my own culture often seemed to depict people of the past. One man could have been a shopkeeper in my neighbourhood, another the doorman of my apartment block.

Within this scheme the walls occupied an ambivalent place. They were the most powerful reminder of the martial power and endurance of the now-vanished society that had built them, but also the stage for the Ottoman Turks' greatest triumph. In a collection of essays on Istanbul, the early Republican poet and author Yahya Kemal wrote of how he spent three years walking the walls 'tasting the conquest of Istanbul'. He goes on:

[T]hat last siege inhabits these stones and cypresses like a ghost that has still not faded. Although this wall had seen so many things before – so many waves of barbarian attacks had broken against its stones, the blood of so many different races had spilled in its moat, so many different colours of enemy tents were pitched before it over the centuries – it is as if all these invasions have been rendered into obscure myths, and only the final arrival of the Conqueror is reality.

I sometimes wondered if their neglected state was the result of this ambivalence; they were a token of possession, important for what they represented rather than what they were – like the bloodied sheet traditionally hung from a house's window to mark the consummation of a wedding night. Probably though, it was simply that they were too big to easily repair, and too important to destroy.

A short walk across the park from the Panorama Museum brought me to the neighbourhood of Merkezefendi, the nucleus of which formed in the sixteenth century around the shrine of a renowned saint who established a centre of prayer, study and healing there. It lay near an older Byzantine holy spring dating from at least the sixth century AD. Various Islamic orders had established themselves nearby in sympathy and competition with this older shrine. The location beyond the walls lent itself to the presence of the mystical and heretical sects that arrived from Anatolia, which found followers in the city but were kept at a distance from the heart of orthodox power.

Merkezefendi was among a dizzying array of places evoked by Turkey's great modernist writer Ahmet Hamdi Tanpınar in his essay, 'Istanbul', written in the 1940s, where he grappled with the wrenching transformation of the city during the course of his lifetime. '[I]t shines among my childhood memories,' he wrote, 'like a heavenly throne that emanates a dark, awe-inspiring spirituality.'

In the course of the twentieth century, however, this entire area fell into a state of neglect, after the religious sects and Sufi orders that had given it life were shuttered and disbanded by official decree. Tanpınar wrote:

> The trees that once made this place of pilgrimage so dark have been cut down, the convent cells around the courtyard have crumbled away, the well has been covered; in short all the elements that

created an air of mystery have vanished. The only remains are
several of the dead in a bare unadorned room like a barracks and
a dervish cell of fasting and prayer, its once-gilded grating worn
away, overlooking the basin of the sacred spring. Behind this grille,
Merkez Efendi would plunge into deep meditation, reading the
Koran from end to end, passing long, lonely winter nights until
daylight, chained to endless prayer, watching the coming and going
of the fish to which, as a child, I was taught to throw food, and
the water from the underground spring the colour of laurel green
with violet streaks and silver, gleams like the eye of a frog.

Tanpınar's essay is at once encyclopaedic in its detail of the city
– its neighbourhoods, festivals, seasons, saints, artists and musicians – but also has a freewheeling richness of association and
description that convey something of the enormity of what
Istanbul lost in the transition from empire to republic.

'In the interval of fifteen years between 1908 and 1923,
[Istanbul] completely lost its old identity,' wrote Tanpınar. '[It]
was swept away by a constitutional revolution, three great wars,
a great number of successive fires large and small, financial crises,
the abolition of the Ottoman Empire, and our eventual accept-
ance in 1923 of a civilisation on whose threshold we had stood
hesitating for a hundred years.'

The misfortunes of the nearby Yenikapı Dervish Lodge offered
one of the most forceful illustrations of this decline. It had been
one of the largest complexes in the city run by the Mevlevi Sufi
order, the so-called 'whirling dervishes'. As a centre of worship
and musical study it had produced some of the most famous
composers and musicians of the Ottoman era. Sufism, a family
of mystical Islamic sects with roots in Anatolia and Iran, drew
on philosophical concepts similar to those of Buddhism, which
may have distantly influenced it. Through their whirling, the
semazen – ritual dancers – sought to shed the ego and reach a

state of perfection. Observers of the ceremony were considered participants in the act of worship. The vitality of this culture was such that after the lodge complex was devastated by a fire in 1906, it was rebuilt and expanded within five years, to include a mosque, kitchen, pantry, dining hall, men's and women's apartments, cells where the dervishes spent time in prayer, as well as a domed *semahane*, a large balconied hall for the performance of the *sema* ritual, the whirling ceremony for which the dervishes were most famous.

But within two decades all this ended with the closure of the Sufi lodges and the ban on activities associated with them. The lavishly appointed complex sank into a state of decay and the community that inhabited and sustained it was forced to disband. It was used as a storage depot and then a student dormitory, before again being devastated by fire in 1961. After that its last habitable portions became an orphanage, before fire again ravaged it in the 1990s.

During its orphanage years, another of Turkey's great twentieth-century writers, Yaşar Kemal, would describe its decrepit state. '[B]eyond the walls, a muddy road ran straight west through the graveyards,' he wrote. 'At the left-hand end of that road was an old building. In the past it was a dervish lodge. A wide courtyard, mud within dirty old fallen walls . . . Its great ornamented ceilings were old, the gilding peeled. Who knows how beautiful, how well-cared for this place was when it was a dervish lodge? Now it is a ruin, and orphaned, outcast children are raised, so to speak, in this hovel.'

On the blustery wet afternoon when I crossed the park from the Panorama Museum to Merkezefendi, all evidence of neglect had been swept away and the neighbourhood stood gleamingly restored. The stones of the shrine of Merkez Efendi once again shone white; fresh wooden window frames lined its once-empty portals, and a small row of stone Ottoman houses nearby now hosted a series of bustling restaurants and cafés. Beyond it my destination, the dervish lodge, was also restored, and now the entire complex was once again occupied, not by the Mevlevi order, but by the Alliance of Civilizations Institute of Fatih Sultan Mehmet University, a recently created academic institution funded using an old charitable foundation set up centuries earlier by Mehmet himself. At the arched marble entrance flanked by low twin domes, students passed in and out through a row of metal turnstiles. Fresh life breathed into what had once been a ruin from a bygone era, a mixture of tradition and modernity: it was a showcase for the AK Party's vision of Turkey.

I had gone to meet cousins Nagihan and Zehra, the former a professor of literature and the latter an MA graduate, also in literature. Nagihan had begun working there in about 2014, but by a strange coincidence their first visit to the place had been a few years earlier, not long after its restoration, when they had watched a performance of the *sema* under the newly re-gilded dome of the *semahane*. The matters that had drawn the cousins there were more earthly than spiritual. Zehra had recently moved to Istanbul to begin her undergraduate studies and was looking for scholarship funding to help support her. The pair had been invited to the ritual by an imam with Sufi leanings whose mosque might be able to provide some money; he was a friend of Nagihan's father, himself a retired imam.

'It was so long!' recalled Zehra, a slight young woman with dark eyes and a roman nose, as we sat in one of the cafés that occupied the row of old stone buildings across from the dervish lodge. 'Just the introduction greeting part felt like one hour. I wasn't bored, I was very interested, but I was like, "When are you going to come to the dancing part?" It made me realise there's a whole ethos behind it . . . I did feel that I was part of it. They walked so slowly that it made me reflect on it. It was a very striking experience for me.'

Nagihan was less impressed. 'I don't do Sufi stuff,' she said flatly. 'I find it quite boring, to be perfectly honest. It goes on for about ten minutes and then it repeats itself. I don't have a Sufi bone in my body.'

About twenty years separated the two cousins, and their convergence in academic pursuits had come through very different upbringings. Nagihan had been raised in the wealthy Istanbul neighbourhood of Etiler, where her father had been a local imam; while Zehra had grown up in the Black Sea province of Trabzon, her father a long-distance truck driver and her mother a housewife; she had just won a place to read English Literature at Boğaziçi, arguably the country's most prestigious university. Having got that far, the money issue seemed a minor obstacle. 'My family's income was not high, but I'd got into the best university in the country so there was no scenario of, like, "Oh, I'm not going to study there." I would definitely have found funding somewhere and my family would work something out.'

In fact it was among the least of the obstacles she had faced in her lifetime. When she was thirteen, she won a scholarship to a selective state high school nearly two hours from her home. In order for her to attend, her parents decided to send her to a private boarding house in the city, one of many such institutions that existed to serve children in her position. Like many of these places, the dorm to which she was sent (and it was the only one to choose from) was run by an Islamic order. The religious character of these places would assuage many parents' fears about sending their children away, but it would also allow the order to proselytise to a young and captive audience. Zehra's dorm had no formal role in the children's education but she and the other girls were nonetheless pressured to read the books of the movement's founder and forced to attend 'study' sessions that sometimes went on for three hours, during which outside teachers – 'or preachers, I'd say' – came in to extol the vision of the movement, which called itself Hizmet, meaning 'service'. In Turkey and abroad, it was known more widely as the Gülen Movement.

Like many sects before it, it had spread in the footsteps of a holy man from the depths of Anatolia. Fethullah Gülen had been born in 1941 near the city of Erzurum, where he had worked as a state-appointed imam. His ideas were inspired by those of an earlier reformist theologian, Said Nursi, and he had begun to spread them through a network of private student dormitories and schools in the 1970s. It was distinctive not so much for the contents of its dogma as its cult-like system of indoctrination, secretive hierarchical structure, and its yen for power.

'You must move within the arteries of the system, without anyone noticing your existence, until you reach all the power centres,' Gülen had told his followers in a leaked sermon recorded in 1999. 'You must wait until such time as you have got all the state power, until you have brought to your side all the power of the constitutional institution in Turkey.'

The movement was extraordinarily successful. By the early 2000s it not only ran hundreds of private tutoring centres, dormitories and educational establishments in Turkey, but had expanded across the world, with schools operating in 130 countries, including a network of 100 charter schools in the United States. Its publicly avowed ideas included interfaith dialogue, globalism and a heavy emphasis on STEM education, along with a slightly incongruous dash of Turkish nationalism. This odd cocktail seemed to have been brewed in order to maximise its reach both at home and abroad. Its male followers were clean-shaven, spoke flawless English, and espoused pro-Western ideas. Its schools, especially in the poorer countries of Africa and Central Asia, gained a reputation for academic excellence that allowed it to forge links with the governing elites of many of the countries where it operated. To outsiders, especially in the West, the Gülen Movement appeared to be a welcome brand of 'moderate' Islam, although to those in Turkey it often seemed that this public face was one contrived to appeal to outsiders, and the worldview of its broader membership – while not radical in their context – contained veins of chauvinism and conspiracy-thinking that were widespread in Turkish society. Gülen himself had been recorded delivering anti-Semitic rants as recently as the 1990s. Now an old man, balding with liver spots and sad swollen eyes as if from a lifetime of crying, he lived in a kind of semi-self-imposed exile. Gülen lived in a closely guarded compound in Saylorsburg, Pennsylvania, granting audiences to close followers and favoured pilgrims.

There was no roll of members and the movement claimed to eschew politics, but those who had left it spoke of a strict hierarchical structure, with followers expected to donate a large chunk of their salaries to the cause. In Turkey, where it ran a huge network of schools as well as a large business, mining and media empire, its well-educated acolytes were able to work their way secretly into the arteries of the state and eventually dominate much of the police force and judiciary. It had also formed an alliance with Erdoğan. In their early years in government the two shared a powerful enemy in the old secularist establishment entrenched in the military and judiciary. The AK Party lacked a cadre of educated, professional supporters who could infiltrate and build its power within the bureaucracy. The Gülenists could provide this, and were able to use their infiltration of the police and elements of the courts to launch a series of mass trials targeting the secularists; these were based in large part on dubious or fraudulent evidence, but they helped break their power. In return, Erdoğan turned a blind eye to Gülenist infiltration of the state and created a benign environment for it to flourish.

At the time when Zehra was staying in the dorm, they were a powerful and unaccountable force that inspired fear and hatred in a broad section of society. So ubiquitous and overbearing had the movement's presence become that many Turks simply referred to it as *Cemaat* – 'the Community'.

Zehra's parents hadn't wanted to send her to a Gülenist dormitory, but there was nowhere else available. They knew what might be in store. Her sister, who was four years older, had just gone to university and herself briefly stayed at a Gülenist-run boarding house. After a short while she had complained and asked to leave because the administrators were imposing a 7 p.m. curfew and forcing the girls to read Gülen's works. When her parents decided to move her, the dorm sent two female staff to their home in order to try to convince them to make her stay. Zehra was at home when they visited, and had found the women unpleasantly pushy, and she thought it was odd that they had come all that way in person.

But her family had no option. If Zehra hadn't stayed at the dorm she couldn't have gone to the selective school, and in the end, she boarded there for three years. Among her strongest memories were what she called the 'crying sessions' where the girls were encouraged to share stories of how they had been oppressed or discriminated against, with the teachers trying to drive them into a state of mass hysteria and weeping.

'They'd say, "Ohhh, we had such a bad experience with the seculars," and they would tell us very emotional stories and they would cry, and they'd expect us to cry as well. I liken it to North Korea – they have crying sessions there.' When her parents called up to complain, they were told these sessions were compulsory.

Perhaps her most bitter recollection related to the occasional visits by students from other Gülen-run institutions in the area. One of the main elements of their organisation in Turkey was a countrywide network of hundreds of *dershanes* – private tuition centres that offered supplementary lessons for middle and high-school children. These offered a way for wealthier families to give their children a leg up in Turkey's rigidly exam-focused education system. These *dershane* students were generally from the wealthier social echelon, and no effort was spared in courting them. Sometimes they would be treated to parties and dinners at the dorm's refectory. The meals were generally awful, Zehra recalled, and the girls were banned from going out to buy their own food. However, on these occasions delicious feasts were laid on. Zehra and the others were excluded.

'All the food smells would come through to us but we weren't allowed to join in. Then they would call themselves religious people. It seems funny, but I was very angry with them. They wouldn't invite us to join in the meals, which is totally against Islam: when there is food you have to share it, but they wouldn't share it with us. That was the thing that hurt me most.'

Zehra never succumbed to the brainwashing efforts – though some girls did. She felt that she had been inoculated against this kind of indoctrination earlier in life. It was not so different from the veneration of Mustafa Kemal Atatürk that was encouraged from the very start of the state education system.

'My whole primary school life was spent memorising what Atatürk did, his stories. I mean, I know everything about Atatürk. Everything! . . . This is not right, small kids should not be taught all this. He might be taught as a national leader but not as everything.' She remembers crying for Atatürk every 10th of November, the anniversary of his death. 'And those were genuine feelings of mine. I'd cry for him.'

When she left the dormitory, however, and came to Istanbul, it still wasn't over. Since she'd won a coveted place at arguably the country's top university, the Gülenists stepped up their pursuit of her.

'They were calling every day . . . They made me so uncomfortable. They'd say, "Oh, we're all about Islam, everything for Islam, why don't you be a part of it? If you're not a part of a *cemaat*, you will get lost in the big city" . . . and so on. I had a hard time in liberating myself from them.'

Sometimes they would organise outings for Zehra without telling her in order to try to steamroller her into spending time with them.

'They'd present me with a *fait accompli*: "Today we are going to Bebek." They would call me and say, "We're arranging something for you, we've already done it, we've arranged it, today at 7 p.m."'

Finally they left her alone, but she had friends who were reeled in. 'They use this [desire for] education: people from Anatolia, from small towns, they want to get education in good places, and they'd say, "Turkey is a very secular country and you might lose your religion very easily, because universities are a nest of atheism." That's how they attract families . . . For me that's the most sad part, because these kids, they wanted to get an education and not lose their identity, and that's why they chose them and then they transform their identity into something else completely, they transform their obedience to God to obedience to Fethullah Gülen.'

Nagihan was about fifteen years Zehra's senior. At the time she and Zehra attended the *sema*, she had recently completed a PhD in comparative literature at Heidelberg University in Germany, and was now trawling the academic job market with mounting frustration. Both cousins wore a headscarf, and while Zehra's university allowed this at the time, covered women were still barred from teaching at almost all universities in Turkey. It was one of the reasons Nagihan had chosen to study abroad after completing her undergraduate degree.

'I finished just as the ban was coming in,' she recalled. 'After I graduated, I wanted to get a transcript and they wouldn't let me in with a headscarf, so I had to get a non-headscarfed friend of mine to get it for me.' For the next five summers she did a part-time MA course in the UK, while spending the rest of the time in Istanbul, where she worked as a translator. That experience made for a stark contrast with her home country, where her headscarf effectively barred her from formal academia. 'It was weird,' she said, 'I would be in the UK for six weeks in the summer: you could enter libraries and universities and do anything you wanted, and then you come home and you can't do anything . . . I wrote my whole PhD proposal just using online library catalogues, because I couldn't go to a single library. It was like Alice in Wonderland, that's what I felt like in England.'

Nagihan had grown up in a very different environment from Zehra: in Etiler, an upmarket Istanbul neighbourhood where her father served as a local imam. Despite having grown up in one of the few pious families in an otherwise resolutely secular neighbourhood, she never had a sense that she belonged to a marginalised group.

'I don't think I ever thought that way, really. I had the sense that we did things differently from the people around us, but I had the sense that Turkey was a religious and a Muslim country . . . I was alone. I didn't have a cliquey understanding of who I was.' She had a large extended family of Black Sea relatives who frequently visited. 'There was this whole clan, and my first sense of belonging was to my family rather than other "oppressed Muslim people".'

The important role her father played even in an ostensibly Westernised neighbourhood also helped. 'I knew that people around us weren't really religious, but it was so funny to see

View of the Theodosian land walls at Edirnekapı during the late nineteenth-century

Modern view of the land walls at Ayvansaray, with the Golden Horn estuary in the background

Ismet Hezer outside his old home in Tokludede, prior to its demolition

Forests of apartment blocks proliferate on Istanbul's Anatolian side

Street dogs being fed on the Grande Rue de Péra (İstiklal Caddesi) in the 1920s

Street dogs sleeping on the quayside at Eminönü in 2021

Medallion showing Mehmet II as a young man

Portrait of Mehmet II in old age by Gentile Bellini

Visitors at Istanbul's Panorama 1453 Historical Museum, which celebrates the siege and capture of the city

Recep Tayyip Erdoğan (top row, second from left) during his youth, when he played striker for the Istanbul club Camialtıspor

Erdoğan as prime minister, conferring with members of his AK Party as mass protests were rocking the country in 2013

Ceyda Süngür – 'The Woman in the Red Dress' – is pepper sprayed by a Turkish police officer during the Gezi Park protests in 2013. This image generated widespread outrage, further fueling the demonstrations

Demonstators at the Gezi Park protests, summer 2013

Celebratory flares over Taksim Square on the final night of the Gezi Park protests

The third bridge over the Bosphorus, named after Sultan Selim I 'The Grim', under construction in 2015. It was one of several infrastructure projects that angered the demonstrators

A modern view of the land walls near to Edirnekapı

them come to my dad to ask for advice: all these women dressed up to the nines, knocking on our door saying, "Can I speak to your father?", and then they would sit down – marital problems or whatever . . . They were seeking that kind of guidance, even though they didn't approve of our way of life.'

Nagihan spoke the kind of British English that some foreigners living in the UK could spend a lifetime trying and failing to acquire; she had no trace of a Turkish accent and could seamlessly insert colloquialisms like 'dressed up to the nines' into her speech without one even noticing. In fact she had only lived there full time for a year. After her five summers of doing the part-time MA, she did a one-year MSt in Oriental Studies at Oxford University. She had an obsessive and critical interest in the vagaries of British popular culture, class and politics, jokingly styling herself a 'Britain expert' in mockery of the 'Turkey experts' who were often cited in international media.

Even after she had finished her PhD in Germany, however, the Turkish academic job market was still closed to her as a result of the headscarf ban. It had existed in various guises since the 1970s, inspired by the same secularist ideology that had suppressed the Sufi sects decades earlier. The scope of the prohibition expanded and contracted over time according to the political climate. It didn't only affect universities: the hijab was banned for employees of public institutions, hospitals and schools, preventing covered women from working in whole swathes of the economy. Any pious woman who aspired to a career was forced to choose between her ambitions and her religious principles. At universities in particular, the force of the ban varied over time. Universities, which had a degree of autonomy, often had more leeway in determining what was permissible for their students, which was why Nagihan had been allowed to wear a hijab during her own undergraduate years in the mid-1990s.

In a neighbourhood like the one where Nagihan grew up, the main element of the community had been raised within Atatürk's vision of a secular Turkey, in which religion was a personal matter, and its public expression restricted within bounds set by the state; this group tended to view any displays of public piety that exceeded those limits – especially the political Islamic movement – as a threat that if allowed to run unchecked could transform Turkey into a place like theocratic Iran. On the other side was the greater proportion of Turkey's Sunni Muslims, who had never been assimilated into this new culture and had to a large extent retained a system of traditions and values in which the Islamic faith occupied a natural place in public as well as private life. For almost all of the twentieth century it was the former group which held the levers of power, set the rules of the game, and overwhelmingly constituted the urban middle class that dominated key professions. However, as Nagihan had perceived as a child, this group was in a minority, and whenever Turkish voters had the opportunity to cast their ballots in a fairly contested election, they usually chose parties that sought to shift the needle in favour of a greater public role for Islam.

For a long time Turkey's Islamist movement framed this debate in similar terms to Ottoman traditionalists back in the days of the empire: a struggle between the native culture and a foreign import that brought moral and spiritual corruption, as well as through the rhetoric of anti-imperialism. That was the narrative of Erdoğan's political mentor and predecessor Necmettin Erbakan, whose own Islamist-led coalition was ousted by the military in 1997. It was called the 'post-modern' coup, because no force was used to topple the government, but a memorandum penned by the country's National Security Council which required Erbakan to roll back a series of policies which senior military leaders were undermining secularism. He was left with little choice but to resign shortly afterwards.

In the wake of that disastrous setback, one of the most striking moves of Erdoğan and the early AK Party was to abandon the anti-Western, anti-imperialist elements of Erbakan's politics. He was not, he told the nation, battling Western corruption or the imposition of foreign culture and values, but for the adoption of rights enjoyed in the West: the freedom of worship and expression that had allowed someone like Nagihan to study in the UK and Germany when she was unable to do so in Turkey.

It was his success that, a decade on from that victory, would create the renaissance of Merkezefendi, and the opportunity for Nagihan and Zehra to pursue careers in academia. When Nagihan got her job at the Alliance of Civilizations, she had not even been looking in Turkey, but was pinning her hopes on Europe or the UK. She knew of a couple of headscarfed female academics who commuted from Istanbul to teach at universities in the Anatolian cities of Malatya and Antep, where it was possible, but there was no one in Istanbul. Then she heard from her sister about a covered woman teaching art at a new institution, and that was how she ended up at the renovated dervish lodge: 'At the time, it could well be that there was this art teacher who was the only one in Istanbul, and I was the second, possibly.'

The ethos of the new university was to try to reclaim Turkish higher education from Western influence. The curriculum aimed to include more Turkish, Islamic and other non-Western philosophers and writers than mainstream Turkish universities. Nagihan was measured about how seriously she took it – she didn't see herself as an ideological warrior, and cheerfully admitted that if Boğaziçi, her and Zehra's alma mater, were to offer her a job, she would probably take it.

'It feels superficial,' she said, 'devoting three weeks of your programme to these Islamic philosophers, but when you compare it to what others are doing, it does feel more important.' She mentioned Tanpınar – who we had discussed, and who she taught on her course – as an example of a writer who was ignored even in Turkish literature courses in Turkey. 'If you're talking about psycho-geography, a student from Boğaziçi will give you names from the US and UK, but Tanpınar was writing psycho-geography as well, to just give an example.'

Zehra was similarly ambivalent about the boldness of the university's effort to de-Westernise the curriculum. 'It's still very Western-oriented,' she said. 'Last summer we did two courses: history of thought across civilisations, and the other was history of world civilisations. We were supposed to study five – Indian, Chinese, Islamic, Greek, and Western – but because all the professors are educated in Western universities and Western philosophies, Indian and Chinese were always skipped over without being studied in depth. The professors just read some books so they could tell us about it. They claim to use a non-Western, non-Eurocentric perspective but in fact it still is . . . The syllabus, the assessment, the process of the course: if you want to make a change, you have to make a change in all aspects.'

Both cousins viewed Erdoğan and the AKP as the force that had made their careers and studies in Turkey possible, but they differed in terms of what they felt they owed him. Zehra had agonised and discussed with her family about putting on a headscarf – her father had urged her not to out of fear it could harm her career prospects; but at the time she had done so just before attending university, her religious identity informed her politics.

'I wasn't a very political person, but because of what had happened to the older generation, my sisters and cousins, I felt that for me to be able to live my religious identity the current government needed to be there, or at least a government that resembled them . . . But later I started realising that, you know, what the government is trying to do is use religion. They are taking advantage of my anxiety over the headscarf, and that was my realisation and why I had to distance myself from them.'

For Nagihan, however, the threat that things could go back to the way they had been before seemed ever-present. 'I think my generation doesn't feel secure and it's very strange when we see younger people in their twenties taking things for granted and they really feel that things will stay the same. Maybe it's post-traumatic stress, but I can never be sure that things will really remain this way.

'I think you only get that perspective once you live through it. They don't have that perspective. They think that this will continue as it is, and when they do see the change, they will get to the point where we are, I think.'

One event in particular had given Zehra pause. In the summer of 2013, demonstrations against plans to redevelop a park in the centre of the city morphed into a mass protest movement demanding the government's resignation. 'At the beginning I was going to go to the protests as well because I was also very annoyed by the kind of language that the politicians were using. But then I saw that it was turning into something very different, into a kind of a civil war or something. And then they were banging pots out of their windows: one day I was going home and there was a lady on the balcony and she saw me and she started banging her pot just at me, looking at me. And I was horrified. And I thought, OK, this is something that is turning against us, against me because I wear a headscarf, like a kind of civil war, and after that I thought this should stop immediately.'

5

The Gate of the Riven Tower

I found a copy of a nineteenth-century engraving which showed one of the square turrets of the inner wall split from head to foot, one half leaning at a perilous angle. The location could be readily recognised as what was known in Byzantine times as the Pempton, or Fifth Military Gate. It lay at the lowest point on the walls, the valley where the Lycus river once flowed into the city, giving it its Turkish name, Sulukule Kapısı – the Gate of the Tower-on-the-Water. The leaning half had long since collapsed, but the contour of the crack could still be discerned in what survived. Nothing remained of the bucolic environs depicted in the engraving – the goats clambering on the grassy footings of the outer ramparts and the sheep heading out to rolling pastures beyond – and it was striking that the element most intended to evoke decay and the passage of time had barely altered at all, for even though the riven tower was largely gone, there were new editions of it in any number of other crumbling bastions along the course of the walls. Every few months a friend would send me an article about their collapse, featuring photos of towers or sections of wall lying in formless heaps of jumbled stone and mortar. Heavy rainfall was enough to do it. The walls seemed to be melting away like ice falling from the face of a glacier, and indeed these articles induced in me a very contemporary anxiety: a feeling of terminal depletion, of time running out.

The most serious collapses were caused by earthquakes, which throughout the life of the walls had resulted in more damage than any invading army. The first came only a few years after their construction, when a pair of large quakes struck the city within a few weeks of each other in AD 447 and 448, causing the collapse of more than fifty towers. The response of the city's people and authorities was extraordinary. In the space of just sixty days, the land walls were repaired and expanded with the addition of the outer wall and the moat, giving them the basic form they would retain thereafter.

What drove this extraordinary effort? Only a few months earlier, Attila the Hun had crossed the Danube into south-eastern Europe, ravaging the empire's Balkan provinces and sacking scores of Roman towns and cities. Now Constantinople itself was vulnerable. The ominous timing of the quakes left little doubt that they were the result of God's wrath; in an act of atonement, the Emperor Theodosius II was said to have donned a simple white tunic to walk barefoot, soles bloody, for seven miles around the city.

But his penance was not a substitute for action. The city, its government and people, mounted the kind of massive collective effort that only imminent and existential threat can provoke. The able-bodied populace was mobilised under the direction of the prefect Constantine and the reconstruction carried out. The feat was commemorated in two inscriptions at the centre of the walls, on the Gate of Rhegion. 'In sixty days, by the order of the sceptre-loving Emperor, Constantine the Eparch added wall to wall,' read one in Greek, while the other in Latin bombastically affirmed that: 'By the commands of Theodosius, in less than two months, Constantine erected triumphantly these strong walls. Scarcely could Pallas have built so quickly so strong a citadel.'

After that, maintaining the walls would remain a top civic priority for as long as the empire had the resources to continue to do so. A system was devised whereby the landlords who owned the territory on which different sections stood were responsible for their upkeep, and in exchange could make use of the lower chambers of the towers during peacetime, a system that continued to function for centuries afterwards.

Earthquakes offer a stress test of human societies. To varying degrees the natural input is always the same – the ground shakes – but the output is determined by the society they strike. They measure its capacity for foresight and crisis response, the effectiveness and probity of its state, and the value it places on the lives of its citizens. In its history Istanbul has faced many of these tests. It lies on the North Anatolian Fault, a grinding junction between two tectonic plates that run lengthwise across Anatolia, with the main portion of the landmass slipping westward at an average speed of 20 to 30 millimetres a year. The fault line is distinctive for its regularity: quakes occur in a sequence from east to west, each slip transferring pressure down the line and setting up the next. In Istanbul, you can see an earthquake coming decades away, and large tremors strike the city at intervals of roughly 120 years.

One such sequence of quakes worked its way along the fault line over the course of the twentieth century, culminating in a

7.4 magnitude tremor that hit the coastal city of İzmit in 1999. Such was the expansion of Istanbul's population over the previous fifty years that even though the epicentre was sixty miles from the city, the loss of life and damage both in İzmit and the Istanbul region were catastrophic. The quake struck shortly after 3 a.m. on the morning of 17 August while people were asleep in their beds. The official death toll was eventually calculated at nearly 18,000, though this was widely believed to be an under-count, and 250,000 people were left homeless.

The country had been utterly unready. Despite Turkey's well-known seismic risk, almost no civic training in earthquake preparedness was in place, no disaster relief agency existed, and no official was designated to take charge in such a situation. A national emergency relief fund was discovered to contain the equivalent of four dollars and forty-five cents. For nearly a week after the earthquake the government and state were paralysed. As TV camera crews captured the devastation, ordinary citizens and private companies took the lead in digging through the rubble to rescue those trapped beneath. The quake laid bare Turkey's lax building standards; survivors combing through the remains of recently built apartment blocks found crumbling concrete and thin or rusting steel girders. Sand from the Black Sea, unsuitable for building reinforced structures, had been used in many projects as a cost-cutting measure. Even when rescue operations got underway, the government seemed more concerned with the damage the quake had done to its reputation. Ministers angrily blamed the media for reporting negatively on their efforts, and even ordered one TV station to close for seven days as punishment. The far-right minister of health in the ruling coalition government provoked fury by first claiming that Turkey needed no external assistance, then that blood donated by Greece should not be used and help from Armenia should not be accepted.

The quake marked a breaking point in Turkish politics. It

shattered many people's trust in what Turks called *Devlet Baba* – the 'Father State' – whose extensive and unaccountable power had always been sanctified by its supposedly paternalistic care for the country's citizens. It showed that the state was incapable of upholding its side of this bargain. In fact, the Marmara quake was part of a string of crises that shook the public's trust in the existing system. Three years earlier, in 1996, a fatal car crash occurred in which Istanbul's deputy police chief, a Member of Parliament, and a far-right contract killer wanted by Interpol were discovered to have been travelling in the same vehicle, along with a cache of weapons, a false passport, and thousands of US dollars. When their car collided head-on with a lorry, the first two were killed and the MP, severely injured, would later claim memory loss. The shocking details of the crash provided a fleeting glimpse into the murky dynamics of Turkey's 'deep state', the web of elected officials, security officers and organised criminals that had long exercised a dark influence over the country's politics. It generated widespread public outrage. Two years after the earthquake, the country suffered a devastating economic crash after a banking crisis escalated to engulf the broader economy, causing skyrocketing inflation and wiping 10 per cent off the country's GDP.

While this was happening, change was afoot in the country's Islamist movement that would prove to be of lasting significance. Following the so-called 'post-modern coup' of 1997, the main Islamist political party had been disbanded and its leaders banned from politics. Erdoğan himself had been removed from his post as mayor of Istanbul and was briefly imprisoned. In response to this setback, he and a collection of other young Islamist politicians regrouped and rebranded themselves under a new name, ditching the Islamist label and styling themselves as 'Muslim democrats' in the manner of Germany's Christian Democrats. Its name – the Justice and Development Party – was a nod to the unaccountability and ineptitude that had come to typify the existing establishment. But it preferred to go by its acronym, AK, or *ak*, the Turkish word meaning white or clean. When the country went to the polls in 2002, all three members of the incumbent coalition government that had overseen the earthquake response were wiped off the electoral map, and Erdoğan's AK Party rode to power with the most decisive parliamentary majority in fifty years.

I would often think about earthquakes when I lived in Istanbul. We were all still waiting for the 'big one' that would soon hit the city. The last time that had happened at the end of the nineteenth century the city was home to under a million people and its buildings were at most two or three storeys high. Now the population was three times that of metropolitan London, but crammed into a smaller area. Estimates of the possible death toll ranged from an optimistic 30,000 – the assessment of Turkey's own disaster management agency – to between 140,000 and 600,000 according to the city's Chamber of Architects and Urban Planners. This broad range reflected a great unknown: even after the introduction of more stringent building quality control in the wake of the 1999 quake, more than half the city's building stock still contravened these regulations. When I had first moved to the city I wondered about the safety of my own apartment, and asked a few of my neighbours about it. I was told that because the building was late nineteenth century it was probably well built, and that our neighbourhood stood on rock, so we were probably safe. But beyond seeking these vague assurances I could never be bothered to look into the issue too closely and after a few months my anxiety dissipated to be supplanted by more immediate concerns: that was how most people lived.

As I learned and read more about Turkey, however, I kept thinking about earthquakes as a metaphor for processes of change in a politically rigid society. During the course of decades in which little of substance seemed to happen, forces appeared to build up that would suddenly unleash themselves in some unprecedented way, leaving a landscape utterly transformed. One of these had been the military coup of 1980, another was the AK Party's election to power in 2002.

Another would take place in the summer of 2013.

The date 29 May 2013 marked the 560th anniversary of the Conquest. Around Istanbul the usual celebrations took place, including a show on the Golden Horn with an historical movie about the Conquest, an Ottoman marching band, a laser show and fireworks display. Istanbul's mayor extolled Mehmet's capture of the city as an event that had brought harmony between religions, sects and races, proclaiming that: '[w]ith the Conquest a message of peace was given to the world'.

Erdoğan expanded on the same theme at the opening of a new archery lodge, where he lauded Mehmet's tolerance of non-Muslim minorities. 'In our civilisation, conquest is not only the taking of lands, countries, cities; at the same time it is the winning of hearts, the conquering of hearts.' This kind of double-edged imagery was typical of his rhetoric: both embracing and dominating, a message of peace couched in the language of war. It was a fitting metaphor: he was indeed serious about winning the hearts and minds of his countrymen, but it was a battle in which he would only ever accept total surrender; the tolerance he spoke of was the conditional tolerance of the weak by the strong.

That same morning I happened to see a few of the people who had rejected those terms. I was walking through Taksim,

the main square on the city's European side, on my way to catch
the bus to the airport for a flight to London. A faint bite of
tear gas caught in my throat and I saw a group of young demonstrators milling about in the half light. I was vaguely aware of
why they were there: they were protesting a government plan
to demolish Gezi Park, a leafy rectangle of plane trees that stood
at Taksim's northern end. A small group of activists had pitched
some tents a few days earlier, and since then the police had been
trying to dislodge them. The previous day they had burned their
tents, but the demonstrators had returned with new ones.

At first they looked a pathetic sight: few in number, bleary-
eyed and forlorn-looking after being violently cast from their
camp in the night, but something about them gave me pause.
They seemed on the surface to be a less-hardened crowd than
the activists I'd typically seen clashing with police. I noticed that
among them were several women with headscarves, which was
unusual. I'd only ever seen headscarved women at demonstrations
supported or encouraged by the government, and never on the
receiving end of police violence. The demonstrators paced about
with the kind of listless indignation of people who had been
turned out of their own homes and had nowhere else to go;
they embraced each other, steeling one another's nerves, wiping
their eyes with milk to ward off the after-effects of the tear gas.

There was an air of outrage and determination that went
beyond what I'd normally witnessed at protests in Turkey, which
often had a theatrical and ritualised quality about them. The
chants usually followed the same dirge-like tune and events
passed off in a predictable manner, the demonstrators marching
to a pre-determined point before reading a press statement to
whichever sympathetic media organisations they had alerted
beforehand; the police would gaze impassively over their riot
shields until the activists, after expending their energy, would
head home as if the whole process were nothing more than a

venting of pressure that ensured the continued smooth running of a machine. Usually you had to go out of your way to witness Turkey's disaffected citizens actually clashing against the hard edges of the state – in the Kurdish regions, for example. Never had I seen this kind of raw confrontation at such a central location in the city.

This is how I pored over my impressions with the benefit of hindsight, for as I hurried through the square on my way to the airport bus all that really crossed my mind was a vague and quickly dismissed curiosity. I boarded the plane and scrolled through my phone seeing how the outrage I'd witnessed was growing and spreading, and as we lifted off and the reception died, I had the uneasy suspicion that I may have picked the wrong day to leave the country. By the time I landed in London and switched on my phone again, I knew I had to book a flight back.

Over the course of the morning more and more people had responded to the activists' calls for support. News about the protest exploded after a photo went viral on social media. It showed a young woman standing in front of a line of riot police; a single police officer had stepped forward and was shooting a jet of pepper spray into her face. The photo captured her in the moment her hair was blowing upwards but before her body had recoiled from the attack. She wore a red dress with a handbag slung casually over her shoulder. She looked utterly unthreatening. The gas-masked police officer, on the other hand, looked both cruel and faintly absurd, reaching forward in a kind of thrusting crouch to spray directly towards her eyes. It was hard to mischaracterise this woman as some kind of terrorist or radical, and the image distilled the sense of state transgression against the dignity of its people that animated those early days of the demonstrations. As the morning wore on, thousands more people flocked to Taksim. The police tried ever more frantically to contain and deter them but every further act of violence only seemed to heighten the outrage.

In the next few days the protests had spread across 79 of Turkey's 81 provinces, and as many as 2.5 million people had joined the demonstrations. The shell-shocked police force withdrew from Taksim after that first day and something happened that I had never imagined possible: the Turkish state ceded control of one of the nation's main squares.

It had begun with the park. Erdoğan had planned to bulldoze it and replace it with the reconstruction of an old artillery barracks that had been the scene of a bloodily suppressed rebellion of Ottoman traditionalists against the Young Turks in 1909. The Republican government had demolished the barracks in 1940 to make way for the park. Taksim was an old battlefield in Turkey's endemic culture war – one on which the forces of conservatism and piety had thus far been broadly defeated. It stood at the top of the hill above Beyoğlu, a bastion of the city's secular night life. In one corner stood the Atatürk Cultural Centre, now shuttered, where previous generations of well-to-do Turks had gone to the opera, a kind of secular temple to Western high culture and symbol of Turkey's Europeanness. The country's Islamists had long dreamed of putting their stamp on Taksim by building a mosque there, and now Erdoğan planned to do this, along with resurrecting the barracks. 'If you have respect for history, research and take a look at the history of that place called Gezi Park,' he declared. 'We are going to revive history there.' The reconstructed building would serve not as a barracks but a shopping mall: a plan that perfectly married the AK Party's twin causes of Ottoman revivalism and neo-liberal capitalism.

The plan's opponents – a vocal group of leftists, liberals and environmental and urban rights activists – were animated less by the symbolic significance of what the government was doing than by the destruction and usurpation of green public space, and the imperious manner in which the government planned to do it.

The previous year had seen a string of instances in which cherished historic buildings in the area had been demolished, usually to make way for shopping malls, including Istanbul's oldest and most iconic theatre house, despite intense opposition. More seriously, a string of massive infrastructure projects were in the process of being forced to fruition which would have worrying implications for the future of the city. These included a huge new airport, which was billed to become the largest in the world, to be constructed on an almost completely undeveloped area of forest and farmland to the north of the city. The ancillary roads to be constructed around it would cut through the Northern Forests, a huge and pristine area of woodland that formed the lungs of the city and was the source of much of its fresh water. Even more worryingly, Erdoğan had recently announced what he called his 'crazy project': a plan to create a new canal to run parallel to the Bosphorus. The ostensible reason was to divert international shipping out of the historic waterway, but the project had no financial logic and would entail massive cost. Hydrologists had warned that it could seriously upset the ecological balance between the two seas it would connect. In both of these projects, there was an additional unstated aim: to open up vast areas of undeveloped land to the north and west of the city – much of it owned by Erdoğan's allies – for development.

Another of these mega-projects was already underway: a third bridge over the Bosphorus. It was something the city's urban planners had long warned against. After the first Bosphorus Bridge, built in 1973, had become snarled with traffic, the second bridge – named after Mehmet the Conqueror – had been built in 1988 to alleviate these issues and bypass the city. Instead it ended up facilitating more urban sprawl and worse traffic. In the wake of its construction new cars came onto Istanbul's roads at a rate of 600 a day, and data from NASA suggested the increase in emissions had raised the city's microclimate by 1° Celsius. It was widely argued, including in Istanbul municipality's own master plan for the city, that a third bridge near the Black Sea would merely result in the same process being repeated again. Erdoğan himself, when mayor, had vigorously opposed it, saying it would be 'the murder of the city'. Now he had forced it through himself. It was to be named after another sultan – Selim the Grim – which in itself generated further controversy, since that ruler had acquired his name through massacre and oppression of the minority Alevi religious group who made up as much as 20 per cent of Turkey's population.

Compared to these projects, which could cause unquantifiable and possibly enormous damage to the environment of the city, Gezi Park was little more than a postage stamp of green space, but somehow it became the line drawn in the sand. The manner in which its fate had been decided typified the increasingly imperious attitude with which Erdoğan had begun to govern. When a court had already rejected the project once, he had airily responded: 'We will reject the rejection.' Then, while the court process was continuing, the demolition started suddenly and illegally, when bulldozers, which were in theory working on another project, began uprooting the trees and scooping away the earth at the park's northern perimeter. This was the spark that lit the fire.

Two years earlier, in the wake of his third, decisive election win, Erdoğan had delivered a speech in which he likened his career as prime minister of Turkey to learning a trade, passing from 'apprentice' to 'journeyman' in his first two terms, and on to this new era in which he had become the 'master'.

Again, it was a double-edged metaphor: the Turkish word *usta* – 'master' – evokes both the accomplished craftsman and the big boss, the overlord. In the early years of his government, when his party had been weak and beset by enemies, he had appeared to earnestly pursue compromise and bridge-building. The AK Party's early parliamentary delegation included Kurds, former members of the centre-left People's Republican Party, secular liberals, academics and members of religious minorities. It seemed to many observers that he was a genuinely consensual politician.

A couple of years earlier the website WikiLeaks had released a massive tranche of US State Department cables sent by American diplomats around the world. Among them had been an assessment of Erdoğan's character made in 2004, shortly after he had assumed power, by Eric S. Edelman, the US ambassador at the time: '[A] natural politician, Erdoğan has a common touch and an ability to communicate his empathy for the plight and aspirations of the common citizen. He projects the image of the Tribune of Anatolia, ready to take on corruption and privilege and to defend conservative traditions.' Edelman listed the new prime minister's weaknesses:

> First, overbearing pride. Second, unbridled ambition stemming from the belief God has anointed him to lead Turkey . . . Third, an authoritarian loner streak which prevents growth of a circle of strong and skilful advisors, a broad flow of fresh information to him, or development of effective communications among the party headquarters, government, and parliamentary group. This streak also makes him exceptionally thin-skinned. Fourth, an overweening desire to stay in power . . .

It was an assessment that would have caused a scandal had it been made public at the time, but now what Edelman had said was plainly obvious. The balance of power had shifted. Constitutional reforms passed in 2010 and the ongoing mass trials had neutralised the old Kemalist power centres in the judiciary and the military, and now the government was beginning to bully and silence hitherto critical media organisations through punitive fines, pressuring the business conglomerates that owned them. Erdoğan had begun to be more open about his desire to remould Turkish society according to his own conservative vision. A year before the Gezi protests he had vowed to ban abortions, and also threatened to limit caesarean sections, which he believed reduced women's childbearing capacity. His government had just introduced new alcohol restrictions to parliament. In the Beyoğlu neighbourhood, a thriving café culture of bars and restaurants along the streets had been forcefully cleared by local municipal police. It was rumoured the reason was that Erdoğan's motorcade had become stuck there and a group of revellers had ironically toasted him. Then a month earlier, at the start of May, the authorities had suddenly banned the traditional May Day demonstrations, an event that had passed off peacefully and festively in recent years despite its sometimes bloody history. In a comment that struck fear into more secular-minded Turks, he had vowed to create a 'religious youth' in the country.

Among the first demonstrators who had pitched tents in the park was a friend of mine: İmre Azem, a filmmaker and urban rights activist. About a year before the events in Gezi Park, he had made a documentary called *Ekümenopolis*, which had become popular among the demonstrators and was widely seen as explaining and prefiguring some of the social and economic tensions that gave rise to the protests. It took its title from a concept first suggested by a Greek city planner called Constantinos Doxiadis, who had rhetorically suggested in the 1960s that the prevalent trends of urbanisation could eventually give rise to the worldwide merging of all cities, an urban sprawl across the entire surface of the planet: the 'ecumenopolis'.

But İmre believed that these urban rights issues were only a small part of what the process was about: the principal impetus of the protests was frustration among the country's secular youth regarding Erdoğan's effort to transform Turkish society into something more to his liking. 'Initially people joined because of the park and the shopping mall that Erdoğan wanted to build, but why it spread so much through Turkey was that a lot of people felt their lifestyle was being threatened . . . Erdoğan spoke with this rhetoric like a father telling his kids what to do, and he continued that all through Gezi.'

The protests started with a burst of reactive anger against police brutality, but they flowered into something very different. After the police withdrew from Taksim Square, an extraordinary coalition of different political and social groups moved in. There were covered women and Kemalists; anti-capitalist Muslims, revolutionary communists and two-dozen CEOs from Turkey's biggest companies. In one corner of the square, Kurdish nation-alists hoisted the banner of their jailed rebel leader Abdullah Öcalan; in the other, a group of far-right Turkish nationalists marched military-style under the banner of the Grey Wolves – a group notorious for their hatred of both Kurdish separatism and the various leftist groups with whom they now shared Taksim. I had never conceived that this kind of tolerance could be possible in Turkey, I think few people had.

There was an air of joyful irreverence. One thing you noticed was the graffiti: humorous, creative and obscene, and much of it referring either to 'Tayyip', the main focus of demonstrators' rage, or to the police and their liberal use of tear gas and water cannon. 'One serving of gas, please,' read one slogan, while another asked: 'Are you sure you'd want three of me?' referring to Erdoğan's exhortations for women to have more children.

The banner was a huge one that simply read: 'Shut up Tayyip'. When he branded the protestors *çapulcular* – marauders – they gleefully coined 'chapulling', an Anglicised version of the Turkish, which came to mean 'fighting for your rights'. Penguins became an unlikely symbol of the rotten, self-censoring news channels after one station opted to air a documentary about the birds instead of covering the protests. One man donned a penguin suit and stood at the entrance to Taksim wearing a sign that read: 'Antarctica is resisting'.

A festival atmosphere took hold. In the park a kind of tent city sprang up, meatballs sizzled on vendors' grills, trees of candyfloss bobbed through the crowd, and buckets of illicit, ice-cold beers were hawked into the square; there were bands playing, pop-up tattoo parlours, tango classes, mass yoga sessions, a lending library, dervishes whirling (one in a gas mask), and a game of giant backgammon with counters of uprooted street bollards made up to look like police and protesters.

When you asked people what the protests were about, the answer depended on who you were talking to: for some it was about defending secularism, for some it was about over-throwing capitalism, for some it was about the environment, or democratic rights, ethnic or religious identity. The answer that felt most true to me – that seemed to make the most coherent sense of the various grievances involved – was one which İmre had given to me at the time: that the protests were a call for a shift from crude majoritarianism to genuine representative democracy in which the rights of every group were assured and respected. 'If we take a vote and ninety-nine per cent of people vote to demolish my house, in a majori-tarian-based democracy they can do it. But in a rights-based democracy they can't do it.' It reflected the tenor of the many conversations I had with demonstrators during those days: co-transformation of urban space without consultation, government interference in lifestyle, suppression of political or ethnic identity.

———

One image from the protests struck me above all others. Early on when I was wandering through the park, I saw pieces of paper Sellotaped to the trees. Written on them were the names of nearly three dozen Kurdish men and boys who had been killed in a military airstrike in the remote south-east of Turkey, about eighteen months earlier. They were not militants, but had been smuggling contraband cigarettes and diesel across the mountainous border with Iraq. Nineteen of the victims were children; the youngest was just twelve. The group, who were trekking on foot with mules, had been spotted by a military drone, and were apparently mistaken for guerrillas from the Kurdistan Workers Party (PKK), the armed separatist movement that had been fighting an insurgency against the Turkish state for more than three decades.

Later it turned out that local military units had been well aware of this cross-border trade, which had been going on for decades on a subsistence level, and was tolerated by officialdom. The men and boys had come from the village of Roboski, a community that was part of the system of 'village guards', a militia armed by the Turkish state to counter the PKK, and so they were in touch with local military units, and always informed them in advance when cross-border trips were taking place. Somehow they were still killed.

Much of the Turkish media simply ignored this awful tragedy, which the military sought to whitewash. As questions were asked, Erdoğan's reaction was to play it down and staunchly defend the military's actions. He offered no apologies and little compassion for the dead or their families, but emphasised that the men were 'smugglers' engaged in illegal activity. The following day he even thanked the military command for their 'sensitivity' in handling the incident, accusing the media of whipping up trouble.

'The planes bombarded the villagers because they thought they were terrorists,' he commented. 'It was a terror zone; compensation has been paid to the relatives of the victims. It is not necessary to make a big deal out of this.'

The suffering and indignity visited on the Kurdish minority was something that much of Turkey had become accustomed to either ignoring or stridently justifying. To see the victims of Roboski honoured and remembered in this way felt extraordinary to me. To understand its importance you would have to know how the problem posed by Kurdish identity cast a pall over the entire modern history of Turkey, over its entire national project.

At the outset of the Turkish Republic, the state sought to mould its citizens not just towards a particular model of religious practice, but also to coerce them in terms of their cultural and ethnic identification. And whereas the state might relax its attitudes to the former over time, the latter it considered of existential importance. The decades-long collapse of the Ottoman Empire, which Atatürk and those around him had witnessed, and the subsequent attempts of the Western powers to carve up Anatolia after the First World War had hardwired a fear of disintegration into the Turkish psyche. The ethnic diversity of the Ottoman Empire, they believed, had been its doom, and while the Turkish state might one day lose the will to unite the country around a secular vision of Islam, its zeal to unite it around the cause of Turkish nationalism would remain undimmed.

Non-Muslims – the Armenians, Jews and the Greeks – might technically fall into this category, but they would always be regarded by the state as outsiders, at best they were guests and at worst grit to be spat out. Pogroms, punitive wealth taxes, and a culture of discrimination reduced their numbers over time.

The smaller Muslim ethnic minorities – Laz people, Circassians, and others – for the most part embraced their new Turkish identity, their old languages and ways persisting harmlessly in the home and village, until after a couple of generations they had all but faded away.

But the Kurds were a different matter. Until the founding of the Republic, the mountainous region of Kurdistan had been a place where Ottoman authority was weak and semi-feudal tribes exercised extensive autonomy. Although the nationalist sentiments that had gripped Anatolia's Christian communities were slower to develop among them, the Kurdish homelands in south-east Anatolia became a site of resistance to the centralising and homogenising efforts of the new state. The first rebellion was mounted within two years of the founding of the Republic and was crushed with relative ease. In 1937, another uprising by the Kurdish Alevis in the mountainous province of Dersim was suppressed by the military over the course of several months in a brutal campaign in which more than 10,000 civilians were killed.

It was not until the chaotic years of the 1970s that a new Kurdish armed movement arose that would prove far more enduring than its predecessors. The PKK was among a plethora of radical Marxist and Communist groups to emerge at that time. What distinguished it from its competitors was its insistence on immediate armed revolution and the ruthlessness of its leader, Abdullah Öcalan, who was willing to murder and intimidate competing groups into submission. At the time of the 1980 coup, during which almost all leftist groups in the country were suppressed, Öcalan had fled abroad to Syria, where he began training a core of guerrillas to launch an armed insurrection with the tacit backing of Syria's Assad regime.

The PKK launched its insurgency in 1984. It was the Turkish state that helped drive the Kurdish populace into its arms;

repression of Kurdish identity had never been as intense and systematic as in the years following the coup. As it flowered into a mass movement, the PKK used both hope and terror to extend its reach. When the Turkish government mobilised and armed a rural militia – the 'village guards' – to oppose it, Öcalan's guerrillas carried out reprisals against communities that had signed up. In one incident in 1987, thirty rebels entered Pinarcık, a village with a population of sixty people that had ignored previous warnings to quit the militia. After a two-hour firefight, sixteen children and six women were dead.

For two decades the entire south-east was declared a special military zone in which normal free movement and constitutional rights were suspended. The army burned out entire villages, causing tens of thousands of people to flee their homes and move to the west of Turkey. Those suspected of helping the PKK were regularly abducted and murdered or faced horrific torture in prison.

This 'war on terror' had a warping effect across society: a brutalised, displaced and alienated Kurdish populace; a generation of young conscripts haunted by being thrown unprepared into a brutal war; a security apparatus with torture and repression imbedded in its muscle memory; and perhaps most insidiously, a broader population disconnected from and desensitised to the humanity of its Kurdish citizens by a barrage of propaganda. Equally, the PKK's own brutally oppressive nature meant that whatever independent expressions of Kurdish politics, culture or identity emerged would be subsumed in its shadow.

Öcalan was captured in 1999 after being forced to flee Syria, was returned to Turkey, tried, and sentenced to death. Although this was later commuted to life imprisonment when Turkey acceded to pressure from the European Union to abolish capital punishment, it marked a major triumph for the state. From captivity he ordered an immediate PKK ceasefire and at his trial struck a conciliatory and slightly grovelling tone, casting himself as a peacemaker. But although his capture and imprisonment knocked the wind out of the insurgency, by that time the PKK had become deeply embedded in Kurdish society.

When the AK Party came to power in 2002, there had seemed to be an emerging consensus within the new government and among a broad range of civil society leaders, academics and journalists that the time had come for negotiation and compromise. Erdoğan's former Islamists, as fellow outsiders to the Kemalist system, seemed more sympathetic to Kurdish grievances than previous governments, and they sought to win over the region through economic development, expanding cultural rights and shared conservative social values. Kurdish voters backed the party in growing numbers. In 2005, Erdoğan went to Diyarbakır, the de facto Kurdish capital of the south-east, and declared that 'the Kurdish problem is my problem'.

But there remained a gulf between the aspirations of Kurdish society and the expectations of Turkish society more broadly. Most Turks believed the country only had a 'terror problem', and the PKK's supporters were presented to it as inhuman monsters that simply needed to be destroyed. Most people were ignorant of the excesses of the security forces, and had no inkling of the depth of PKK support within the Kurdish population or the degree of anger and grievance that lurked there. And even if they had, many were inculcated with the mortal fear of dismemberment that had haunted the Turkish Republic since its birth. Any price in blood was worth paying to stop that.

Erdoğan himself had launched a potentially historic peace process with the PKK, but his attitude towards the issue – such as his callous words following the Roboski tragedy – sometimes called into question the depth of his commitment to solving it. My own belief was that lasting peace could only come through an acknowledgement of Kurdish suffering and grievance on a societal level. That was why those paper signs on the trees of Gezi Park struck me with such force.

During the first week of the protests, Erdoğan, who had been on a trip to North Africa, was uncharacteristically quiet. In his absence, senior members of the government struck a conciliatory tone. Speaking at a news conference in Ankara, Deputy Prime Minister Bülent Arinç apologised to the demonstrators who had initially occupied the park.

'The use of excessive force shown against the people who initially started this protest with the motive of protecting the environment was wrong. And it was unfair. So I apologise to those citizens,' Mr Arinç said at a news conference in Ankara, but added: 'I do not think we need to apologise to those who create destruction of public property in the streets and who try to prevent the freedom of the people in the streets.'

Abdullah Gül, the president, was even more dovish. 'Democracy does not simply mean elections,' he said in a statement. 'It is natural for people to reveal their objections or different views through different means such as demonstrations. Therefore, I consider the recent incidents in our country to be part of this fact. The state has got the well-intended message.'

Hearing these words and seeing the extraordinary solidarity of the different groups in Taksim Square it was hard not to be hopeful. It was possible to imagine a path forward for Turkey rooted in compromise and dialogue between the opposing factions in society.

Those hopes died on 7 June, when Erdoğan's plane arrived back in Istanbul from North Africa. In a piece of carefully arranged political theatre, party officials had vocally urged his

supporters not to turn up to greet him, while making sure the
Metro stayed open late so they could. Even so, there was no
mistaking the size and passion of the crowd that turned up in
the dead of night to welcome their leader home. By the time
he and his wife climbed on top of a campaign bus, more than
ten thousand had gathered.

His words in that moment were measured compared to his
later rhetoric. He opened with a carefully weighted message
of peace and love. He greeted Istanbul, the city that made
him, 'again and again, with all my heart: every neighbourhood,
every street, every district'. He greeted all of Turkey, and what
he called Istanbul's 'brother cities': Sarajevo, Baku, Beirut,
Skopje, Damascus, Gaza, Mecca and Medina. He was every
citizen's servant, he said, irrespective of his or her ethnicity,
origin, or ideology. 'We are against the majority tyrannising
the minority,' he said, addressing President Gül's earlier
comments. 'But we are definitely against the minority tyrannising the majority.'

Turning to the protesters, he labelled them vandals, looters
and the pawns of terrorists. He lambasted the public and media
figures who had supported them: 'They said they were journalists, artists, politicians and they acted irresponsibly by provoking
this lawless behaviour.' The project for Gezi Park would go
ahead, he vowed, and the protests must stop immediately. What
made the moment so chilling was not so much the tone of his
speech but the response of the crowd. Each time he paused to
soak up their adulation, a chorus rose in counterpoint to his
words: 'May the hands that strike the police be broken!' they
roared. 'Tell us and we will crush Taksim!'

Within a week the protest camp at Gezi had been violently
cleared out. Over the course of the protests, eight people were
killed during the police crackdown and thousands were injured.
The months that followed would be characterised by running

protests, mass arrests and prosecutions. Erdoğan soon abandoned the relatively restrained rhetoric of that airport speech; he appeared to believe that the protests were an orchestrated attempt to overthrow him directed by shadowy internal and external enemies, and vigorously stoked the nation's culture wars. One of those who died in the protests was a fifteen-year-old boy named Berkin Elvan, who was hit in the head by a tear gas canister. He passed away after lying in a coma for ten months. At a political rally shortly after his death, Erdoğan accused the dead boy of terrorist links and encouraged the crowd to boo his grieving mother, who had accused him of being responsible for his death.

Years after the protest was over, civil society figures who had played a role in them were still languishing in prison. Perhaps the single tangible victory of the demonstrators was that the artillery barracks was never rebuilt and Gezi remained a park – albeit one with a constant and large police presence – but the government would later realise the long-cherished Islamist dream of erecting a mosque to loom over the square.

Watching Erdoğan's speech on television in my apartment, I felt then that I was witnessing a turning point – or perhaps just a final falling away of my own illusions. Erdoğan was gearing up for a fight; there would be no compromise or healing dialogue between the opposing factions of Turkish society, no subsuming of old enmities within the scope of a democratic system. After that time, the relationship between Turkey's state and a huge section of its population seemed to me like a man with his foot on another man's neck: as the man on the ground becomes more angry and desperate to be released, the man pinning him down presses all the harder, fearful of having to face the consequences of that anger. Probably it had always been like that.

What I would come to appreciate more clearly over time was that there was a vast swathe of Turkey's population who

had watched the unfolding protests, filtered through the lens
of the pro-government media, with horror and anger. They
did not see the extent of the police brutality, but they did see
the images of burning cars, smashed-up bank branches, masked
demonstrators lobbing petrol bombs, and calls for the government to resign. Some, like Zehra, were subjected to harassment
or abuse. The message they took away was one of hostility,
chaos and the attempted overthrow of a democratically elected
government.

Still I find myself thinking about Gezi: perhaps that's why I
have digressed into the past to describe it at such length. Within
the scope of the time I lived in Turkey, it stands as a portal to
a better world, bounded by the geography of Taksim Square
and the span of those two weeks in which the Turkish state
withdrew from it. When I think of the distaste and fear the
protests aroused in people like Kader or Zehra, I cannot help
but think that if they had been in the actual square perhaps
they would have seen it differently, found some kind of connection. I tell myself it is naive, but part of me believes that place
of connection is still there and that at some point in the country's future that gateway can be opened and its road travelled.

6

The Golden Gate

At first I struggled to reach the Golden Gate. Even though it was huge and I could see its marble bastions looming from a distance, every approach seemed to be blocked. From the inside, access was barred by the old Ottoman fortress of Yedikule that had been built onto the rear of it, and which was closed as part of a long-running renovation. From the outside, the southern approach was blocked by the deep cutting of the Halkalı train line, and from directly in front it was obscured by an old closed-off cemetery that lay in and around the sunken terrace of the moat. Only from the north could I approach via a track that led off the road to the nearby Yedikule Gate, where there was an arm barrier with a 'no entry' sign. Ignoring this warning and following the track along the wall brought me to the private realm of the *bostans* and the gate's locked outer portal. A fresh pile of manure lay heaped next to it, steaming in the late autumn sun. A little further down the track was a rough wooden foot gate guarded by a chained dog, and beyond this I could see an immaculately tended stretch of gardens extending out beyond. Chickens pecked and clucked at the entrance, and the smell of a wood fire hung in the air. In the distance a man and woman working their plots looked up briefly at the sound of the dog barking; I waved to them and they returned to their labour.

Peering through the narrow gap in the closed outer gate I saw a courtyard of weeds, bushes and wildflowers from which rose a triple archway with a large central portal flanked by two lesser ones. This had been the triumphal state entrance to Constantinople built in the days of the Byzantine Empire's glory, the largest and most magnificent of its gates. Over time the gate's celebratory function had diminished and its defensive role increased: the triple portals had been reduced and the frames of progressively smaller doorways were visible in the masonry until the once-soaring arches had become no more than posterns. The gate had taken its name from the plates of gilded brass that once adorned its exterior; these, of course, were long gone, as was the great sculpture of the Emperor Theodosius riding a chariot of four elephants that once stood above the central portal, and the inscription below in gilded lettering that had celebrated his defeat of a usurper. 'He rules a golden age, who built the gate of gold,' the now-lost inscription had proclaimed. The only evidence that survived of it were the rivet holes in the masonry where the letters had once been fixed.

The ruins of Byzantium stretch from Spain to Syria and from Crimea to the banks of the Nile; at its peak, the eastern empire encompassed almost the entire coastline of the Mediterranean and Black seas, stretching from the edge of the Sahara to the steppes of Russia. It persisted for more than a millennium from the splitting of the Roman Empire in AD 395 to the final siege and capture of Constantinople. It was not an offshoot or a descendant of Rome, but a continuation of its institutions and culture, and although these evolved over time (Greek supplanting Latin, the Orthodox Patriarch trumping the Catholic Pope), its people continued to call themselves Romans and nearly six hundred years later the few remaining Greeks of Istanbul were still called *Rum* – Romans – by their Turkish neighbours. And yet despite the might and power it once commanded, and its importance to the development of both European and Middle Eastern culture, Byzantium seems to occupy a meagre place in the popular imagination of the West.

'[T]he fate of the Greek empire has been compared to that of the Rhine, which loses itself in the sands, before its water can mingle with the ocean,' wrote the great eighteenth-century historian Edward Gibbon in *The History of the Decline and Fall of the Roman Empire*. In his sprawling 3,000-page opus, he glossed over the last eight hundred years of Byzantine history post AD 500 in a small portion of the space he had devoted to the previous five centuries – and then only grudgingly. He was utterly scathing in his assessment of the Byzantines, characterising them as superstitious, feeble-minded and corrupt. '[T]he subjects of the Byzantine Empire, who assume and dishonour the names both of Greeks and Romans, present a dead uniformity of abject vices, which are neither softened by the weakness of humanity, nor animated by the vigour of memorable crimes.'

Gibbon's notorious judgement has been blamed for deterring historical interest in the Byzantines throughout the nineteenth and early twentieth centuries. And indeed, viewed in through broadest lens, its history does have the feel of a long, slow death played out over centuries. But this is an illusion created by our own perspective. For many generations, Byzantium was a bastion of strength and beacon of art and learning sitting astride two continents, whose capital attracted the awe and envy of its neighbours, both east and west. It maintained its power in the face of almost unrelenting aggression from the various tribes and peoples who sought to overrun it from every direction; it outlasted the threat of the Persian empire in the east and the first Islamic Caliphate in the south, defied raiders and would-be conquerors from the Russian steppes, and for a long time held off the growing power of the Christian states of Europe, and shielded them from these other threats. In its libraries and academies there survived a vast corpus of Classical literature, mathematics and philosophy that would otherwise have been lost to the world. In the empire's dying years, the migration of Byzantine scholars to the Italian states has been credited with a key role in fostering the atmosphere of intellectual ferment that gave rise to the Renaissance.

But even if we do not justify Byzantium on its merits, or if we accept Gibbon's judgement on its people's moral and intellectual deficiencies, a greater objection can be made to his claim that their story does not give the reader 'an adequate reward of instruction or amusement'. The Byzantine story is that of a people who spent generations contemplating their own doom and strenuously defying it, for whom the threat of destruction was ever-present and who thrived in spite of it.

Perhaps what made the Byzantines so revolting to Gibbon, writing during an age of endeavour and advancement, was that they themselves seemed to share his assessment that the summit of civilisation had been crested; their role, as they saw it, was not to advance it but to preserve it until the coming of Doomsday. There was a widespread belief among the Byzantines that their empire would be the last on earth, and their city the last city before the Second Coming of Christ and the arrival of Judgement Day, which they believed to be imminent.

As epitomised most forcefully in the structure of the walls themselves, Byzantium was a society concerned with preservation. To more sympathetic observers than Gibbon, it was this quality – set in the context of their inexorable and total decline – that made them tragic and compelling. 'In Istanbul it is hard to escape a recurring sense of loss,' wrote the late poet and writer John Ash, who wrote lyrically on Byzantium in his history-travelogue, *A Byzantine Journey*. '[N]o civilisation fought harder than the Byzantine to preserve the past for future generations, yet so much that was great in its own art and architecture has vanished.'

From the moment when the empire calved away from Rome, its existence was characterised by a paradox of power and vulnerability, and a kind of siege mentality that is epitomised in the stones of the land walls and, at their heart, the unusual structure of the Golden Gate: a hybrid between triumphal arch and fortress with its great twin bastions, both ceremonial and functional in form, an expression of might and insecurity.

There is some doubt as to whether it was built at the same time as the land walls or slightly earlier, but either way, both were constructed at a time when Constantinople enjoyed great wealth and power and was also haunted by the threat of disaster. During this period, at the end of the fourth century and beginning of the fifth century, the Roman Empire was fragmenting in the face of wave after wave of incursion, and towns and cities across the empire were building fortifications to defend themselves. Rome was sacked by the Gauls in AD 390, and five years later, the split between east and west, which had been growing since Constantine had moved the capital to Constantinople in AD 330, finally became complete. The west fared worse. Rome was sacked again by the Visigoths in 410, and after that the Western Empire limped on for another few decades before collapsing entirely. This was the climax of the so-called 'Barbarian Invasions', during which a host of mainly Germanic and Slavic tribes began encroaching on Roman territory. Historians from Gibbon onwards have debated whether they were the cause of Rome's decline, if they merely exploited it, or if both were correlated with some other factor. Some have suggested that changes in the North Atlantic Oscillation, an atmospheric pressure system which affects rainfall across Europe and caused particular periods of drought in northern Europe, may have triggered population upheavals, for these were not just expeditions of conquest but wholesale movements of people.

However, the eastern portion of the empire, with Constantinople at its heart, retained its power and integrity even as the threat of marauding armies menaced it. From its origin as a small trading city, the eastern imperial capital was experiencing a boom in population and wealth and had become a thriving metropolis. Themistius, a prominent statesman and rhetorician of the time, extolled its expansion to the city's senate when he became its prefect under Theodosius I in 384.

'No longer is the vacant ground in the city more extensive than that occupied by buildings; nor are we cultivating more territory within our walls than we inhabit; the beauty of the city is not, as heretofore, scattered over it in patches, but covers its whole area like a robe woven to the very fringe.' Constantinople, he proclaimed, was 'a factory of magnificence', full of 'carpenters, builders, decorators and all kinds of craftsmen' and he correctly predicted that on its current course a new and broader circuit of walls would soon be necessary. Thus, at a time when settlements across the empire were fortifying themselves against external threats, Constantinople built its great walls both to address this danger and to accommodate its burgeoning population. The threat was real, and would be exemplified most completely later in the century by Attila the Hun, whose horde devastated Roman towns and cities in the Balkans and was only deterred from attacking Constantinople itself by the newly built walls.

The successes of the empire in the centuries that followed were told in the triumphal processions that passed through the Golden Gate. Through it marched Heraclius in AD 628 after ravaging

Persia and sacking its royal palace; before him went the True Cross, recovered from the Persians, and behind were four elephants, the first to be seen in the city. Constantine V held a triumph after annihilating an invading Bulgarian army in 763. Theophilus held two in 834 and 837 after driving back the Arabs, John I Tzimisces in 972 after defeating the Russian prince Svyatoslav in Bulgaria (the Bulgarian king who had been aiding, and whose territory he promptly annexed, was paraded in a manner more like a vanquished opponent than a liberated ally), and Basil II held one after his battles against the Bulgarians between 1000 and 1018, during which he extended Byzantine territory to the banks of the Danube for the first time in four hundred years.

It was in the decades after this that the Byzantine decline began to set in. Chief among a series of body blows to the empire was the Battle of Manzikert in 1071, when the imperial army under Emperor Romanus Diogenes was routed and destroyed by the Seljuks, opening the way for the Turkish colonisation of Anatolia and eventually robbing the Byzantines of their principal base of taxation and manpower. In 1204 the city was captured and looted of its riches by the Fourth Crusade, heralding nearly six decades of Latin occupation – a disaster from which the empire never recovered. Constantinople was eventually recaptured by luck, when a small Byzantine force raiding near the city received intelligence that its Venetian garrison was absent. Learning of an open postern through which a few men might sneak, they took the opportunity to seize it. After confirming this miraculous news, the emperor in exile, Michael VIII Palaeologus, entered the Golden Gate and was crowned anew at the Hagia Sophia. In 1261, this was the last ever triumphal entry through the gate. He took over a ruined city denuded of its riches, uniting it once more with a state whose territories were now shrunken and fragmented.

By the time that the young sultan Mehmet II was planning his assault on the city, an air of irretrievable decline had long settled over Constantinople. The city was more like a ruin than an imperial capital. Its population, which had once numbered a million inhabitants, had shrunk by the eve of the siege to no more than 50,000, emptied out by successive waves of plague and its ebbing fortunes. The sack by the Fourth Crusade in 1204 had dealt the most damage, with the European invaders plundering the city and carrying off most of its wealth to Venice. The fourteenth century was a catalogue of disaster, in which the empire – or what remained of it – was riven by civil war, invasions by the Ottomans and the Serbs, and the Black Death, which devastated Constantinople's population. By the early 1400s the city resembled a series of villages spread out among orchards and fields within the compass of the walls, and the thriving trade its position once afforded it had shifted to the Genoese colony of Pera on the other side of the Golden Horn. The Byzantine domain, which once stretched from Italy to Syria, now barely extended beyond Constantinople itself, and included only a few villages and fortresses along the coast and some territories in the Peloponnese.

Visitors described a sad and desolate place dominated by ruins, churches and monasteries, whose impoverished inhabitants were gripped by a morbid piety. According to the Spanish adventurer Pero Tafur, who visited the city in the 1430s and penned his account after its fall, its common people were 'sad and poor . . . [and] go continually about the city howling as if in lamentation, and thus they long ago foreshadowed the evil which has befallen them.' The Emperor John VIII, with whom Tafur struck up a close friendship, was 'a bishop without a see'. His description of the Byzantine royals calls to mind a family of eccentric English aristocrats clinging to their rotting family pile. The imperial palace, he wrote, 'must have been very magnificent, but now is in such state that both it and the city show well the evils which the people have suffered and still endure.' Inside it, he continued, 'the house is badly kept, except certain parts where the Emperor, the Empress, and attendants can live, although cramped for space.' During hunting trips together, John VIII tried in vain to convince Tafur to settle and marry in the city.

The churches and monasteries alone retained the ability to impress – especially the great basilica of Hagia Sophia – and European visitors toured these, describing in awed and credulous tones the various relics enclosed in them: the iron lance that pierced Christ's side, a stone bearing the miraculous tears of the Virgin, the gridiron on which St Lawrence was broiled alive. Ruy González de Clavijo, another Spaniard, was shown both arms of John the Baptist, which resided in separate churches; the left, he complained, was just withered skin and bone, but the right was 'quite fresh', though lacking a thumb. He had arranged to see other more special relics but was unable to 'because the emperor had gone out hunting, and had left the keys of the church with the empress, but he forgot to give her the keys to the place where these relics were kept.'

<hr />

In the decades before the siege the city's rulers, acutely aware of their vulnerability in the face of growing Ottoman might, had wrestled with how to reverse their fortunes. They had pinned their hopes on Europe, which despite complicated and often antagonist relations, was the only realistic source of aid. Byzantine emperors had for some years been travelling cap in hand round the continent in the hope of securing military aid against the Turks. In 1400, Emperor Manuel II toured the European courts as far afield as England, giving gifts of the city's coveted relics and treasures in exchange for money and soldiers. He stayed two months during winter with Henry IV, and although he and his retinue of knights and clergy impressed the English with their exoticism and piety, they evoked mainly pity.

'I thought to myself how sad it was,' the Welsh chronicler Adam of Usk recorded, 'that this great Christian leader from the remote east had been driven by the power of the infidels to visit distant islands in the west in order to seek help against them.' Henry gave him the considerable sum of £2,000, but was unable to provide soldiers, which was what the empire most sorely needed.

In an effort to unlock real aid from Europe – the most probable source being the Italian powers – Byzantine rulers began toying with the idea of healing the old schism between the eastern and western churches. The divide between Orthodox and Catholic was four hundred years old, although its roots were deeper than that, and they rested on cultural and political differences that had only widened over time. The bones of contention were partly doctrinal, resting on the relationship between the Father, Son and Holy Spirit as expressed in the liturgy, but at the heart of the rift was the Papacy. Orthodox Christians had been willing to grant the Patriarch of Rome a notional primacy over his counterparts in Constantinople and elsewhere, but the Pope had wanted more, demanding that the Orthodox formally recognise his authority over all Christendom including Constantinople, which the Greeks could never countenance. Enmity between the eastern and western churches was great, and the common people and clergy, for whom the hateful memory of the sack and occupation of the city by the Fourth Crusade was still vivid, deeply loathed the Latins and their creed.

The idea of healing the rift was at first a rhetorical ploy more than a sincere proposal: it was a prospect the Ottomans seriously feared, and the Byzantines dangled it before them in the hope of deterring their foe from pushing them into too desperate a position. However, in the 1430s, the Byzantine emperor John VIII decided to attempt to heal this rift in earnest. The result came at the ecumenical Council of Florence, during which a delegation of senior Orthodox clergy spent nearly two years hammering out an agreement with their Catholic counterparts at the end of which unity was declared. The Greeks had given way on the key question of the Trinity and the primacy of the Pope, but these were fudged so that while acknowledging them formally, the Orthodox weren't required to insert them into their daily creed.

At this time, there had developed a deep divide between Constantinople's ruling elite and its people. The emperor, nobility and civil servants had a keen idea of how weak the city's position was, and thus from desperation and expediency they supported the union. But the common people and clergy vehemently rejected it almost as soon as it was made. They tended to the belief that the fate of the city was in God's hands and that by accepting what they saw as a heretical creed, their rulers were not buying it a lifeline but sealing its fate. Others among the elites and clergy, remembering the Fourth Crusade – which had in theory been launched to seize Jerusalem from the Saracens before it diverted to attack Constantinople – feared that 'help' from the Latins would be as sure a way of forfeiting their sovereignty as surrendering the city to the Turks. Opposition to the union was so intense that it proved impossible to consecrate in the Hagia Sophia, as the agreement had stipulated, and the key clergymen who had been present for its negotiation either renounced it or fled abroad. And so the worst possible outcome resulted. The Pope, in whose eyes the Byzantines had failed to honour a sacred agreement, was unwilling to offer the city anything in the way of help, and the people of Constantinople, who had rejected the union, were demoralised in the belief that their own rulers had perjured their souls and hastened their downfall.

It was against this grim backdrop that Constantine XI Palaiologos, the last Roman emperor, took the throne in 1449, though he was never formally crowned. He was a supporter of the union with Rome, and although for centuries coronations had taken place in the Hagia Sophia, it was felt that the crowning of a unionist emperor in the great church would provoke such serious disorder that it was never attempted.

Two years later Mehmet II would ascend to the Ottoman throne. In certain respects the two men were utterly unalike: where Mehmet was an unproven youth with grand dreams and ambitions, Constantine was a grizzled soldier who had spent his life fighting the Turks and was pragmatic and dutiful by nature. We know almost nothing of his appearance, but he was a typically multi-ethnic product of the ruling classes of the time: he had a Serbian mother and a half-Italian father, and his various siblings, uncles and aunts had married into the royal and aristocratic dynasties of Italy, Bulgaria, Russia and the Ottomans. The facts of his life suggest a leader who was decisive, capable and inspiring on the military front but less surefooted when it came to political matters; a man of prodigious energy who was resolute in the face of the significant setbacks that he faced even before becoming emperor. In some respects he was more similar to Mehmet's father Murat: a reformist who sought to reverse his people's misfortune. Indeed, during his years as the despot of Morea he had been a persistent thorn in Murat's side. He had built a strong fortress – the Hexamilion – across the isthmus of Corinth to guard his territories, which comprised the modern Peloponnese, and attempted for a number of years to reassert Byzantine power in northern Greece. After crushing the Crusaders at Varna, Murat finally marched on Constantine's stronghold, bringing to bear the force of gunpowder artillery to swiftly breach and storm the Hexamilion, before going on to pillage the Morea and carry off as many as 60,000 of its inhabitants into slavery. Humiliated, Constantine had been forced to accept vassalage.

He was forty-four years old when he became emperor on the death of his brother John. As soon as he ascended to the throne, and with greater urgency after Mehmet's own accession, he set about trying to shore up Constantinople's sorry defences. This involved a diplomatic effort to secure a royal wife from abroad who might bring helpful dynastic links, as well as overtures to the European powers and a desperate programme of repair on the dilapidated city walls. In all of these endeavours he was largely unsuccessful, not through deficiencies on his own part so much as the meagreness of the hand he had been dealt.

At the same time, he grappled unsuccessfully with the rolling crisis in Constantinople caused by the union of the two churches. As Mehmet tightened his noose around the city, it remained in a state of rancour, suspicion and spiritual doubt. The city's Orthodox patriarch, who had supported the union with Rome, had fled in the face of unrelenting popular fury, leaving behind a headless church and an uncrowned emperor. Ill feeling festered on every side; the Byzantines had sworn to an agreement that they refused to consummate, and the Latins in the city, whose diaries and statements form the bulk of the surviving accounts, condemned them as dishonest and treacherous for making the union in bad faith.

The Pope, who still wanted the decisions of the council to be enacted, sent an envoy to try to win the people over: Cardinal Isidore of Kiev, a Byzantine by birth who brought with him a company of 200 archers as a show of good faith. Their arrival in the city, whose people were now aware of the imminent threat from Mehmet, shifted popular opinion somewhat. The main leader of the anti-unionist cause, a monk named Gennadios, issued a series of harangues against the population. He warned that the Apocalypse was nigh, that the city was lost, and that its inhabitants had doomed their souls in the vain hope of help from the Franks.

Nonetheless, the service of union between the two churches was finally proclaimed in the Hagia Sophia in December 1452. After that, the faithful of the city, fearful for the purity of their souls, shunned it as if it were 'a pagan altar' or 'a synagogue of Jews', in the words of the historian Doukas. In a proclamation pinned on a monastery door shortly before the service of union was performed, Gennadios declared:

> Wretched Romans, how you have been deceived! You have departed from hope, which rests in God, by trusting in the power of the Franks. As well as the City itself, which will soon be destroyed, you have lost the true religion. O Lord, be merciful to me. I give witness before Your presence that I am pure and innocent from blame in this matter. Be aware, miserable citizens, what you are doing this day. With slavery, which is hanging over your heads, you have denied the true faith handed down to you by your forefathers. You have confessed your impiety. Woe to you when you are judged!

In the end no further aid came from Rome, and little from any other quarter. Around the end of January, however, morale was buoyed by the arrival of Giovanni Giustiniani, a professional soldier from one of Genoa's ruling families. He brought with him 700 trained fighting men, armed to the teeth and wearing steel plate armour. They were 'full of martial passion', according to Doukas, and arrived 'in two huge ships which were carrying a large supply of excellent military equipment'. Constantine was so impressed by Giustiniani that he appointed him to lead the defence and promised to gift him the island of Lemnos, should they succeed in holding the city. He and his men took up position alongside the emperor at the section of the land walls known as the Mesoteichion, opposite where Mehmet would pitch his own tents and set up his largest guns.

Even so, the Byzantines still had precious few resources with which to defend their city. Their numbers were so thin that the defenders abandoned entirely the high inner wall of the Theodosian walls and only manned the lower outer wall, which was less dilapidated – it was a decision that would later be criticised by some of the survivors. One saving grace was that the defensive chain which closed off the Golden Horn had been lowered and the Byzantine and allied fleets were safe within and able to protect it, meaning that the sea walls facing the Horn could remain unmanned. Soon before the siege began, George Sphrantzes, the advisor to Constantine, was asked by the emperor to take a count of all the fighting men available and found that apart from the foreigners there were no more than 4,773 Greeks.

'I completed my task and presented the master list to my lord and emperor in the greatest possible sadness and depression,' Sphrantzes recalled. 'The true figure remained a secret known only to the emperor and myself.'

7

The Gate of the Dervish Lodge

If you walked towards the walls from gleamingly restored Merkezefendi, through the old cemeteries, you would arrive at Yeni Mevlevihane Kapısı – the Gate of the New Dervish Lodge – named after the place that now hosted the university where Nagihan taught. In the Byzantine era it had been named after Rhegium, a town on the lagoons outside the city where its road had led to, and was richly adorned with inscriptions including those commemorating the swift reconstruction of the walls following the earthquakes of AD 447. As you passed through the gate you arrived in the neighbourhood of Mevlanakapı and beyond it Kocamustafapaşa – Paşa for short. It was a world of tight-packed streets with a motley of decaying houses and low apartment blocks. The contrast with Merkezefendi was not just one of atmosphere and urban fabric, but in the prevailing social and political ideology. Paşa had been a bastion of the left since at least the 1960s, when the neighbourhoods immediately within the walls were still more like a string of villages set in a patchwork of market gardens than a solid urban fabric.

In the 1950s and 1960s it became a location for dormitories associated with the nearby Istanbul University medical faculty, and was a place of settlement for workers arriving in the city. The students, workers and unions stamped a left-wing identity onto the area, which the centrifugal violence of the 1970s later cemented. The neighbourhood was home to the offices of a well-known socialist newspaper, and later its affiliated TV station. There had also been a Greek, Armenian and Jewish population there; while these emigrated over time, they were replaced by other minorities, firstly Alevis and later Kurds, both groups which tended to gravitate towards left-wing politics.

Immediately to the left of the gate within the walls was Kaledibi Sokak – 'Foot-of-the-Tower Street', a single row of houses pressed face to face with the inner wall. They were simple one- and two-storey buildings, often with small courtyards with fruit trees and gardens within them. They were built from a mixture of wood, bricks and concrete breeze blocks, thrown up and extended by their occupants over the years. When I went there for the first time, chickens and ducks still stalked the streets.

It was in one of these houses that a young woman named Yurdanur began her married life in the mid-1990s. When she'd first arrived in Istanbul from her hometown in the southern province of Malatya, the house had seemed like a welcome challenge to her – easier at last than that presented by her husband – and she threw all her energy into making it beautiful.

It was an arranged marriage. Yurdanur was twenty-one, a skinny young woman who weighed not much more than forty kilos and had almost no education. Her elder sister had graduated from high school, studied economics at university and become a manager at a textile company, but when Yurdanur was still in primary school her family had fallen on hard times and her father decided to keep her at home. Her husband Sadık, seven years her senior, was from the same village but had moved to Istanbul a few years earlier, and had bought the house cheaply after finding a job handling paperwork at one of the local docks.

The pair had never spoken to one another before their betrothal. In fact, Yurdanur's heart had been elsewhere: she had hoped to marry Hüseyin, the son of her step-uncle. The two had been exchanging written messages through his younger brother; their mothers knew they liked each other, and there had been some discussion about a match, but her aunt – the wife of her step-uncle – had fought against it on the grounds that Yurdanur suffered from a minor facial paralysis which her aunt feared could make her unable to bear children. Hüseyin offered to run away with her and get married anyway, but she refused due to the shame it would bring on her family.

As it turned out, Sadık too had been pining for another. At some point during their wedding Yurdanur learned from one of Sadık's young cousins that he had been close with another girl – the next-door neighbour, with whom he'd wrestled and had pillow fights as a child – and after Yurdanur pressed further, the girl revealed that Sadık had been unable to marry her because she'd run off with someone else while studying at university. About ten days after they moved into their new home, Sadık had asked if he could read her some poetry he'd written. The poems were about love and nature – she thought they were beautiful, but then she noticed that in the same box there were photographs of this other girl.

'How could you bring these into our home?' she'd demanded, horrified, and he'd torn them up in front of her.

Recalling this years later, Yurdanur giggled with an ease that suggested she was long over it.

'I still bring it up with him,' she said, 'I won't let him forget it!'

We sat on the balcony of their home on Foot-of-the-Tower Street.

It was an unseasonably warm winter's day and the low-rise streets and open ground created the familiar feeling that we were not in the city but perhaps in Yurdanur's home village of Arapgir, for spread out before us were the jams, dried fruit and nuts the family had brought back from there after their last visit. It was an illusion broken only by the contrails of airliners crisscrossing the wide blue sky. Yurdanur detailed the provenance of everything on the table.

'These kind of raisins are found nowhere else in the world, only in Arapgir, and we produce them and dry them there,' she told me. 'These are dried plums, dried apricots, dried chickpeas from Arapgir . . . This is dried mulberry pulp. We boil the fruit with sugar and we call it *malız*. We pour it into big containers and we then whip it up and pour it onto special fabrics we call "curtains", and then we peel it and we call it *sor*. Then we cut and preserve it. There are a lot of Malatya markets in Istanbul but I don't buy anything from those places. We go to our home-town in summer or autumn – we last went there with my husband in November and we bought all we need in terms of nuts, butter, legumes and so on.'

Yurdanur remembered Arapgir in her youth as a warm and diverse place. It was home to a mixed community of Sunni Muslims, Alevis and Armenians. Before the genocide of 1915, it had been predominately Armenian and the site of a major cath-edral, but even during Yurdanur's childhood several Armenian families remained, though over time they left. There was no tension between the different creeds as far as she recalled; she and Sadık were both Alevis. Often described as an Islamic sect, Alevism was better understood as a fusion of pre-historic Anatolian beliefs encompassing shamanism, Zoroastrianism and other creeds with a thin over-glossing of Islam. Its adherents did not attend the mosque, but a community prayer house called a *cemevi*; men and women worshipped together and dancing formed a part of their religious ceremonies. Women were not required to cover their heads, consumption of alcohol was not prohibited, and its members did not observe the Ramadan fast. They had been the subject of persecution in Turkey for long before the Republic, most intensely during the sixteenth and seventeenth centuries, starting with the reign of Sultan Selim the Grim, whose army launched campaigns of massacre and suppression against Alevi communities, which had begun to fall under the influence of the Ottoman Empire's eastern rival, Safavid Iran.

The advent of the Turkish Republic brought a different kind of persecution. The nation's peculiar brand of secularism (in which the Muslim faith was not so much divorced from the state as taken over and run by it) attempted to impose a uniform brand of Islam on the whole population. While the country's small remaining Christian and Jewish communities were able to continue to attend their own schools and worship in their own churches, Alevis were considered Muslims, and had no such dispensation. Added to this state-backed cultural suppression was a rising atmosphere of intolerance that grew through the late twentieth century. Many Sunni Muslims began to regard Alevis as heretics. During the violence of the 1970s, during which Alevi communities almost universally aligned with the left, political enmity acted as a proxy and catalyst for sectarian hatred. During that period several notorious massacres took place, including in Kahramanmaraş, where a marauding mob of rightists went on a five-day killing spree in 1978, murdering more than a hundred Alevis after a series of tit-for-tat attacks between rival factions over the preceding days. Among the most raw and painful of these was an attack by an Islamist mob in 1993 on a hotel in the Anatolian city of Sivas, where artists, writers and musicians had gathered for a symposium on the life of a famous sixteenth-century Alevi poet. The mob – who were angry at the presence of a leftist intellectual who had attempted to publish Salman Rushdie's *Satanic Verses* in Turkish – broke through police barricades and torched the hotel, killing thirty-seven people, including a number of prominent intellectuals, poets and musicians.

But Istanbul was a friendly place to Yurdanur. Her village seemed to have transplanted itself to her new neighbourhood; friends and acquaintances from Arapgir were all around her. When she had first arrived, Sadık's house had been a simple bachelor's den, a small single-storey building constructed mainly of wood and divided into two basic rooms which served as a bedroom and living room, with an adjoining area for the kitchen, bathroom and toilet.

'When I first came my husband asked me, how do you find it? I went inside. I thought to myself: "This place is like a partridge nest." But I didn't say that to my husband . . . I said it was very nice.' The couple brought with them Yurdanur's dowry, which consisted of a mattress, some kitchen utensils, a carpet and a refrigerator, which was delivered a few days later.

'I set up the house, I cleaned it – it took me about ten days,' she recalled. 'When his friends came to visit, they later went and told their mothers and aunts, saying they never saw a house like ours . . . I made it so beautiful.'

Sadık, however, proved tougher to please; he seemed to find fault with everything she did. Soon after their wedding, his parents came and stayed with them for four and a half months, and he berated her in front of them at every opportunity: this dish was too salty, that dish too heavy, and so on. The difference in their family cultures also caused tension. Before she'd married, Yurdanur had worn trousers, manicured her nails, and sometimes put on make-up. In Sadık's family the women never did these things and he promptly forbade them. She said: 'I asked why?

He just said, "No, I don't want it." I saw that if I insisted we would grow apart . . . I said to myself, be patient, Yurdanur. I said, "OK, if you don't want it, I won't wear it", and I gave away all my trousers.'

The first ten years were miserable.

'If you had asked me, in those first ten years, if I'd had financial freedom would I have left my husband, I would have said yes.' After fourteen months of marriage, when Yurdanur became pregnant, she recalled feeling ambivalent; it made her feel more trapped.

'In our eastern tradition you leave your father's house in a wedding dress and your husband's house in a shroud,' she said. 'You have to keep silent about everything. If my father had sent me to school, and if I was someone that could stand on my own feet, I would never have put up with it. You're obliged to stay with him because you are dependent on him and when you have children it's even harder. You think about your children's happiness and ask yourself, "How can I ruin their stability?" And so you have to put up with it for your children.'

So she kept on. During this difficult time, their tiny house on Foot-of-the-Tower Street came to seem like a steady rock in their difficult family life. She and Sadık, these two strangers, might struggle to create the emotional architecture of a relationship between themselves, but they could repair and improve the physical fabric of their home. They started soon after their first daughter was born. There had been so many mice in the house that Yurdanur was scared they would nibble off the newborn's nose and ears. Sadık had done all the building work himself: digging out foundations, strengthening walls, replacing brick with concrete. Over time they knocked through the thin wooden walls on the ground floor to make one large living room, extending the kitchen, and adding an additional floor with two bedrooms upstairs for themselves and the children, and eventually the broad balcony, until the home was utterly transformed from what it had been.

Somehow, over the course of that time, their marriage also began to transform. It helped that they felt sustained by the community around them: other friends and neighbours from Arapgir, some of whom were facing similar or worse struggles.

'When I came here I didn't feel like a stranger,' she said. 'I had relatives and neighbours. There were a lot of people from my hometown. You shared [your troubles] with your neighbour – we supported each other. I would listen, I would think, and if I saw that it made sense I tried to implement it . . . It's women's solidarity. I had a sister-in-law, she was living close to me; we were like two sisters. We are still the same. There were a lot of times when we supported each other, both materially and spiritually. We were really happy with our neighbours. You don't share everything that happens between four walls to the outside – there are things that you experience just within the four walls – but there were things that you shared as much as you needed to. Sharing is for comfort. You cry, you laugh, you relax, you unwind.'

After that first decade their relationship began to improve; each began to learn and accommodate the other's character. Sadık softened, Yurdanur became more confident. She began to dress as she pleased.

Eventually she discovered that her life was happy: she and Sadık had three children in a community that they loved, in a home that had grown with them in the little street by the walls with its low houses and gardens, its chickens and ducks, in the heart of the greatest city in the world.

'Everything about this house is beautiful to me,' she told me as we sat on the terrace. 'Perhaps it's not much, perhaps you may look down on it, but it is a nice home for us. We worked hard for it. We cannot recreate our lifestyle here anywhere else except our hometown. We have seen so many children of our neighbours growing up here. We took care of each other's children. Our children used to go out playing together. We had grandmothers here who have now passed away . . . My son can listen to loud music anytime he likes and no one complains. If someone else does it, I wouldn't mind, I would sing along. It's that kind of beauty.'

There had long been rumours that the neighbourhood would be subject to a redevelopment project, but the talk had been going on for so long that they had stopped believing it would really happen. And so it came as a shock to her when one day in early 2014, an invitation came from the local municipality telling them that their home would be taken from them and they would be moved to an apartment block out on the fringe of the city.

A few doors down from Yurdanur's home on Foot-of-the-Tower Street was another house. At the same time that she was struggling through the early years of her marriage, its occupant was engaged in a different battle. Cem was a young man in his twenties, handsome and six foot three inches tall. As a teenager he'd been athletic and one of the country's top breakdancers – he'd been selected as a backing dancer for Michael Jackson when he performed in Istanbul in the 1980s. Now, emaciated and weighing under 50 kilos, he was in the depths of a heroin addiction. The house had no electricity or heating and he shared it with a handful of other addicts. Winter was on the way, and he would quite possibly not survive it.

Cem had grown up in Paşa. His father's family ran a tavern near the Çapa hospital and his grandfather on his mother's side was a successful leather merchant. His early childhood had been spent on the streets, happily and innocently enough at first

– cycling, playing marbles, throwing balls – but those streets carried him, as if on a conveyor belt, to the world of the older boys, the teens who had been like him a couple of years earlier but now hung out on the corners drinking wine and beer. He and his friends naturally looked towards them. They began running errands, fetching beer from the shops, hiding stolen money, knives and so on. He began drinking at around thirteen, when he and his friends would take their bicycles to other neighbourhoods and steal from shops. A year or two later they started mixing booze with a prescription drug from Cyprus called 'akineton' that the local dealers sold. It made them hallucinate and they thought it was great. He became an 'ear' for the illegal gambling dens in the neighbourhood, watching out on the street corners for the police, and later graduated to become the lookout on the door. His parents knew he was heading in a bad direction but were unable to do anything about it. Every night Cem's father worked in the tavern until two in the morning, then came home, slept and returned to work at 11 a.m. He barely saw him. His mother couldn't control him and by his early teens he'd learned to dominate and bully her. The worst she could do was tell his father, who might beat him, but that was it.

He muddled his way through to the end of high school. He was expelled from three different schools, usually on the grounds of truancy, and finished a year late. He spent the next two and a half years hanging around the neighbourhood without getting a job; he could get away with it because his family were well off. His father, who paid a bribe for him to graduate from high school, believed he'd grow out of his dissolute ways. He hung out on the streets, drinking, fighting, and stealing. Other than that, he was a member of a youth supporters' group for Fenerbahçe football club, where he would act as a scalper, and did his break-dancing. Then came his obligatory six months of military service: the last hope, the longed-for boon for parents of wayward children. His father believed it would sort him out.

But the year happened to be 1991. Turkey at that time was engaged in a brutal insurgency with the Kurdish separatist PKK, a war directed by the generals but fought by young conscripts like Cem. He did thirty days training in Hatay in the south of Turkey and then was sent east to a fortified gendarmerie station in Şemdinli, close to northern Iraq. From there, he and the other conscripts were sent across the border again and again to lay ambushes for the guerrillas who had made their bases in the mountains. More often it was they who were ambushed.

Cem spoke fluently and in impassive, matter-of-fact detail about his life, but when he reached this moment his account became elliptical and disjointed. '250 left, 134 came back. All those intimate friendships, sharing a common fate, all those people being martyred. It's not healthy. You could break up with your lover, get sacked from your job or go through a traffic accident and these are some traumatic incidents and can haunt you and make you react to things in different situations but this was not something I could put to one side . . . the operations in northern Iraq. We went out to ambush every day, it was mandatory.'

He arrived and left Şemdinli by helicopter. There was no decompression time. He arrived back in the airport in Istanbul, where an old friend met him, wanting to show off the brand-new car his father had given him. Cem got in and asked what the plan was. He wanted to drink and find some women and smoke weed. He'd saved a lot of money during his military service and there'd been nothing to spend it on in Şemdinli. At some point during the evening his friend gave him something new to smoke, a brown powder that he called 'angel dust', and it made him vomit. His friend said he'd bought it from the Africans in Aksaray, the sprawling immigrant district in the belly of the old city. A few days later he went with him and bought more. The Africans seemed amazing to him. They handed off the dope like dealers in an American movie: dropping the stuff on the ground and then taking the money in separate transactions.

Later, it was impossible for him to disentangle his descent into addiction from his experiences on military service. 'When I came back I wasn't healthy. I was in a spiritual quest just to forget those days.' The city didn't seem to have changed in the time he was gone, but all his friends said he was different. It was months later that he realised he was using heroin. He'd been without it for longer than usual, and woke up one morning in excruciating pain.

'I still don't know a proper Turkish word to describe that kind of pain and I've never met someone who could put up with it . . . You have stomach ache, diarrhoea. You feel like your bones are giving away. You're incredibly aggressive. You could be so aggressive that you could contemplate killing someone. You have to find money.'

He called his friend and asked him why he was feeling so shitty, and his friend said it was the medicine they'd been taking. He asked him what medicine, and he told him heroin. He begged his friend to give him some more, and he said: 'Come over and smoke some, if you have the money.' It shocked Cem that his friend would demand money from him in this, his hour of need. It was a moment of realisation of the world he had fallen into.

'We didn't have that kind of a relationship. Everybody says that in this circle, but our friendship and history called for not ever saying such a sentence. That's when I said, "Oh boy, you're fucked. Now you're in trouble." In the end, I found the money, went there, smoked it and became a normal person again. It could take fifteen seconds to switch from that state to this, all that pain and the cramps and stomach aches and it disappeared with one puff in less than fifteen seconds. That's the day I realised I was an addict.'

———

Not long after Yurdanur had heard about the municipality's scheme to take her home away, a young man showed up on her doorstep with a plan to help her and her neighbours. He wanted to start an association that would bring together the people of the neighbourhood so they could resist the project with a collective voice.

Fırat was twenty-four years old: stocky and bearded with beetling eyebrows and a deadpan sense of humour. He had been inspired to activism by the Gezi protests, and even years later – when he'd gone bald, got married, and had a child – he would still say that Gezi Park had changed his life. He'd grown up in Paşa, not far from Foot-of-the-Tower Street. Inspired by the crumbling ancient buildings around him, he wanted to become a restoration architect, and at the time of the protests was an undergraduate at a university on the Aegean coast. As soon as he'd seen what was going on in Taksim he'd returned to Istanbul and was there on 31 May when the police ceded the square to the demonstrators.

'It was beautiful,' he recalled of that first night. 'After that, I didn't leave the park. I stayed there. I took on responsibilities, I made new friends. I slept on my feet.' He was part of the group that hung the first banner from the top of the Atatürk Cultural Centre, a huge sign that read 'Stand Tall'. The whole thing had happened by chance. He was a member of the Turkish Communist Party, and the party's leadership was going to send a huge banner for the demonstrators that would read 'Government, resign!'. But someone messed up and sent one saying 'Stand

Tall!' instead. After the correct banner arrived they wondered what to do with the other one, and someone suggested hanging it from the cultural centre.

'The security guards were still there,' Fırat recalled. 'We wanted to go up and at first they wouldn't allow us. Then we begged a guy to let us in and asked him to pretend he didn't see us, and thanks to him, things turned into something else and the banner was seen by everyone.' Within a few days the whole building was festooned.

For Fırat, that summed up the freewheeling spontaneity of Gezi, the sense of freedom and possibility. But what struck him even more was the *politeness*. 'Normally, people living in Istanbul are really disrespectful while you're walking on the street. But during Gezi, people used to turn and apologise if they bumped into someone while walking. It may seem like a small thing, but even for two weeks the notions of earning money, success and so on just disappeared. It was sort of like a commune life . . . You don't have to exceed anyone, you don't have to make it anywhere. I am not an anarchist, but it takes you away from your ego and greed. That's what it's like in Istanbul, in that crowd, on the Metrobus line: bumping into someone and pretending that person doesn't exist just for your own comfort . . . whereas in Gezi an environment came into being where people apologised to each other. That's what stayed with me.'

Fırat's journey through life had not been an easy one. When he was still young his father, who had a successful career as a contractor outfitting hospital buildings, separated from his mother and left her to raise him and his two younger siblings alone, plunging them into poverty. His mother became a cleaner, and Fırat remembered her intentionally leaving home with wet socks so that the people she worked for would take pity on her and give her another pair, which she'd then give to the children. If they gave her breakfast, she'd carefully wrap the cheese in aluminium foil and bring it home to them. On one occasion, Fırat's younger brother had an earache and was crying with pain for days, but his mother couldn't afford to take him to hospital. This situation left him with a sense of indignation that never left him.

Fırat reckoned that socialism was in his bones; or, as he put it, it was the natural ideological stance of anyone with a sense of compassion or social justice. But it might also have been partly because he'd grown up in Paşa. Many of his childhood friends had flirted with extreme organisations such as the Marxist–Leninist DHKP/C, which was committed to armed revolution and considered a terrorist group by both the US and the EU. He never went down that road, but he was an angry and impatient child with what he called an 'ugly stubbornness'. When he was thirteen his father remarried, and he refused to visit him because he wouldn't sleep under the same roof as his stepmother. A couple of years later when his mother also remarried and moved to Şanlıurfa, usually known as Urfa, far away in south-east Anatolia, he refused to go with her on the same principle, even though he didn't really blame her for remarrying: she needed to for her own security. 'It wasn't about houses, yachts or apartments,' he said. 'It was just about getting by.'

He remembered when a van came to take her belongings away; his younger siblings went with her. 'I was carrying things to the van and crying at the same time. And then she was gone. I stayed on in the apartment for a month. The landlord took the deposit. After one month, he came over and asked me if I was able to pay the rent and I said no. I didn't have a job, I'd failed my first year of high school . . . I took my bag and left.' And so he found himself homeless at the age of fifteen. For the next twenty nights he slept at the nearby Çapa hospital. During that time he met a university student who helped get him a job filing customer contract applications at a mobile phone store.

After a few days working there the guy noticed how dishevelled he was and pressed him about his situation. He took him out for a drink and after a couple of beers, Fırat opened up.

'He invited me to stay at his place. I told him I didn't want to bother him but he insisted . . . I've experienced many great things in my life but the best moment was that hot shower and soft bed. It was that night. I started to live with him for some time after that. He spoke with me and asked what I wanted out of life, what my expectations were and he told me that whatever it was I wanted, I had to study first.'

So he spoke to the vice principal of his school, explained his situation, and was allowed to re-register. But he also needed to pay his own rent and feed himself. He worked nights in a range of jobs: as a janitor, a waiter, a chef, a decorator, a construction worker. At one point he had a job painting dye onto polyester buttons for a textile company. The school authorities were understanding of the fact that he had to work to support himself and couldn't always make it to class on time. Some days he would arrive early and sleep in the classroom before everyone else arrived, and one geography teacher presented him with an alarm clock as a joke. Fırat was furious: 'My situation wasn't voluntary. He apologised after that and we became closer. That was the advantage of the school, the teachers were really good people.'

Most of the children in his neighbourhood never finished high school; many never even finished primary school. But in the end, Fırat graduated with grades good enough to enrol on an undergraduate course in restoration architecture, just as he'd dreamed of. He was about to take up his place at university when his mother returned to Istanbul pregnant, having got divorced from the husband in Urfa. Fırat was working as an apartment caretaker at the time. He'd converted an earthquake bunker in the building where he worked into a small flat and was living there rent-free, and so he was able to help support his mother and her newborn baby, but it meant he had to delay university for a year.

He'd finally taken up his place at university, and was in the process of graduating, when the Gezi protests erupted. It may have been serendipity, but it happened at a time when he had begun to search for ways to become more politically involved. He was aware of the assistance he'd received on his journey through life: the support of his teachers, of neighbours, of the young man who took him in when he was homeless. It gave him a sense of the importance of family, in the broadest meaning of the word: the networks of support and solidarity that allowed someone to overcome obstacles and thrive.

'A person has to be able to think about his country – I say country but I mean environment, neighbourhood, city – and not hold these problems as different from what he has going on at home. When you think like this, you look around for friends and you act together. There are people already in this struggle, in some cases you take their guidance or follow in their footsteps. After some point, joining a cause becomes a necessity. You want to take responsibility, you want to be a part of something.'

He had already joined the Communist Party, but Gezi energised him, gave him fresh sense of purpose. 'Gezi was the first place in my life that made me feel like I was human. It was the first place where I really tried to make the world better, where I really believed it and worked for it . . . The human condition is clear in Turkey: we live to fill our stomachs and help others make money. Life never fulfils you, you never get to do the things you want. You can ask a hundred people and perhaps five or six of them do what they like, the majority do not. You work at a job you don't like, you live in a place you don't want to live in, you are subjected to politics you disagree with, to laws you don't want. Nothing is the way you want it.

When the objective should be to be human, you only get to be a device . . . So when I said I felt human for the first time there, what I mean is that I felt I was doing something right, that I was doing something for myself, for the people alongside me, for the generations that would come after me. It refreshed my faith in things.'

And so after the police moved in and broke up the protests, Fırat, like the thousands of other young people who had been energised and inspired in those two weeks, returned to his own neighbourhood and began to look at what he could do. That search would lead him to Foot-of-the-Tower Street and to Yurdanur and the residents there, who were now struggling to keep their homes.

———

A heroin addict could often fund the first six months or so of their addiction through the goodwill of the people around them, and so in the early days Cem borrowed from his friends, family, neighbours: anyone he knew who was trusting and well-disposed. Then he started to empty out his loved ones' homes of valuables. At his sister's house, he took her dowry items – glass crockery, fine teapots and so on – and exchanged them directly for drugs.

'They would rip you off spectacularly,' he recalled. He'd given a dealer 1,000 liras-worth of goods for a single packet of heroin worth about 10 lira. Around the same time he started dealing weed to fund his habit, acting as a middleman. If he knew a dealer was selling a bag for 75 lira, he'd charge a customer 100 lira and keep another cut of about 5 liras-worth for himself.

At around that time he met a woman and they fell in love. It was quick: within four months of meeting each other they were married. She was a professional volleyball player and lived a clean life.

'We met, and I was using heroin, and I told her I was using heroin on the second day,' he recalled. 'That's how our love started. She thought she could save me: it was that kind of connection. I had a feeling of finding someone and getting support from her. I had a feeling of finding pity too: pity me, love me, that kind of thing. She thought that together we could save me with our love.'

By this time Cem's family had worked out he was an addict. They found heroin in the house a couple of times and when they'd confronted him he became aggressive and denied it. His father tried to stop the marriage from taking place, but the pair eloped and got engaged anyway. Within a couple of months he'd taken all the gold coins which friends and family traditionally give couples to mark their union, sold them, and replaced with counterfeits.

Not long after that he checked into AMATEM, a state-run rehab centre. After three days of withdrawal he couldn't stand it, checked himself out, and was using heroin again within an hour of leaving. That was in 1993, and over the following years he reckoned he went there twenty or thirty times, and around ten times to private rehab clinics. He never got clean for any length of time, and began dealing heroin, buying 10- or 20-gram bags and splitting them up to sell to other users.

His wife never used, but she began to be sucked into his world. His family had persuaded them to move to a summerhouse they owned about four hours outside the city. Both their families would send them money, and every two days they would come back to Istanbul; he would make her wait at a café, and then he'd go and buy twenty or thirty packets. Then they'd spend a night in a hotel, and return to the summerhouse the next day.

At some point he managed to get clean for a year and a half, but during that time he and his wife argued so much that they split up and he ended up living in a hotel near Taksim, where he started using again, this time injecting rather than smoking. It was better, he said, because you used less that way. He and his wife continued to see each other on and off, spending time together when he was clean.

She became pregnant and they had a daughter. After that both their families worked hard to keep them together. They moved back to Paşa, but the familiarity of being in his old neighbourhood only made him want to use more. 'I wanted to save our marriage, but I was too far away from being a person who could take such a responsibility or make it work. I woke up in the mornings – there's a process, you know – you have to find money, you have to find junk, you have to use.'

Eventually when their daughter was two years old his wife's family intervened and called an end to it, and they split for good, but by that time he was away from the house so much that he barely cared.

That was how he ended up squatting in the derelict house on Foot-of-the-Tower Street owned by a friend of his who was in prison. He'd virtually stopped eating and was 'five minutes from death', in his words: 'just injections and no veins left'. At one point he'd seen a doctor, who told him he would probably die that winter if he didn't make a change.

By this point his family had cut him off, but there was one line of support they kept open: he could go at any time to his father's restaurant and have a meal there. He went there to see the manager, Muharrem, and begged him to take him back to AMATEM: 'It was a period when I was tired of this. Something happened and I thought I could stop it. He said I will pick you up tomorrow morning at 8.30, be here.'

At first he thought they wouldn't take him after all his previous failed visits. He finished his stash that night and they went to AMATEM in the morning. 'They said they would accept me in three days' time. I was extremely happy, happy like I'd won the lottery.'

During those three days he kept using. He even hid a stash of money so that if he quit, he could immediately start again.

Early on during his stay at AMATEM he wanted to leave but didn't have the physical strength to do it. But after ten days had passed, he felt stronger and wanted to stay. Normally patients were discharged after ten days, but he begged to stay and staff agreed to re-enrol him in the alcohol section in order to allow him to remain for another seven days.

One day before he left he called his family and asked if they'd have him back, and they said they would allow him on the condition he remained clean. He did urine tests every few days to show them he was, and he began going to therapy two or three times a week. For the next year he did everything the therapist told him to: he never left home, he did not use a phone, and he went to sleep by 11 p.m. every night. When he began to go to Narcotics Anonymous, it felt like a turning point.

Before that he had never believed staying clean was really possible in the long run: 'When you are using, you never see anyone who's clean . . . there are only people who are having a break. I went [to Narcotics Anonymous] and saw people who stayed clean and they told their experiences. I went there every night for three years: I had never seen such a thing. Can you recognise a former heroin addict on the street in broad daylight? You can't but you come here and see ex-addicts. When you are using you never see one. But I saw there were people getting on with their lives: translators, actors, bankers, doctors – and I've met them. They come to the meetings and they stay clean. Just sharing their experiences. When you continue doing this, you stay clean. When you stay clean, things look up.'

Yurdanur and Sadık's house would be purchased by the municipality, and its value would be converted into equity in a newly
built apartment at a place they hadn't heard of called Kayabaşı,
built by TOKİ, Turkey's Mass Housing Administration, which
had partnered with the municipality for the project. Foot-of-the-
Tower Street would be erased and replaced by a park with cafés,
playgrounds and cycle lanes as part of a project to restore the
areas along the walls.

They had gleaned all this by checking the public plans submitted
by the municipality and from talking to their neighbours who
had already been approached. Then in early 2014 they were invited
to their own one-on-one meeting in the office of the deputy
mayor, who confirmed the whole thing and presented it in the
most glowing terms, as if the offer of the loan and the new apartment were a favour being bestowed upon them.

'We are not going to abuse you,' Yurdanur recalled him as
saying. 'We have agreed with TOKİ, and TOKİ is willing to
help you. It is going to make you a gesture.' He said that the
difference in value between their existing home and the apartment would become a loan that they would pay off over ten
years. 'We just listened,' Yurdanur recalled. The couple had
decided to feign approval in order to elicit as much information
as possible. 'Whenever we had to respond we just said, "How
lovely! What a wonderful offer!" He was very excited. "Could
you tell this to the people in the neighbourhood?" he asked us.
"How are you getting along with the people in your neighbourhood?" We said we had good relationships. He said he didn't
want them to come here all together at once, there can be
hot-blooded people and they may disturb the mood.'

Privately they were seething. They felt confident they could
keep their property because they and their neighbours all had
clear deeds and property rights. Many of the houses were
ramshackle and a hodgepodge of different styles and materials,

but they were not *gecekondu* – 'built at night' – an expression that referred to the illegal housing which had driven the expansion of Istanbul through the mid- to late twentieth century.

'I own a house, I don't owe anyone any money, I have children and they're in school, we have a routine and are settled here and – thank God – we want for nothing,' said Yurdanur. 'And what are they saying? You buy my house and leave me without a home and completely wreck my situation, and I will be working non-stop for ten years to become a homeowner again? And you don't even ask me if I am able to pay it.' To make things worse, Sadık was undergoing cancer treatment at the time.

'My husband is retired. He has health problems. We still have routine checks at the hospital . . . The price they put on the house means nothing to us. Even they give us billions, it's not about the money. We want to live where we are now, within our own culture.'

A few weeks later, the mayor himself, Mustafa Demir, hosted a meeting at which he invited people from across the neighbourhood to hear about the plans. It was then that Yurdanur, Sadık and other affected residents made their feelings clear: they would fight the plan with every means at their disposal.

It was around that time that Fırat came into their lives. He had heard about the project and had the idea of creating a neighbourhood association to fight against it. Yurdanur and Sadık knew of a house on the same street that they could rent and use as a centre for it.

And so the Walled Neighbourhoods Living and Support Association came into being in one of Foot-of-the-Tower Street's low houses. When I visited on a wet autumn day in 2015 it was full of activity. Residents gathered in the courtyard to listen to live music, as well as speeches about the threats facing their neighbourhood. In a makeshift classroom at the back a small group of children were having extra maths lessons. Fırat had heard from a friend about the urban renewal project to demolish the houses along the walls, and this was the issue he'd decided to focus on. He went around the affected area with a friend, going door to door to raise awareness and find support.

'Everyone was complaining about it,' he recalled. 'We spoke to them, asking about their situation, to see if they wanted to give their houses away, and they all said they didn't. If someone was considering giving their house away, it was more about selling it at a decent price so they could buy somewhere else. They didn't want to be homeless.' Fırat soon approached Yurdanur and her husband Sadık – they were known as people who were respected and influential in the community, and from there, he tried to build support for some kind of collective action. Some people were sceptical of their motives.

'It was because before us men with briefcases visited them asking about prices and how much they were going to give them, etc. This is what I told them: I live here, my house is not in the gentrification area but I grew up here. My memories are here, this place has a history and it's true for all of us. It's precious for all of us.'

In the end many of those affected by the scheme were won over, and the idea for the association evolved organically during these conversations to encompass more than just the expropriation issue. Many of the families Fırat spoke to were worried about schooling. Over the previous few years the government had pushed through a series of wide-reaching educational reforms that critics had linked to a pronounced drop in levels of reading, maths and science in Turkey's OECD rankings. Among the most controversial of these was an expansion in religious vocational – or 'imam hatip' – schools of the kind Erdoğan himself had attended. The government claimed to be responding to demand, but sceptics saw it as part of Erdoğan's professed desire to raise 'pious generations'.

These schools offered a curriculum of increased religious instruction including Quran study, classical Arabic and courses on the life of the Prophet. Nationally, they still only accounted for about 14 per cent of pupils enrolled at high-school level, but children could end up being placed in them against their will if they performed poorly in national entrance exams since the schools were often among the least competitive academically. They catered to families who were fearful for their children's moral education, but those of a secular mindset, or those who cared more about their job prospects, were often appalled at the idea of their children going there.

In Fatih, several large state schools had been converted into imam hatips, and children were frequently assigned to them against their or their parents' wishes. Fırat's brother Ercü had attended one for a year and left Istanbul to go and live with his aunt in order to go to a different school. His sister had also been placed in one and decided to quit high school altogether and do home schooling rather than go there. In Mevlanakapı, the issue was particularly fraught, because many of the residents – like Yurdanur and Sadık – were Alevis, and they already objected to the religious element in the main national curriculum, which subjected their children to Sunni doctrinal teaching.

And so the idea arose that rather than simply form an association on a single issue, they would address education and whatever else they might help with. One of the residents who owned one of the threatened houses agreed to rent it to them for a discount price, and that's how the Walled Neighbourhoods Living and Support Association came about. There was a political agenda, albeit in the background: the association was run in part by a committee and volunteers from the Turkish Communist Party of which Fırat was a member, although others from the community got involved too. Among them was Deniz, a university student who was not in the party, but lived locally and had a background in volunteering with children. She and Fırat worked together and became a couple, and they painted and cleaned up the run-down association building together.

'You can see things have spiralled out of control,' Fırat said with a grin as he showed me around. At its height, the association was teaching four classes of seven students across a range of subjects. Volunteers from the party taught the lessons. Some were qualified teachers, others professionals with postgraduate qualifications – a doctor teaching biology, an engineer teaching physics. Initially these classes were for eighth grade students but as demand increased, they opened basic classes in maths and literacy for third- and fourth-grade students. They ran Turkish classes for Syrian refugees. Some evenings they hosted movie nights for around twenty to twenty-five local women, who were often stuck in their homes with few avenues to socialise. Occasionally they hosted outside speakers, including a Harvard historian Cemal Kafadar, whose talk was attended by about two hundred people and drew in visitors from outside the neighbourhood.

The association basically took over Fırat's life. He'd discovered that it was impossible to build a stable career as a restoration architect: 'The employer buys this place and it's a three-months' contract and you agree but then once that three months is over, you are unemployed again. It has no guarantee, you only have a job until the project is finished; when it's done, you don't have one any more. Only the big firms with international partnerships give you an employment guarantee and they seek five years' experience. In an environment you work half a year, the other half is unemployment and it's very difficult to gain that five years of experience.'

Their fight against the expropriations seemed to be bearing fruit. When the municipality invited the various residents back for individual meetings, they gathered first at the association and then all went together to the municipality to see them as a group. They were shocked. A few weeks later the municipality contacted them again and requested a meeting with them, not as individuals, but as an association. It recognised them as an interlocutor. It felt like a step towards victory.

———

Cem had not seen Muharrem, the manager of the family restaurant where he had gone to eat during the worst days of his addiction, since the morning when he had dropped him off at the rehab centre for the final time. As we entered the restaurant one quiet afternoon the pair embraced and Muharrem looked him up and down in speechless amazement.

'You haven't changed in fourteen years,' said Cem. 'How does a man not age in that time? You have the same suit. Everything.'

'I've gained a few kilos . . .' he replied.

'I've gained forty.'

Muharrem ushered us to a table and ordered tea. 'It's something else to see you again, to sit next to you. Back in the day, you wouldn't even speak . . . This one suffered so much, to see him like this now, it's one for the books. What can I say, to be able to survive from this filth? Impossible. I was putting food in front of him and he didn't even eat.'

'God bless him,' said Cem. 'Every day he'd say, "Come and eat here, don't pay money to anyone else." That's a big favour. I came to this place and took money and God bless him, he was such a big brother to me, and not just for one day or two days. Not everybody takes a junkie into his shop, you know what I mean?'

Nowadays Cem almost never came to Paşa; staying away had been part of his rehabilitation. He returned now only to run addiction clinics and NA sessions. That had become his career:

an addiction counsellor whose rare journey, eloquence and insight about addiction had led him to collaborate with university academics, police and government officials in trying to combat Istanbul's burgeoning drug epidemic. His experience as an addict of twenty years who had now been clean for more than ten made him almost unique among those working on the issue in the city.

About three years earlier a new opportunity had presented itself. Cem was working with a group of academics and psychologists who were making presentations at state-run rehab centres, the state-run clinics where he had got clean. They were stressing the importance of long-term follow-up treatment and intervention that went beyond the centres' ten-day treatment stints. Officials from Esenyurt Municipality, one of the districts of Istanbul, approached him after one of these presentations and said they were looking to start their own project: a live-in centre where addicts could go to keep clean after they got clean. Esenyurt was Istanbul's largest district with a population of nearly a million people, a sprawling area of high rises with a population almost entirely formed of recent migrants, and a case study in the kind of community breakdown that was afflicting the city. Research published in 2021 based on an analysis of city wastewater found that Esenyurt had the highest heroin use of anywhere in the city. The same study, which compared overall drug use levels with ten other major cities, put heroin use in Istanbul the second highest after New York.

The AK Party mayor of the district had made combating the problem a key priority, and had spent a huge sum of money checking more than four hundred addicts into private hospitals in an attempt to get them clean, but with no tangible results. The new live-in rehab clinic would be the first of its kind in the country, and Cem agreed to help on the spot, helped set it up and had been working there ever since.

What they were doing barely scratched the surface of the drug problem in Esenyurt, and did nothing to address its root causes. The scale of the problem was dramatically larger than when Cem had been an addict. 'There is a wave of addiction now,' he said. 'The other day I saw a fifteen-year-old girl, and another boy who died: seventeen years old. I could not even hospitalise them at AMATEM because I needed to take them to the child polyclinic first.'

When he compared Esenyurt to Mevlanakapı in his childhood, the obstacles to escaping addiction seemed far steeper than those he faced. People were poorer, less educated, with more dysfunctional and less supportive families, and immersed in a culture where drug use and addiction were so prevalent that it was hard to escape.

'Addiction in the ghettos is a deeper kind of addiction. It is harder to solve it there than among more cultured people. It is a family disease. It's not a disease you can heal from by yourself. The mother and the father need to heal too and the wife needs to heal too, and then you can have a chance at healing . . . If something is missing, it is harder for the addict to stay clean. The families know nothing: the child is trying to stay clean, but parents are rehashing the past, saying, "You did this, you stole this, you couldn't do this, you are an animal," and then push the child more away.'

Another problem, he believed, was the collision of rural and urban cultures brought by migrants who had come to the city but were unable to adapt themselves to city life. They sought to live as they had done in the villages, but had children whose dreams were formed by the social media age, who craved money and wealth and believed they wouldn't have to work for it – which in a place as cut-off and deprived as Esenyurt was a recipe for disillusion and despair.

Still, at the live-in centre they managed to get people clean and keep them clean. At any one time between fifteen and twenty recovering addicts lived there. 'There is no money in Turkey or the whole world that can give me the satisfaction this gives me,' he said. 'This week I helped a couple of them to find work, and these are people who stay clean. The effort they make to stay clean from day one to today makes me sit here comfortably. I can help them get better and I know with my message and my experience they can stay clean and they appreciate this and are grateful to me.'

Cem had a fiancée now, a woman he had met about seven years earlier while she was working at the rehab clinic where he attended NA. The clinic had offered him a job and that was when they got together. She knew all about his past. He was also seeing his daughter regularly, a couple of times a week. He still feels a great sadness about his past: 'A lost youth, not seeing your own child grow up. Family relations frozen . . . Certainly the thing that makes me saddest is the lost years. Years spent on nothing. The harm I've done to myself. Knowing you can never be a normal person. It's hard to be an addict. You constantly have to avoid certain things, to not react against certain things and to live with a strict discipline. This can be difficult. If I could go back, I'd keep my marriage because I am a domestic man. I would have loved to see my child grow and take her to school. Would have loved to spend more time with her. These are the things that remain in my past and I beat myself up about them. Now I am at a different place. A better place where I am relaxed and in comfort. Thank God, I am happy today.'

8

The Gate of Martyrs

There were many ways to arrive at the walls, each with its own mood that changed according to the weather or the time of day, such that the city never ceased to strike me anew. So it was one November morning when I headed to the expanse of cemeteries near the gate of Edirnekapı. I took the last stage of the journey on the Metrobus, an articulated coach that travelled in cordoned-off lanes like a train. It was one of the city's cheapest and most efficient forms of transport and was packed at almost any hour. That morning Istanbul was submerged in a damp sepia fog, and as we crossed the bridge over the Golden Horn the carriage was flooded with mist-diffused light, bright and comprehensive. I watched people look up from their phones to the windows. Outside were the familiar contours of the old city, its domes, towers and minarets rinsed of colour and rendered into silhouettes. It was the kind of moment at which Istanbul excelled: the sudden shift from the mundane to the numinous, along with an unexpected sense of community, as if we were all connected through the act of partaking in something precious and free.

I felt this most intensely when I took one of the old open-decked ferries across the Bosphorus or to the islands: the smell of the sea, the wind on your skin, the cry of seagulls; the flights of shearwaters skimming across the unfolding skyline; tankers rolling past with the majesty of leviathans, so huge and close they were hard to encompass; the fug of the lower decks in winter, the tea and *simit* vendors and the salesmen who hawked novel, dangerous-looking kitchen implements, turning the cabin into a theatre as they demonstrated them for the entertainment of the passengers. I felt it too on the *dolmuş*, the private mini-buses that plied set routes around the city, a hybrid between bus and taxi. You passed your fare forward through the hands of the other customers to the driver, who glanced down and thumbed through the notes and coins even as he forged his way through the traffic. Hurtling across the Bosphorus Bridge in a *dolmuş*, cramped as a space shuttle, bonded to my fellow passengers through the quaint act of passing money, the city stretching away beneath us: I felt in those moments an unfamiliar feeling that I was part of it, one of its people, that I belonged there.

The Edirnekapı Metrobus station was, in its way, just as characteristic of the city's moods and atmospheres: a breathtaking piece of utilitarian violence wrought on the urban topography. It stood in the central reservation of the O-1 highway, which ran straight through the cemetery in a concrete-walled cutting twenty metres deep. From there, bombarded by the roar and fumes of ten lanes of traffic, you ascended to ground level via an open metal staircase that led to a footbridge. Soon after I'd left it, however, the sound died away and I was once again cocooned in a fog that shrouded the gridded avenues of the cemetery. Cypresses and palm trees loomed out of the whiteness, the silence pierced now and then by the wing claps of crows and shrieks of parakeets. Large sections of the Edirnekapı cemetery were given over to martyrs, with separate areas for the army, navy, air force and police. Among these were the dead from the Russo-Turkish Wars, the Balkan Wars, and the Gallipoli campaign. The collection of graves I was seeking were among the most recent additions to this tally. Lined up along the cemetery's south-eastern edge were a row of pristine tombs covered with flowers and topped with Turkish flags. Unusually, these were not soldiers, but civilians. Their lives all ended on the same date: 15 July 2016.

On that Friday evening, Tolga Ecebalın had been in Eyüp Sultan visiting his fiancée. He was a slim, clean-cut young man, twenty-seven years old, divorced with two young children. He worked as a shop assistant in a shoe shop. He had grown up in Lonca, a run-down, pious neighbourhood near the Eğrikapı Gate. His wedding day was about two months away.

A few miles away, Servet Acun, a police officer whose station was in the heart of the old city, had arrived at his home out on the lagoons, finished dinner with his wife and was sitting drinking tea with her while watching the television.

On the Anatolian side in Ümraniye, the Açıkkollu family were preparing to celebrate the birthday of their son Fatih, who was turning seventeen and about to enter his final year at high school. It was just the four of them: parents Gökhan and Tülay, Fatih, and his sister Zeynep, who was seven. Tülay had bought Fatih a cake and a North Face T-shirt. They were going to give him these later in the evening after they'd finished dinner, so as to make a small surprise of it.

For these people and millions of others around the country, who were settling down to a quiet evening, the night's events began in a similar way: the arrival of messages from friends and colleagues telling them to switch on the news because something strange was happening. The two bridges over the Bosphorus were blocked by soldiers, and traffic had ground to a halt. Initial news reports mentioned a possible bomb threat, but within minutes it became clear that wasn't it at all. Soldiers and tanks were on the streets at different points around the city, and there were reports of gunfire in Ankara, with fighter jets and helicopters in the sky. At that point, the whole country knew what was happening: it was part of a playbook seared into the nation's psyche through traumatic repetition. For the fifth time in six decades Turkey's military, or a faction within it, had decided to overthrow the elected government.

Servet Acun had received a warning before the news broke: messages on a police WhatsApp group told him that soldiers had entered an Istanbul police station and were disarming the officers. The Açıkkollu family, meanwhile, sat glued to the TV screen and their phones. Viral videos showed the tanks rolling towards Istanbul's Atatürk Airport. Soon, Prime Minister Binali Yıldırım appeared on television, confirming what everyone had realised. He shied away from using the word 'coup', calling it instead an 'unlawful act by some people outside of the military chain of command', and vowed it would be thwarted: 'Those who made this attempt, those who made this madness, will pay the heaviest price.' When the presenter pressed him as to whether this could be called a coup attempt, he still demurred, saying: 'It would not be right to call it a coup yet; it is true that there has been an insurrection.' His unwillingness to use the word may have been due to the aura of inevitability that hung over Turkish coup d'états.

It was clear, however, that this time round things were different. Unlike in previous coup attempts, events were unfolding in real time and across an array of media that the putschists seemed unable to control. Yıldırım's defiant statement was just the first indication that things were not going according to their plan. Across social media and news channels, the AK Party and various state agencies were urging people to resist. The country's citizens and elected government were not stepping dazed into whatever reality the plotters had prepared for them; they were fighting back.

It was around this time that Tolga Ecebalın headed out into the sultry night with his fiancée to join the thousands of others who had begun streaming onto the streets to defy the soldiers. So too did Servet Acun, who put on his uniform, took his handgun and all the ammunition he could find, and headed out on his motorbike towards Fatih.

There was a point in the evening when what was taking place ceased to have the cinematic feel of a breaking news story and became something immediate and terrifying. For most, this moment came with the sound of fighter jets roaring low over the skyline. In Ankara, they bombed the national parliament building, but in Istanbul they seemed only intended to intimidate. Sonic bombs rolled out across the city, rattling and smashing windowpanes. The Açıkkollu family heard the crashing sounds, and then the noise of people chanting in the streets, and then sporadic gunfire in the distance. Fearful of stray bullets, they moved from the sofa and huddled on the floor in front of the television.

For Servet Acun, the night's events took on a dreadful reality as he was speeding towards the old city. As he drove along the main highway, the carriageway began to fill up with demonstrators who had come out to oppose the coup. They were chanting and waving flags; cars had stopped on the road and were beeping their horns in solidarity. He felt excited, exhilarated at first, until suddenly he was confronted by a scene of carnage. A tank had ploughed through the traffic and protesters, crushing both cars and people. Dismounting, he came to the body of a young woman; she was still alive but had been run over by the tank and had devastating injuries. For a moment he considered putting her on his motorbike and taking her to hospital but he saw that this was impossible. She died there on the ground, and he carried on towards Fatih, forcing his way through the crowds with a growing sense of horror and anger.

By this time the coup plotters had commandeered a state TV station, and forced the presenter to read a statement by a body calling itself the 'Peace at Home Council' which accused Erdoğan's government of corruption, authoritarianism and misrule and said it was assuming control of the country. 'The government, which has lost all its legitimacy, has been dismissed from office,' it declared.

Only a few minutes later, Erdoğan himself appeared. Speaking from an unknown location, he addressed the nation via video call on a mobile phone shakily held up by a TV presenter. He looked harried, a faintly dishevelled figure in a tightly framed shot with a curtain behind him, as if in a passport booth. Occasionally his image was replaced by incoming call notifications that the presenter frantically cancelled. It was the most fragile of connections to the nation, a digital equivalent of a trickle of water, but it was all he needed.

'I would like to call out to our people,' he declared. 'I am inviting them to the squares and airports of our provinces. Let's gather as a nation at the airports and squares. Let this minority come with their tanks and weapons and do whatever they may. Until today, I have not seen a force greater than the people's will.'

As Servet Acun got closer the road was blocked by abandoned trucks and tanks and it became hard going, but finally he passed through the land walls at Vatan Caddesi, the wide avenue that cuts into the heart of the city, and when he arrived at the main Police Security Directorate that lay on one side of it, he found a colleague on duty and asked where he should go. All he wanted to do was find the soldiers and confront them. He was pointed to the main municipality offices a few hundred yards down the road, where protesters were facing off against a group of soldiers who had occupied the building. He rode on through the thickening crowds until suddenly he felt bullets whistle past his ears. He slid from his bike, as he and all those around him dropped to the ground.

When he looked up he saw that some of those around were lying still, while others were struggling to get up. He was at the edge of a park adjacent to the municipality building that was strewn with the remains of Byzantine masonry. He crawled to a nearby tree, took cover, and began to return fire, trading shots with the group of twenty or so soldiers across the road. A few civilians had guns and were firing back as well, and protesters continued to run forward, shouting and chanting, though he urged them to get away.

Among them was Tolga Ecebalın. At some point in the evening he had called his father, who still lived in Lonca, which was nearby. He had also headed out to resist when news of the coup attempt broke, and had flowed with the growing crowds towards the park and the confrontation with the soldiers. When Tolga heard what was happening, he immediately headed there, ignoring his father's warnings to stay away. By this time the tarmac road beside the park was shining with patches of wet blood. The crowds, still defiant, were chanting. They scattered whenever the soldiers opened fire, then crept back in to pull away the dead and injured towards ambulances waiting nearby.

Sometime during this repeated cycle of advancing, coming under fire, and falling back, Tolga was among those who fell. He was hit by a bullet under his right eye. His father was about fifty metres away when he saw a body fall to the ground, and in a split second he realised it was his son. By the time he got to him the crowd was already carrying him to a nearby ambulance. He was declared dead within the hour.

Similar scenes were being played out at various points around the city, where demonstrators and police were confronting the soldiers. But the tide was turning. A spokesman for the armed forces came on air to disavow the coup attempt as the action of a rogue minority. Loyal army units had begun to mobilise, and many of the rank and file soldiers involved in the coup attempt – most of whom, it would transpire, had no idea what they were involved in – began to waver. Erdoğan was reported to have escaped a helicopter attack by rogue special forces on the hotel where he was holidaying on the Mediterranean coast, and had boarded a plane bound for Atatürk Airport, which had been reclaimed by the police and army. All over the city, those involved in the uprising began to surrender or flee.

When Erdoğan's plane landed in Istanbul in the small hours of the morning, he was met by a scene that mirrored his arrival during the Gezi Park protests: again it was the middle of the night; again he was greeted by thousands of rapturous supporters; and again it was a moment laden with foreboding. 'Strike for strike, death for death,' the crowd chanted, and: 'We want executions.' It was not hard to understand their anger. Through the course of the evening videos had circulated of the atrocities perpetrated by the putschists: tanks crushing cars and civilians, soldiers gunning down unarmed protestors, and shooting at those who tried to rescue the wounded. One clip showed a helicopter gunship opening fire on a group of people dashing across a road near the presidential palace in Ankara. Some 250 people had died resisting the coup attempt, and another 2,200 were wounded.

Erdoğan was clear about who was behind the coup attempt: the movement of Fethullah Gülen: once his ally, now a bitter enemy. The accord between the AK Party and the Gülen Movement had broken down spectacularly about three years earlier. This falling out had been a complicated and opaque process, but in essence the two turned on one another to fight over the spoils after their common enemy – the secularist establishment – had been defeated. At the end of 2013 Gülenist prosecutors launched a series of graft investigations in which they wiretapped top figures in government, including Erdoğan, implicating him and his entourage in a web of corruption. These cases became public knowledge with a wave of arrests and the leak of damning phone evidence intended to disgrace the government into resigning. Erdoğan had survived, however, and counter-attacked, seizing the Gülenists' powerful media empire and business assets and attempting to purge the police and judiciary of their presence.

Speaking at the airport, he said the coup was the work of the 'Parallel State' – his preferred shorthand for the Gülenists since their falling out, and added that the coup plotters had 'been taking orders from Pennsylvania', the US state where Fethullah Gülen himself was still living in self-imposed exile. The Gülenists, he said, were a 'virus' that must be purged from the state once and for all. It was a sentiment with which Turkey's fractured opposition, who had long feared and despised the Gülen Movement, could certainly agree. For the government's opponents, the failure of the coup attempt was a cause for overt celebration, but private unease. Very few people had wanted the putschists to succeed: had they done so, they would have overthrown a government with a passionate and deep base of support and sparked such fierce counter-resistance that they may have tipped the country into civil war.

However, there was a growing fear shared by many Turks over

how broad-ranging the government's revenge might be, how far it might extend beyond the Gülenists, and whether the insurrection would become a pretext to carry out its own coup, suborning the state apparatus to its own control once and for all. In his airport speech, Erdoğan had described the coup attempt as 'a gift from God' in the sense that it would allow him to purge the military of disloyal elements once and for all. It was a phrase that his opponents would not forget.

The final, defining images of that bloody night were played out on the Bosphorus Bridge, the great suspension bridge that spanned the city's Anatolian and European sides and where hours earlier, the first inklings of trouble had been detected. The sun was rising on a new day when the soldiers who had been holding the bridge finally surrendered. Crowds had flocked there during the course of the night, and some thirty demonstrators had been killed in the confrontation. Now, in the bright morning light, set against the panorama of the city, the soldiers huddled on the ground in a tight knot, hands shielding their heads, as furious young men beat them, kicked them and whipped them with belts.

For some people that night never seemed to end at all. Servet Acun had remained at the municipality until the soldiers there were finally routed and fled at about four-thirty in the morning when police used an armoured vehicle to advance on them. During the course of the night he had broken a finger and injured his knees by throwing himself on the tarmac. When he went to the hospital, he was so shaken that for a long time he still believed the soldiers were coming and refused to put his pistol away. The sounds of fighter jets swooping over the city made him jump at every moment.

Gökhan, Tülay and Fatih Açıkkollu stayed up the entire night watching events unfold. Fatih's birthday present was forgotten and his cake remained uneaten. Even when Tülay and Gökhan finally went to bed at around six in the morning they had trouble sleeping. They did not know it yet, but their family life as they knew it had ended that night; for them there would be no return to normality.

The Açıkkollus had particular reason to feel anxious. Both Tülay and Gökhan were followers of Fethullah Gülen. Gökhan, who had grown up in Istanbul, had joined the movement when he attended a Gülenist-run *dershane* during high school. Tülay had joined when she was an undergraduate studying theology at Ankara University. Her family had tried to set her on a career in healthcare, and she had attended a vocational high school to train as a nurse. But the first time she witnessed childbirth, the passion it aroused in her was more spiritual than medical.

'I realised it was something miraculous,' she recalled. 'Something far beyond the normal human bodily system . . . When I saw this, the question of creation intrigued me a lot: the creation of the universe, the creation of mankind. It is the perfect system.' Her own family were observant Muslims, but they were not, in her words, 'conscious': 'They did not have the knowledge to ponder on this subject, to give opinions, to answer my questions.'

It was while she was studying theology in Ankara that she came into contact with the Gülen Movement. She called it by the name which its followers preferred: *Hizmet*, meaning service. She was struck by its inclusivity. 'They valued people for being human. They were not obsessed with beliefs, lifestyles, or wanting to change them. I wanted to know the source of this. How can you look at life this way? How can you be so kind to people? Then I started to read the sources they read and which enriched them. It was very good for me, they were things that fitted with my philosophy of life.'

She met Gökhan through friends involved in Hizmet. He was

a friend of the fiancé of one of her classmates. They were attracted to each other even though they were quite different in temperament: 'I am very active, and impetuous; my husband is cautious, but we were very agreeable in terms of ideas . . . We attached importance to the same values.'

They got married a year later, just after graduating from university; she was twenty-three and he was twenty-four. For the next few years they taught at Gülenist-run *dershanes* in different central Anatolian cities, according to where the movement sent them: five years in Nevşehir, three in Aksaray, four in Konya. Gökhan's a combination of anxiety and grit. He had a history of panic attacks and was hard-working and diligent in his professional life working at the *dershane.*

'He devoted most of his time to his students,' said Tülay. 'He used to say that because they took care of him, he should take care of his own students too. He had a sense of loyalty.' He longed for the family to move back to his home city. 'Even on television, when he saw a scene about Istanbul, he would hit his knee with his hand, and he would always say: "I miss Istanbul so much it hurts."' Eventually they managed to get transferred to a *dershane* there around 2010, but Gökhan was becoming burnt out. He had developed type 2 diabetes, and the couple decided to stop working at *dershanes* and transfer to the public education system, where the work would be less intense. They did the necessary exams, and eventually got jobs in Ümraniye, where Gökhan taught history at a public high school and Tülay taught religious culture and ethics at a middle school. It was a comfortable life. They rented an apartment in the area, and Tülay enjoyed feeling part of a community; both teaching and living in the same neighbourhood, they became friendly with many of the families whose children they taught.

The day after the coup attempt the family returned to their normal lives with a sense of apprehension. They had seen images of badly beaten coup officers being paraded on television. Watching events unfold, Gökhan had been suspicious that it was not a genuine coup attempt at all but something staged by Erdoğan to justify seizing more power and cracking down on his opponents. Why had it been carried out so early in the evening, rather than during the dead of night, like previous coup attempts? And why had the plotters not taken basic steps like locking down all media outlets in the first moments? The Gülenists had already been in the government's sights since their long alliance with Erdoğan's AK Party had broken down two and half years earlier. The government had seized and liquidated its major media empire, Feza Publishing, which had included the country's highest-selling daily newspaper, *Zaman*, and also confiscated Bank Asya, a major high street bank affiliated with the network.

But in the wake of the coup attempt, the government's rhetoric assumed a violent new tone. Gülen's followers were a 'virus' that would be 'purged from society'. Within days, the movement had been added to Turkey's terror list; the previous euphemism of a 'parallel state' was abolished in favour of the more aggressive Fethullahist Terrorist Organisation, or FETÖ for short. A state of national emergency was declared, and the government began to arrest thousands of suspected Gülenists working in the police, military and courts.

The Sunday after the coup, the Açikkollus crossed over to the European side of the city to attend Gökhan's brother's wedding, a quiet affair at a municipal registry office. Crossing the Bosphorus Bridge, they saw workmen hosing it down after the chaos that had unfolded there two nights earlier, and Tülay wondered if they shouldn't be preserving the scene to gather evidence. The following day they went to her hometown in

Konya, as they did every summer, to spend it with her family. A few days later they learned that the Hizmet-run private school that their children attended had been shut down by the government.

'We were asking ourselves which school we would send the children to; we had already paid the school fees . . . Could we get them back?' Tülay recalled. 'These were mild concerns compared to what else was happening, of course, but when we heard about it at that time, it put us in a state of worry.'

And so the following Friday, a week after the coup attempt, Gökhan returned to Istanbul alone to try to resolve the issue and if possible recoup the school fees. Tülay spoke to him the following evening, when he told her that he'd been unsuccessful. The police had cordoned off the school, he wasn't allowed on the premises and there was no one from the administration he could speak to.

Just after seven the following morning she received another call, this time from an Istanbul number she did not recognise. It was an officer from the anti-terrorism department informing her that her husband had been detained. The officer refused to give further details and then hung up. The images of the beaten putschist soldiers once again flashed through her mind, and she felt a rising sense of panic. Gathering all their belongings, she got in the car with the children and her elder brother, who agreed to accompany her, and they returned to Istanbul, driving through the night to reach their apartment early Monday morning.

They arrived to find it ransacked. 'The flat was no longer a home . . . All the things we had in the cupboards, the sofas, the bed bases, whatever was in the bookcases, they threw every-where . . . I had pots on the balcony where I grew plants, they even spilled the soil in those pots. It was like we were hiding ammo in our house and they were trying to find it.' Even the contents of the fridge had been strewn about the place. As she set about cleaning up the mess, she realised that every electronic device in the house was gone: her husband's computer, the memory cards where they stored their family photos, their hard drives, an old digital camera, even a small computer game console of her son's. They had also taken paperwork, including her bank account statements. What alarmed her more, however, was something they had left behind: her husband's diabetes medication.

Her fears multiplied when she spoke to the building manager, who was one of her neighbours. There was a legal requirement during police searches to have a civilian witness present, and the woman had been called in to perform this role. She had watched as the police had begun to beat and interrogate Gökhan while searching the apartment. The woman was badly shaken. She said they had become so violent that she had begged to leave rather than witness it.

For the next four days Tülay kept on calling the number that the police had rung her from, to no avail. No one would tell her where her husband was. She told them about his panic attack disorder and his diabetes.

'I said that he should take his medication, he should use his insulin, that he may go into a diabetic coma. I explained all these dangers, but they did not care at all. They said doctors would look after him if he had such a disease and then hung up the phone.'

Finally, at the end of the fourth day she was told that he was being held at the anti-terrorism detention centre of the Vatan Police Security Directorate.

Vatan Caddesi – 'Homeland Avenue' – was a broad, arrow-straight thoroughfare cut into the heart of the old city between the Sulukule and Topkapı gates. The avenue had been built in the 1950s by Prime Minister Adnan Menderes – it was later renamed in his honour but the original name had somehow stuck – and for a time it was used for official processions and celebrations associated with the Conquest, as if the clearing and opening of this broad stretch of the urban fabric represented another triumph over the past. The Police Security Directorate was part of a large complex of state buildings about six hundred metres from the walls. It was the main police department for Istanbul, and the place where detainees from across the city would be taken and processed.

It was about two in the morning when Tülay Açıkkollu approached the building with her elder brother to deliver her husband's insulin and a clean set of clothes. Even though it was nearly two weeks after the coup, there were still demonstrators camped outside, chanting slogans against the coup suspects held within. Her brother was worried that if she went into the building and had to show her ID they would arrest her too, so she waited outside while he went in alone. The crowd was in a mood that was both celebratory and angry, and the police had set up a barricade to keep the demonstrators at a distance. On the areas of grass outside abutting the road people were cooking barbecues, holding banners and shouting slogans denouncing the traitors inside. Overwhelmed at the scenes around her, Tülay broke down in tears, and a plain clothes police officer approached her, gave her water, and made her sit down. He asked her if her husband was detained inside and then asked if he was a soldier or a police officer. 'Just a teacher,' she replied, and he told her that in that case she shouldn't worry as they would probably just take his statement and release him.

At one point while she was waiting, she watched a frail old man approach the police at the barricades and ask to speak to a 'superior'. At first they tried to brush him off but he was insistent, and someone was found. 'Let me in, I have names to report,' he announced. It was a moment that appalled Tülay. 'It shocked me to my core. Who were those people? Were they his neighbours, his friends, his family?'

Eventually, Tülay was able to get the number of a lawyer who had been automatically assigned to represent her husband by the Bar Association. She ignored her many calls before finally answering by text message to say that she had not yet met Gökhan, and that the police had yet to take a statement from him. She said she could not speak by phone and would only communicate via text. Tülay realised she was scared of being seen to assist the family of a suspected coup plotter, even if he was her client. The next day the lawyer texted again to say that she had now met and talked to Gökhan. Overwhelmed at this news, Tülay called her again and again until she finally picked up.

'Are there any signs of beating on my husband's face and body?' Tülay asked. 'Did my husband tell you about anything?'

At this the woman was silent for a moment. She ignored the question, replying instead that his statement had still not been taken, and that she was working to make sure that it was. He had mentioned, she added, that his glasses had broken and he was having trouble seeing; if she had a spare pair then Tülay could seek permission from the prosecutor's office to give them to him.

This only deepened her fears; his glasses were robust and wouldn't have easily broken. It was a clear sign he had been beaten. She told the lawyer this and said she wanted to lodge a criminal complaint, but the lawyer said it was too early to do such a thing: wait until they had taken her husband's statement. The last she heard from the lawyer was a few days later, when she texted to say that she had again met with Gökhan, that his statement had still not been taken, and that he had sent a message telling her he loved her.

On the morning of Friday 5 August, thirteen days after her husband's detention, Tülay was feeling hopeful: she had been frantically looking for a new lawyer who might willingly represent him, and the previous day she had found one; he was planning to try to visit Gökhan that morning. Just as she approached the bridge, she received a phone call. It was the police telling her to go immediately to the Haseki Hospital, which lay near the security directorate. She was in the car, caught in the scrum of traffic around the Bosphorus, and couldn't turn quickly and so she called her brother and asked him to go there. Then only a few minutes later she received another phone call from the police: don't go to Haseki, go to the Institute of Forensic Medicine.

She immediately understood what this meant. 'Of course in that moment I sensed that my husband was dead. They were taking him to the forensic institute for autopsy; and of course, my world collapsed.'

———

Tülay stood outside the room where Gökhan's corpse lay at the Institute of Forensic Medicine. She was told he had died of a heart attack. Gökhan's parents and Tülay's brother were there, and she remained outside while the other three identified his body. They then broached the formalities of receiving it and arranging the funeral so that burial could take place within twenty-four hours of death, as faith and custom dictated. Since her husband had been a public servant, a coffin and hearse would be provided by the municipality. An official asked if they meant to bury him in Istanbul, and they replied that naturally they did. In that case, they were told, they could not hand over the body because it was to be interred at the Traitors' Cemetery.

Tülay had never even heard this term before, never even conceived of the existence of a 'traitors' cemetery'. In fact, it was an idea put forward by the Istanbul mayor, Kadir Topbas, only a few days earlier in the wake of the coup attempt. Supposedly it stood in the neighbourhood of Tuzla, on the fringe of the city, adjacent to an existing municipal cemetery for street animals.

Tülay was aghast: 'My husband's statement was not even taken: how come he can be buried in a traitors' cemetery? Of course, we did not accept this. I said, "My husband is a teacher. How can you declare him a terrorist? How can you declare him a traitor? My husband had no role in this coup attempt."'

The official seemed sympathetic but would not back down. He told them that if they wanted to get Gökhan's body, they would have to go to the prosecutor's office and obtain a letter confirming that this was a normal funeral. This launched the family on a fruitless round of bureaucratic wrangling from which they returned empty-handed and begged again to be given Gökhan's body. The official agreed to hand it over on the condition that they bury him away from Istanbul. They agreed, and decided they would take him to Tülay's hometown in Konya. The official refused even to embalm his body for the ten-hour car drive in sweltering heat, although in the end he agreed to lend them the necessary chemicals and injection equipment, so that Tülay's brother could do it himself. And so they drove to Konya, Tülay's brother with the coffin in his car, she and the children travelling separately, and there they buried him.

The details of what had happened to Gökhan during his thirteen days in custody emerged a couple of months later. Tülay had filed a criminal complaint concerning her husband's death, a prosecutor was appointed and a judicial investigation launched. After that a package of documents was sent to her lawyer, including a list of medical and police reports covering her husband's entire period in custody.

The story of his final two weeks could be glimpsed in sparse, handwritten notes written by doctors who examined him daily. Ironically, this was a system put in place to prevent torture. They described his complaints of being in pain as a result of beatings, of physical and verbal abuse, as well as noting his frequent panic attacks. There were multiple trips to the hospital, where he was prescribed tranquillisers and treated for low blood pressure as a result of his diabetes. In the first report, written the morning after he was detained, he complained of 'lesions and bruises on his back . . . sweating, dizziness, chest pain'. In subsequent reports he continued to describe being beaten. '[H]e reported he was slapped on the face on both cheeks,' one read, 'a kick to the chest, head banged on wall, insults, panic attack, bruises and scrapes on face, minor injury on head, tenderness on chest, feeling terrible due to psychological pressure, can't sleep, consultation for tenderness in chest and panic attack consultation.' The reports generally concluded with the examiner's assessment of his general condition as 'OK' or 'no emergency'. The following day, for example, the consultation noted: 'heavy insults under detention for six days, coercion, hundreds of slaps to the face, cursing, kicks on his back, marks on his back, bruises, chest ache, no vital danger.'

The day after that, the daily report noted: '. . . head injury and ache, back bruises and ache, chest ache and bruises, sensitivity, right side of glasses broken, panic and fear, extreme terror'. He was sent to hospital again, prescribed a second tranquilliser on top of the one he was already taking. After a while he began to refuse examination, and was described as being 'depressed'.

A couple of days later he again reported being kicked in the ribs, although it was unclear if this was a fresh incident or a reference to the ongoing pain in his right rib. It was the following day, 5 August – three weeks to the day after the coup attempt – that he died. The autopsy report, which was also included in the documents, gave his cause of death as a heart attack and noted minor bleeding in his eyes, nose and mouth, as well as a broken rib and chest injuries, which were ascribed to resuscitation efforts. Along with these documents came a notification of the prosecutor's refusal to proceed, concluding that his death had been as a result of prior health complications, that treatment had been given to him while in custody, and that therefore no one was criminally responsible for his fate.

No evidence would ever emerge linking Gökhan Açıkkollu to the coup attempt or to any criminal activity at all – except for membership of the Gülen Movement, which had now become a designated terrorist group. Nearly two years after her husband's death, Tülay received a letter from the Education Ministry, which had suspended him in the wake of the coup, reinstating him in his job, apparently unaware that he had died. She published the letter as a sign of vindication, and his case drew sympathy and attention in some sections of the media. After this, the police's case against him was leaked to a pro-AKP newspaper. Other arrested Gülenists had allegedly named him as an 'imam' of the movement, a figure of influence who had regular meetings with senior members. It was also claimed he had a messaging app on his phone called 'Bylock', which the government said was being used by Gülenists to communicate securely. In the paranoid and vindictive atmosphere following the coup, having this app on your phone – it was freely available online – was treated as a priori evidence of criminal activity, and formed the grounds for the arrest of as many as 75,000 people.

Tülay denied her husband ever had any involvement in the coup attempt, or foreknowledge of it, nor any special role in the movement beyond his past administrative work in the *dershane* study centres. Her legal battle to bring those responsible for his death to account would continue unsuccessfully through the Turkish courts before ultimately going to the European Court of Human Rights, where she was still awaiting a hearing when I last spoke to her. Turkey's Human Rights Foundation, which backed her husband's case, issued its own report on the autopsy, which stated that even if Gökhan did die of a heart attack, his mistreatment in prison must be considered as a contributing factor.

His family's lives were devastated by his death and other consequences of the coup attempt. His son Fatih clammed up and refused to discuss what had happened. He had been planning to study computer engineering at university, but now wanted to become a lawyer to fight for justice for people like his father. It meant changing his final high school subjects, but he threw himself into this with zeal and secured a place on an undergraduate law degree the following year. For a while, seven-year-old Zeynep would become angry if she heard anyone use the word 'Daddy', even if it was Tülay addressing her own father. Then later she told her mother that she missed saying 'Daddy', and began carrying a picture of him everywhere she went.

Tülay herself was called in by the police after publicising his case and put under investigation. Her personal and professional life collapsed. As a follower of the Gülen Movement, she had been fired from her job and barred from working as a teacher in the wake of the coup attempt. Because she'd worked in a local school, everyone in the neighbourhood knew her well, and in the past would call on her with worries and questions about

their children. Now everyone shunned her, turning away whenever they saw her in the street.

The only exception to this was a Kurdish family who lived
in the same building and had a small daughter. The father was
also a teacher and helped get Zeynep enrolled in a local school.
When they saw her they would always make a point of asking
how she was and offered her their sympathy. The two families
were utterly different in their social habits and customs; before
they would probably never have bonded but now they became
close: 'They said, whatever you need, day or night, knock on
our door.' The family had attended rallies for the pro-Kurdish
party, and in the broad crackdown on dissent that followed the
coup attempt, they too feared they might be targets. While their
children were playing in the playground, the father told her
about the persecution his own family had suffered in the past.

'That's when I thought I understood why Kurdish people take
to the mountains, because the law is finished. Everyone is trying
to create their own law now.'

There was a certain irony to this. When they had enjoyed
power in the judiciary and police, the Gülenists had been particularly zealous in targeting the Kurdish nationalist movement, had
spearheaded a series of mass trials targeting Kurdish political
figures, and were rumoured to have helped derail tentative peace
talks initiated by Erdoğan in 2009. In the future, they would
increasingly find themselves trying to make common cause with
groups they themselves had played a role in oppressing. The
movement had used quite sophisticated tools of propaganda and
disinformation to pursue its enemies; falsified evidence, the
blending of truth and lies, and faked witness testimonies were
all part of its toolkit. Even in the wake of the coup attempt
those higher up in the movement never admitted these tactics
or showed any contrition for how they had behaved in the past,
and the kind of empathy and understanding reached by Tülay

and her Kurdish neighbours would never be replicated on a larger scale.

Eventually life in Turkey became intolerable for Tülay. It was like 'living as if you were dead', she said: unable to work, unable to socialise, no future for her or her children, scared by the sound of the doorbell, by the constant fear of arrest. She knew she was probably barred from leaving because she was under investigation, so she paid a people smuggler to take them to the Greek border, where they were met by a young Afghan man, who ferried her and the children across the Evros river. From there she travelled on, eventually claiming asylum and receiving refugee status in a European country. I spoke to her online from a location she would not disclose, since the Turkish government had on occasion abducted Gülenists and returned them to Turkey for prosecution. Life in Europe was hard, she said. The children were adapting, but she had lost her self-confidence and sense of purpose – she struggled with the language, couldn't find work, and was dependent on the charity of others. And she could never get over what happened to her husband.

'Death is God's order,' she said. 'One day we will all die. But I could not accept the way my husband died. I could not accept that he was killed after being mistreated, persecuted and tortured in this way. The litigation process is still ongoing, but there is no law in Turkey, and when the law arrives, when those responsible are tried, when those people are sentenced, maybe then I will be more relieved.'

The coup attempt itself would also remain troublingly opaque. Nobody seriously doubted the Gülenists had some hand in it – although Gülen himself denounced the coup and denied any involvement. Turkey demanded his extradition from the US but never submitted detailed evidence to support its request. The Gülenists may not have been the only group behind the attempt since many of the senior plotters had no known history of involvement with the movement. Later it would emerge that Turkey's intelligence agency had discovered the plot, prompting the putschists to rush into action five hours earlier than they had planned. This would explain why the attempt was so poorly executed. But what exactly did the government know in advance? When did they know it? And what did they do with this knowledge?

The most extreme allegation – the one made by the Gülenists themselves – was that the coup attempt was a kind of 'Reichstag Fire', an event the government had staged for its own political benefit. A more nuanced hypothesis was that they had received enough forewarning to insulate themselves against the plotters, and then allowed it to go ahead in order to create the pretext for seizing more power and purging their enemies. If this had been the case it would have been a breathtakingly reckless gamble, allowing potentially fatal attacks to go ahead on its own people, up to and including Erdoğan himself. A further explanation was that the government had received enough forewarning to weaken the plot but not forestall it, buying off potentially hostile factions in the military and security services by engaging in negotiations that they couldn't ever allow to become public.

Erdoğan's description of the coup attempt as 'a gift from God' would continue to hold a sinister resonance for his opponents, as the government embarked on a nationwide crackdown on dissent that would reach far beyond the military or the Gülenists and would be the harshest era of oppression since the 1980 coup. The government would formally arrest more than 77,000 people accused of involvement in the Gülen network, and 180,000 would be sacked from jobs in the civil service, military, or public education, totalling nearly 10 per cent of the country's public employees. Within a year of the coup, the government had expropriated nearly a thousand businesses with a total value of more than $11bn. The country was placed under a rolling state of emergency which would continue for two years, and which gave the government broad authoritarian powers. Regular decrees issued from the presidential palace ordering the closure of thousands of associations, publications and charities and the suspension of tens of thousands of people from state jobs. These extended far beyond suspected Gülenists, and especially included organisations and individuals on the left and involved in the Kurdish movement. More than 170 media organisations were shut down by decree.

The Gülenists, who had once seemed untouchable and were long detested by the country's opposition groups, were now reviled on all sides. The AK Party – which had done more than anyone to encourage and support the Gülenists during their erstwhile alliance – now had the embarrassing and awkward task of renouncing their past affiliation to the nation. An atmosphere of paranoia took hold within government-supporting circles. Many people had taken money from the Gülenists or collaborated with them; many people had relations, friends or colleagues who had been sucked in by them. Ripples of fear spread out through society.

Among those with long personal experience of the Gülenists was Servet, the police officer who had raced to the old city on his motorbike to confront the coup plotters. He had signed up for the police eight years before the coup attempt, at the age of eighteen, and become a serving officer after two years in cadet school. Servet was Kurdish, from the province of Mardin in the south-east of the country. He'd had a comfortable upbringing.

His extended family owned several food distribution companies and were 'quite important in the south-east,' he said coyly when we met at a tea garden near a motorway in a remote neighbourhood of the city where he now lived. A comfortable career had awaited him in one of the family businesses, but he'd opted for a different route. As a child he'd dreamed of being a police officer, inspired by a soap opera called *Yılan Hikayesi* – 'Snake Story' – that followed the exploits of a heroic police detective called Memoli. Memoli was dashing, charismatic and smart. Servet wanted to be like him, to catch bad guys and protect people. More than that, however, he wanted to be independent and to forge a life that didn't rely on family connections.

'I arrived here by my own path,' he told me proudly.

But life as a police officer had been far from what he'd imagined. There had been no arrests, no investigations, no detective work. In fact he had spent most of the past six years filing paperwork in the financial department, mainly in relation to counterfeit money cases, putting together files while others did the investigating. He felt he was going to waste and being denied opportunities; unlike most of his colleagues he spoke fluent Kurdish, which could have been useful in the counter-terrorism or organised crime units to which he applied but was never admitted.

He believed he knew why. Ironically, it was the very thing he had eschewed by joining the police in the first place: connections. In this case, advancement into the investigative arms of the police hinged on one's closeness to the Gülen movement, whose followers dominated the upper echelons of the anti-terror and organised crime departments. He'd been aware of them since his cadet days. They ran private extra tuition courses to help applicants pass their police exams – sometimes they would give poor students free tuition, and there were persistent allegations that they would help their followers cheat their way into the force by giving them the answer to exam questions in advance. One way or another, they had created a system of patronage and obligation that had crept up the ranks of the police force over the course of many years.

To Servet, they had corrupted the very ideals that had pushed him to join the police. 'A system of merit should serve the police and the government: that is how I was raised. Police officers should be objective, they should not have a specific political affiliation. They shouldn't have that kind of liability.' This factionalism in public service was so ubiquitous that his defiance of it would strike many as naive. In a sense there was nothing unusual about what the Gülenists were doing; religious sects and political movements had long sought to spread their influence in different arms of the state and bureaucracy. There was even a word for it, *kadro-laşma*: 'setting up one's own cadre in public offices'.

However, the Gülenists brought an intensity of focus to this task that outstripped all others. Servet viewed the movement as a kind of pyramid scheme, in which gratitude and obligation flowed up to the top ranks, allowing those at the top to amass power through the loyalty of those beneath them. 'When you first start the job, you donate a fifth or a sixth of your income [to the movement],' he said. 'Normally you would say, are these people idiots? Why would they give their money to the organisation? But the man has a history, a deep gratitude. He thinks, "If I am a police officer now, I have become one thanks to you." And generally the mentors do not change, they call you and say "You came along these roads, we are raising more people like you, why don't you support us monthly?"'

These bonds were constantly reinforced by various social events and activities. 'On weekends, for example, when there were work hours, they'd say: "Let me take you to breakfast for free" or "Why not come for a picnic?"' They'd made some overtures to Servet, but it was soon apparent that he would never be one of them. 'I am not a religious person,' he said. 'I was not into their lifestyle. That's why they didn't really welcome me.'

Before its dramatic fallout with the government, there were many who had regarded the movement's growing influence as benign, or even beneficial. Its followers were often urbane and well educated, and they were believers, which was important to many pious Muslims who had felt threatened by the secular state in the past. 'Back then, people thought they were good eggs: they were believers, they would not accept bribes, they were solid. They filled the police stations with them thanks to these kinds of arguments.'

Servet's own assessment based on Gülenists he'd known in the police was that rather than swivel-eyed fanatics, many were opportunists, people searching for an easy way forward like so many others who had sought advancement through connections. 'They were people who would like to have a position or a title up there somewhere, who want to reach a goal easily rather than doing it with their own sweat and tears.'

<hr>

After the coup attempt was defeated, Servet felt relief and vindication, but as time went on these emotions were replaced by other, more ambivalent feelings. He was feted as one of the heroes of the night, embraced by the government, invited to endless ceremonies and presentations, and called upon to relive the events for television cameras and documentary films; he was even received and thanked by president Erdoğan himself. He was now a *gazi* – a veteran of a holy war – decorated with honours and awards demonstrating the nation's gratitude, as well as a pension and free public transport for life.

The events of the night itself were taken up by the government, and the state and media organisations it controlled and portrayed as a seminal event in Turkey's history, a kind of new inaugural moment for the nation. Endless documentaries were made, ceremonies held, schools, streets, bus stops renamed, monuments built. Glossy coffee-table books with photos from the night and explanations of its significance began to adorn the waiting rooms of state offices and institutions. The Bosphorus Bridge, which had played host to such dramatic scenes, was renamed the 'July 15 Martyrs' Bridge'.

However, Servet's heroism had exacted a heavy toll. His physical injuries were minor but he was plagued with anxiety and insomnia that continued for years afterwards, despite psychological treatment. Loud noises sounded like gunshots, and details of the night seared into his memory kept resurfacing. There had been a man standing near him, shooting at the soldiers with an old hunting rifle, and he often seemed to hear the loud crack of its report, making him jump. Eighteen civilians had died in the confrontation outside the municipality, and he'd seen many of them fall. There had been one man with a thick beard yelling 'Allahu Akbar' over and over again. He was dangerously close to Servet, who was drawing the soldiers' fire. He was shouting at him to move away and take cover when the man collapsed on his back. At first he looked uninjured and Servet thought he must have fainted. His chest was clean and there was no blood, but when he turned him over he saw he was dead with terrible injuries. 'That scene is always in front of my eyes,' he told me.

The constant reminders of the night's events were hard to bear, but he attended all these events and spoke to the media because he believed it was important to educate the public about them, to warn against the dangers of giving over parts of the state to factional groups such as the Gülenists, and to advocate for the rights of those who had been injured and the families of the dead. Aspects of the public eulogisation of 15 July began to bother him.

It was painted as a great victory, but not so much for the country as for the AK Party and Recep Tayyip Erdoğan, whose appeal for people to flood onto the streets was being portrayed as being decisive in defeating the putschists. The distinction between rising up to defend the country and rising up to defend a particular politician or political party was key for Servet, it was at the heart of what he had always believed in.

Over time, events related to the coup took on an air of celebration he found hard to stomach. 'A victory has been won but when they invite me somewhere for this, I feel sad,' he told me. 'Those eighteen civilians haunt me. There should have been mourning. We tend to celebrate martyrdom like it's a holiday – that's a part of our culture – but it makes me sad. It shouldn't be a celebration, it should be a commemoration.'

Meanwhile, the sense of disillusionment he had felt with the police before the coup attempt had not gone away – in fact it deepened. Servet was told to rest for two weeks under doctors' orders, but he insisted on turning up to work on the very day after the coup attempt. He was worried about the risk of further attacks by Gülenist elements, however almost all of the group's followers disavowed the failed coup attempt, and in the coming months all those suspected of membership were purged from the police forces. The Gülenists were driven out but over time their influence was replaced by other religious brotherhoods – the Suleymanists and the Menzilists – who were more in favour with the government but similarly factional and nepotistic in their practices. Four months after the coup attempt, he quit the police.

‒‒‒‒

From the Edirnekapı cemetery, where I saw the tomb of Tolga Ecebalın, the young father who was among those killed in the park where Servet had confronted the putschists, I walked to the neighbourhood of Lonca, to visit his shrine. Lonca was a closed, suspicious place. It lay in a long valley between Eğrikapı and the lively, gentrifying district of Balat, but was more run-down and neglected than either. It was described to me as a Roma neighbourhood, like Sulukule up the road. But while Sulukule wore its Roma culture on its sleeve, the people of Lonca were more prickly and reticent, as if asking them about it was an attempt to divide them from their homeland. In the past, when I'd made the mistake of doing so, I was told that they were 'Turkish citizens and Muslims', as if to say that this was all that mattered.

Outside a small three-bedroom breeze-block house I met Tarkan Ecebalın, a slight man in his late fifties with walnut skin and a short salt-and-pepper beard. He had worked all his life as an *esnaf* – a street vendor – a trade he had inherited from his father. He would take his handcart around different parts of the city, selling produce according to the season – watermelons when it was hot, *köfte* or stuffed mussels when it was cold. He had soulful, watery eyes that seemed to be brimming with inspiration or tears. It was about six months after 15 July that I visited the family home, the entirety of which Tarkan had turned into a kind of museum dedicated to his son.

'Can you feel him?' Tarkan asked quietly as we stood in the living room of the house. All around us were mementoes from Tolga's life. There was the pair of blood-spotted trainers he wore on the night of his death; the ring from his finger; the prayer beads, cigarettes and lighter that were in his pockets when he fell; the flag that had been draped over his coffin and the roses that were thrown onto it. There was a wealth of objects from his daily life: his collection of watches and cufflinks; his toothbrush, nail clippers, razor and hair wax. These were all labelled and on view in a glass-fronted cabinet. His clothes were displayed on mannequins lining the walls, from the tuxedo he'd worn at his engagement party, to his Fenerbahçe football shirts. His PlayStation stood beneath the television with his favourite game – 'God of War' – lying next to it. All over the walls pictures commemorated both his life and the night of his death.

A class of local children were also visiting. They trooped from room to room with wide-eyed expressions while their teacher intoned on the events of that night. In the new mythology of Turkey, 15 July was a stepping stone in the country's emancipation from the colonial influence of the West and its re-establishment as a global power. The Gülenists were a cat's paw for the United States which, along with other shadowy enemies, had tried to do away with Erdoğan and bring Turkey to heel just as they had done with the Gezi protests and in previous coups. Erdoğan called it Turkey's 'second independence day'. Tarkan Ecebalın said it was the 'second conquest of Istanbul'.

'God wrote it,' he told me of his son's martyrdom. He believed signs had pointed to and prefigured it. When Tolga had been born, he had been wrapped in a red and white cloth – the colours of the Turkish flag; he had been in a marching band as a child, and there was a photo of him again wearing red and white, his finger pointed upwards – a symbol of martyrdom; and a few days before his death, his mother had thought she noticed a speck of something under his eye where the bullet would hit him and had asked him to rub it away.

Tolga had attended the local Ulubatlı Hasan primary school, named after the famous Janissary who was said to have been the first to scale the walls during the Conquest and raise the Ottoman standard before being cut down by the defenders: another martyr, another sign, perhaps? He hadn't excelled at high school, according to the short biography displayed on a brass plate in the house, written by his father, but in his son's voice. 'I learned about life elsewhere,' the text read. 'I learned right and wrong, I learned the flag and the Quran.'

As Tarkan talked there was a tension in his voice and his face, a struggle between exultation and grief, pain battling with pride that his son had been elevated and sanctified in the eyes of God and the nation. One of the exhibits in the shrine was a chip of rock, which Tarkan said he had been given by a workman doing repairs around the Ka'aba in Mecca. He and other family members of the martyrs had been sent there by Erdoğan as a token of gratitude for their sacrifice. He said it was hard to describe how he felt there.

'If you have tea and put sugar in it, it becomes sweet, and if you put lemon in it, it becomes sour, and when you put these in together you get another taste which is neither sour nor sweet,' he said. 'I met people there who had suffered as I had, and meeting them made me feel strangely better. We were staring into one another's eyes and sharing the same loss and the same pain but also joy, because our lost ones were in Heaven and as it says in the Holy Quran martyrs are not dead, they are alive, only we cannot see them.'

To me, Tarkan Ecebalın's shrine to his son bore an inescapable resemblance to another place in the city: the 'Museum of Innocence' that the writer Orhan Pamuk had created as a counterpart to his eponymous novel. It stood a short distance from where I'd once lived in Beyoğlu and I'd often taken visiting friends and family there. Like Tolga's shrine, it was a collection of everyday objects ostensibly dedicated to the memory of a single individual; it too occupied an entire house which, in the world of Pamuk's novel, had once been the home of the young lover of the book's narrator. One of its most memorable displays was a cabinet of crushed cigarette butts with the girl's red lipstick still smeared on them, pinned to a board and labelled like entomological specimens, and this jumped into my mind when I saw an exhibit in Tolga's shrine: an unsmoked cigarette still perched on an ashtray where it had sat at the time of his death.

These similarities were all the more remarkable because in other respects these places inhabited two different worlds: the pious, nationalist, impoverished neighbourhood of Lonca and secular, cosmopolitan, middle-class Beyoğlu. Pamuk had published a manifesto of what he believed future museums should look like, making the case that they should be small and personalised, telling the lives of individuals in the context of their actual homes and lives rather than of grand national narratives. 'The future of museums is inside our own homes,' it concluded. In a sense Tolga's shrine fitted Pamuk's manifesto perfectly. It was lovingly curated in a way that revealed both the personality of the person it evoked, and the world that they inhabited.

The story I took from it was of a life and death enmeshed in the myths that made up the modern Turkish nation. As Tarkan had enumerated the various signs that prefigured his son's martyrdom, I wondered how many other millions of Turkish young men were marked in this way, and if any of them died, could one trace these same signs prefiguring their death? The symbols of sacrifice, the shedding of blood, the embracing of the flag were part of the way in which the Turkish state had conditioned its young men to expect and embrace the prospect of sacrifice through death. When confronting a challenge or enemy, Erdoğan's followers would often say that they had 'come here in their funeral shrouds', meaning they were ready to die for their faith.

'The young, the old, they closed their eyes and went out to defend the country,' Tarkan said of that fateful night. 'That was the only thing that we considered. We wouldn't be here if the coup had been successful. We couldn't have made this house a museum. We couldn't have spoken here.' Turkey, he believed, was under unprecedented assault. 'If you put a big rock in the sea so the waves keep hitting it, eventually they will weaken it. This is what is happening in Turkey at the moment. There are waves crashing against us from all directions and even though they are huge blows Turkey is still intact, and thanks to Tayyip Erdoğan, it has become even stronger and better. Any other country would already have been swept away.'

I had been in England with my fiancée when the coup attempt took place, planning our wedding. We had intended to get married in Istanbul but had moved it after a spate of almost monthly terrorist attacks by Kurdish and Islamist militants. In March a suicide bomber had blown himself up, killing four people on İstiklal, the city's busiest pedestrian thoroughfare, only a hundred metres from my flat. The blast had rattled my windows as I sat at my desk. In June, armed attackers wired with suicide vests launched an assault on the airport that left 41 people dead and 239 injured.

About two months after the coup attempt and a few days before the wedding, my future father-in-law revealed that he had become the target of a judicial investigation. He was a doctor and medical professor in his early eighties, and heavily involved in opposition political activism; at that time he was serving as president of the Istanbul branch of the Medical Chamber. In Turkey, these kind of professional associations had always been highly political. The boards of the chambers were elected by medical workers, who tended towards the left of the political spectrum. In the stifled atmosphere that came to prevail in the wake of the coup attempt it was an isolated and embattled institution. As part of his role on the board, my father-in-law and his colleagues supported the thousands of doctors who had been thrown out of their jobs or imprisoned on dubious political grounds, and also protested about the increasingly onerous labour conditions placed on medical workers.

The chamber also took a vocal stance calling for a ceasefire in the reignited Kurdish conflict. It argued that war was a public health issue and so as doctors they had a duty to highlight its cost and advocate for a peaceful solution. In the increasingly oppressive atmosphere, advocating for peace was seen as tantamount to supporting terrorism. Only a few months earlier, a large group of academics had signed a petition condemning the war in the south-east and calling for negotiations to resume. In response they had been hounded by the government and judiciary. A large number of these people were being prosecuted, or were fired from their jobs, and a few were arrested or forced to flee abroad. My father-in-law would be tried for the crime of 'inciting the public to hatred and enmity' and 'undermining the unity of the nation', offences carrying a possible two-year prison sentence. These charges were based on a newspaper article in which he had been misquoted in a way that seemed to suggest he supported the PKK.

Following our wedding, we returned to Istanbul for the first time since the coup attempt and the city seemed like a different place. Billboards had been commandeered by different branches of the state in order to issue proclamations of defiance or veiled threats. 'We curse acts of treachery,' read one message sponsored – bizarrely – by the national airport authority. Erdoğan's purge was in full swing, and almost every day we watched news reports of synchronised police raids on homes, at night or in the early morning, with suspects led out handcuffed before news cameras. Dozens were detained at a time, their homes ransacked for evidence, devices taken and pored over for anything that might be used to accuse them.

We were living with my father-in-law at the time, and the anxiety provoked by his predicament seeped into our daily lives. He seemed unfazed. He was where he wanted to be, having arrived at a point in his life where he no longer felt vulnerable; his children had grown up and made their own lives and he had no dependents. He was surrounded by people younger than him who faced the same risks but with their lives ahead of them, with far more to lose – why should he not put himself in the line of fire? However, he was also in his eighties and had a pacemaker, and if he was arrested he could expect to languish in an overcrowded prison for months without any kind of hearing, given that Turkey's judicial system had virtually ground to a halt under an avalanche of cases, and with many judges and prosecutors themselves behind bars. We expected to be woken any night by a knock at the door. I threw away things that I worried might be used against him if the police raided the house: a gas mask I'd used while reporting on the Gezi protests, several books relating to the Gülenists, various leaflets and books given by Kurdish municipalities during trips to the south-east. I agonised over what to do with my computer and my old notebooks, which had contacts and phone numbers in them. My father-in-law's case would grind on for a couple of years, and was eventually dismissed after he had stepped down from his role at the Medical Chamber, but at that time the threat of his arrest, as so many others were suffering a similar fate, felt very real.

The radically altered atmosphere in the country triggered in me waves of fear, despondency and alienation. At times I harboured a burning anger that I felt was professionally inappropriate and to which I did not feel entitled as a foreigner, even one whose marriage into a Turkish family made me more intimately connected to the country than ever. I began to worry my work could get me thrown out, or could hurt my wife; I'd never had an activist's zeal, and I felt compromised by fear. Contacts and interviewees I spoke to were increasingly nervous about criticising the government or being quoted in print. A couple of foreign journalists I knew were kicked out for straying across the contracting red lines that now governed reporting, and in some instances Turkish friends who worked for opposition media were questioned or arrested. Others began to talk about leaving.

A few months later, we too left Turkey and moved to England.

II. OMENS

Tell me please how and when the end of this world will be?
And how will men know that the end is close, at the doors?
By what signs will the end be indicated? And whither
will pass this city, the New Jerusalem?

Epiphanios, tenth-century Orthodox monk speaking
to St Andrew the Fool-for-Christ

Many of the strong and brave are laid low
The dying die; the living that remain are ours.

Dadaloğlu, early nineteenth-century Ottoman bard

9

The Prophesied Gate

Sometime around the end of 1452, one of the largest volcanic eruptions of the past two thousand years occurred at Vanuatu in the western Pacific Ocean. The oral histories of the people of the archipelago speak of earthquakes, tsunamis, and an entire island sinking beneath the waves. Many thousands of times more powerful than the atomic bomb dropped on Hiroshima, the explosion may have ejected more than nine cubic miles of material into the air, transforming the 600-metre-high island of Kuwae into a 400-metre deep underwater crater. Most of the evidence for this eruption has been gleaned from the effect it had on global weather through the vast quantities of dust, sulphur dioxide and other chemicals released into the atmosphere. Its trace has been found in ice cores from Greenland to Antarctica and from tree rings preserved in the oak panels of British paintings; in the Yangtze river valley it snowed solidly for forty days, in Sweden crops failed, and on the western side of North America the growth rings of the ancient bristlecone pines show signs of exceptional frost.

The dust from such large eruptions is known to cause striking optical effects across the globe for months afterwards in the form of unusually brilliant sunsets resembling flames on the horizon. This was the case following the Krakatoa eruption in Indonesia in the summer of 1883, the effects of which were visible in New York the following November.

'Soon after five o'clock the western horizon suddenly flamed into a brilliant scarlet, which crimsoned sky and clouds,' the *New York Times* reported. 'People in the streets were startled at the unwonted sight and gathered in little groups on all the corners to gaze into the west. Many thought that a great fire was in progress.' Similar reports were made two days later in Oslo, where the local newspaper reported that a 'strong light was seen yesterday and today around five o'clock to the west of the city. People believed it was a fire, but it was actually a red refraction in the hazy atmosphere after sunset.'

A few months after the Kuwae eruption, in Constantinople – a city now besieged by Mehmet's forces – the population anxiously looked to the skies for signs of their coming doom and observed one evening 'a frightful sign' in which 'the entire city was illuminated'.

'The sentinels, who saw the light, ran to see what had happened, for they were under the impression that the Turks were burning the city,' recorded one eyewitness account. 'They cried with a great voice. Many people gathered and saw on the church of the Wisdom of God [Hagia Sophia], at the top of the window a large flame of fire issuing forth; it encircled the entire neck of the church for a long time. The flame gathered into one; its flame altered, and there was an indescribable light. At once it took to the sky.' The belief among the people and the clergy was that this was the Holy Spirit departing the city and leaving its people to their fate.

This was just one of the omens reported in the final days of the siege. The various eyewitnesses and contemporary chroniclers describe storms, strange fogs, earthquakes, a lunar eclipse, oysters that when opened dripped blood, and even rumours of 'a dragon laying waste to the fields' beyond the city.

In light of all this it is hard to say if the fearful citizens of Constantinople really were observing optical phenomena linked to the Kuwae eruption, or if it was merely the fevered foreboding of a people whose fatalism had reached the level of a psychological affliction. When I read about Kuwae and the siege, the possible link between the two appealed to me in a way that I struggled to explain. In rooting the superstitions and forebodings of the Byzantines to a geological event, Kuwae seemed to offer both a partial explanation for those forebodings and also to deepen their mystery. It connected the distant doomsday of the Byzantines to the climatic forces we now feel bearing down on us with our own secular sense of guilt, apocalyptic dread, and illusions of powerlessness in the face not of God, but of a natural world now poised to punish us.

The people of Constantinople had long been mired in a web of prophecies and omens, which had only become more pessimistic and stifling as their long decline entered its terminal phase. One popular apocalyptic text at the time, attributed to the fourth-century bishop and martyr Methodius, laid out a bird's-eye history of the world from Adam and Eve to the Last Judgement, predicting that the events leading to Doomsday would begin when the 'children of Ishmael' overran the Christian lands, before being fought back from the grind of victory to be defeated by the last Roman emperor. After this the sea would rise up and swallow Constantinople and Christ would descend to enact judgement on humankind. *The Apocalypse of Pseudo-Methodius* was lent weight because it seemed to eerily prefigure the seventh-century rise of Islam and Arab conquest of the Middle East; in fact it was written after them by an anonymous Syriac monk and falsely attributed to the long-dead Methodius. The text's vision of the defeat of Islam and the coming of Doomsday were likely written to steel the nerves of Christians in the region who were then converting in large numbers to the new faith.

When the text arrived in Constantinople, translated from Syriac to Greek, the new version was laden with references more specific to the Byzantines and their city. One of these was the prophecy that foretold the city would be invaded through the Xylokerkos, the Gate of the Wooden Circus, one of the main public entrances to the city, later known as Belgradkapı.

'Woe to you, [City of] Byzas, that Ishmael will conquer you,' it warned. 'Since every horse will cross over and the first of them will set up his tent opposite you, Byzas, and will begin the fight and crush the Xylokerkos gate and enter until the [Forum of the] Ox.' In a sign of how seriously this prophecy was taken, the Xylokerkos was bricked up by the Emperor Isaac II at the end of the twelfth century in case it might relate to the German emperor Frederick Barbarossa, whom it was feared would lead the Third Crusade against Constantinople, and it remained so up until the final siege, in which it would play little role.

Its name, however, would later become muddled with that of another gate, the Gate of the Circus or the Wooden Postern, which stood at the other end of the land walls and whose role, according to the account of Doukas, would prove far more consequential. The location and even existence of this gate has not been definitively established, although Alexander Van Millingen, who published a detailed and invaluable survey of the walls in 1899, identified it as a small postern sandwiched between the walls and the Palace of the Porphyrogenitus, or Tekfürsarayı, which abuts them. And so the prophecy, perhaps, had a way of asserting itself with a little help from Doukas or the various sources he consulted when compiling his history.

The thicket of omens and prophecies in which the Byzantines appear to have been tangled risks blinding those of us who try to look back at that time. The events that unfolded during the course of Mehmet's eight-week-long siege of Constantinople have come down through the accounts of eyewitnesses and contemporary historians who were often themselves traumatised by what they had been through, and for whom ideas of predestination were a natural part of their outlook on the world. The descriptions of signs, omens, prophecies, the operation of fate and divine punishment that permeate these narratives can create the impression that Mehmet's victory was inevitable, and risk obscuring the intensity of the human struggle that surrounded it. Mehmet might easily have lost; he nearly did. During those eight weeks both sides were torn between conviction and uncertainty, hoping for victory and fearing defeat in a contest that was as much psychological as physical and that played out amid rising brutality. Its outcome was uncertain until the very final moments.

The surviving testimonies describing those events come overwhelmingly from the defenders. Among them were a Catholic cardinal of Byzantine birth, an Italian bishop, a Venetian ship's doctor, a young Classics student from Brescia, and an enigmatic Russian monk who was captured and inducted into the Ottoman army before escaping; there are almost no Greek eyewitness accounts. On the Ottoman side, meanwhile, the sources are slim, the main one being an account of the siege published in 1488 by an Ottoman courtier who fought at the siege as a young man.

This handful of accounts would survive, some mutilated by

time – translated and retranslated, corrupted, added to and altered. In recent decades historians have worked diligently to unearth and unstitch them from their later embellishments. Nonetheless, those that come down to us collectively paint a picture that is both vivid and broadly consistent in its details.

———

At the start of April 1453, the Catholic bishop Leonardo of Chios stood on the walls of the city and watched the army assembling there with fearful appreciation. He had arrived in Constantinople a few months earlier as part of a delegation sent by the Pope led by his friend, the charismatic Greek-born Cardinal Isidore of Kiev, who had recruited him on Chios when Isidore stopped there en route to the city.

Over the preceding days Mehmet's army had begun to assemble, prompting Constantine to close the gates to the city on 2 April. The Ottoman forces had stormed or blockaded the few remaining Byzantine strongholds outlying the city, and were cutting down trees and levelling roads in preparation for the artillery. The most conservative of the eyewitness accounts numbered his army at around 160,000 men. Of this number only a minority were fighters – perhaps around 60,000, which included 15,000 of the elite Janissary corps. The rest were cooks, hawkers, workmen and an array of others required to service such a large force, as well as hangers-on and camp followers who had come in hope of plunder.

Leonardo was impressed by the orderliness and efficiency of the preparations as the Ottoman forces moved into place their cannons and siege engines, protecting themselves from any defenders' fire with hurdle-like structures of woven branches. 'A Scipio, a Hannibal, or any of our modern generals would have been amazed at the discipline which they showed in arranging their weapons, and the promptness and evidence of forward planning which their manoeuvres showed,' he would later write in the long letter he dispatched to the Pope a few weeks after the siege.

A zealous partisan in the schism between the Eastern and Western churches, his account frequently digresses into bitter condemnation of the Greeks, whose refusal to embrace Catholicism he believed had sealed their doom. He fumed at the fact that within Mehmet's army were many who were, or once had been, his co-religionists. 'I can bear witness that Greeks, Latins, Germans, Hungarians, Bohemians and others from all the kingdoms of Christendom were to be found among the Turks, and followed their faith and their works,' he railed. '. . . Oh, the wickedness of denying Christ in this manner!'

Of these some had been forcibly converted to Islam and others were levies sent by the Ottomans' Christian vassals. Several other contemporary accounts mention the ethnic diversity of Mehmet's force: it was far from monolithic, and most were not zealous in the cause beyond the promise it offered of plunder and riches. Among their number, there may have also been a young Russian monk named Nestor-Iskander, who had been captured by the Ottomans, circumcised and inducted into the army. The chronicle of the siege that would bear his name, written in Old Slavonic, would be so mangled by later additions that historians can only guess at its original elements, but it has been argued by some leading scholars of the siege that Nestor-Iskander, having somehow escaped his captors, entered the city and wrote a diary of the siege while aiding the defence, which forms the nucleus of his account.

Another of those present was Ubertino Posculo, a twenty-two-year-old student from Brescia who had come to the city to learn classical Greek. Ten years later he would publish an epic poem in Latin recounting these events. Despite being penned in a florid Virgilian style, with the names of various nations involved substituted for their imagined classical counterparts, it nonetheless contains a precise and detailed account of key moments by someone who fought in the defence and would have witnessed much of what happened.

He described the moment Mehmet's great cannon was first fired at the walls: 'The first enormous bombard strikes the Roman walls with a fast flung stone through the black and smoke-filled air, and struck them with a horrible sounding blow. The walls quaked with a rumbling . . . At the first blow, the walls stood unmoved and only weakened . . . But after the bombard struck a second time, the immovable wall was unable to withstand a boulder of such a great weight; it yielded and caving in makes a wide hole falling earthward in a dense mass.'

The extent of the destruction wrought by the Ottoman artillery in those opening days is dwelt on in every account of the siege. There are conflicting accounts of the effectiveness of Mehmet's giant bombard, which Leonardo suggests ruptured early on, but others describe as operating with devastating effect.

'Sometimes it demolished a whole section, sometimes a half-section, and sometimes a larger or smaller section of a tower or turret or battlement,' wrote Kritovoulos, the Greek historian who was not an eyewitness and compiled his account later. 'And there was no part of the wall strong enough or resistant enough or thick enough to be able to withstand it.'

Leonardo described how a tower near the Caligaria Gate, which was close to where he was posted, collapsed after being hit by one of the larger cannons so that the rubble filled the moat, opening the way for the attacking army. He was so fascinated by these terrible weapons that he even found one of the cannonballs and measured it himself with his arms, finding it to be eleven hands in circumference.

The noise, smoke and destruction of the cannon terrified the people of the city, but they did not have the immediate and overwhelming effect Mehmet might have hoped for. A few years earlier, his father Murat had reduced and stormed the strong Hexamilion wall, which Constantine had built, in just five days, using far more modest artillery and by undermining it with explosives. The difference in this case was largely due to the energy and experience of Giustiniani, the Genoese commander who had so impressed Constantine when he arrived with his company of heavily armed soldiers shortly before the siege. As Murat had done at the Hexamilion, Mehmet repeatedly dug mines to try to blow up the walls from beneath, but among Giustiniani's company was a man named John Grant (Bishop Leonardo describes him as a German, but modern scholars reckon him to have been Scottish) who was expert at sapping, and oversaw the digging of countermines through which the Ottoman tunnels were smoked out or flooded. Every attempt to undermine the walls in this way was foiled. Giustiniani pitched his tent alongside that of the emperor at the area known as the Mesoteichion, where the walls were weakest due to the lay of the land. It was where Mehmet's own tents were pitched and where the Ottoman bombardment was heaviest.

Experienced in siege warfare, Giustiniani sprang into action each time a section of wall was damaged or destroyed, marshalling the defenders to gather material and create stockades of wood, rubble, and earth-filled barrels across the breached sections. The resulting barricades were able to absorb the impact of the cannonballs far better than rigid masonry, and could be swiftly rebuilt. Leonardo recalled him as being tireless in these efforts: 'Whenever the weight of a huge stone brought down the walls, he, nothing daunted, repaired them with faggots and earth and barrels piled together.' Posculo described the operation of the repairs in more detail: 'They order bundles of branches to be brought there; they dig out the ground and pile up a mound beneath the sky. Once the rampart is built, a long wooden beam, wooden planks, and mud are brought in with wagons from every corner of the city and they patch up the hole.'

Over the course of the siege his leadership came to be of pivotal importance to the effectiveness and morale of the besieged force. 'The whole city had confidence in him and his bravery,' recalled Jacopo Tetaldi, a Florentine merchant who fought among the defenders. Leonardo described him as 'the guardian of all our fortunes'.

Two miles away at the mouth of the Golden Horn, a very different contest was unfolding at sea. The Byzantines had a motley fleet of ships in the harbour, protected by the great chain that for centuries had been drawn across it at times of siege. Their ships, which were mainly trading or cargo vessels from the Italian states, were not dedicated warships but were nonetheless formidable with high strong sides, built to resist and fight back against pirate attacks. Many of these had been forced or enticed to remain in the harbour to aid the defence. Among their crews was Nicolò Barbaro, a ship's surgeon in his fifties serving on a Venetian galley. He wrote what would be the most detailed and lengthy eyewitness account of the siege, a day-by-day diary in which he recorded events as they unfolded, focusing mainly on what occurred at the harbour.

Barbaro noted the arrival of the Ottoman fleet on 12 April, and estimated it to be about 145 ships, of which twelve were large galleys and the rest were various smaller types, mainly *fustae*, low boats crewed by teams of rowers. It was the first time the Ottomans had attacked the city from both sea and land, and their fleet was dauntingly large. Despite their advantage in numbers, Ottoman naval technology was still inferior to that of their opponents; their ships were smaller, lower in the water, and less sturdy than their European counterparts, and the Ottomans made no immediate move to attack the chain, but moored in the Bosphorus, out of sight of the Christian fleet, near where the late-Ottoman Dolmabahçe Palace would later stand. Their primary function was probably to deter outside assistance rather than to attack by force.

For Barbaro and the other seamen, the entirety of the siege was spent in a state of tension and readiness, awaiting a possible attack on the chain. Watchmen on the walls of the Genoese colony of Pera, which lay on the other side of the harbour and maintained a delicate neutrality, reported any movements in the Ottoman fleet that might indicate an attack, whereupon a trumpet would be sounded and the crews rushed to arms. '[W]e waited every hour for the Turkish fleet to come to attack us,' wrote Barbaro. 'So each day we were in this difficulty, and in great fear . . . having by day and by night to stand to our arms.'

The main hope of the besieged city was that help would arrive in the form of a relief fleet from the Italian states, and so on 20 April there was great excitement when four large vessels – three Genoese cargo ships and a Byzantine transport, were sighted approaching from the Sea of Marmara under a strong southerly wind. They had come with men, arms and grain for the beleaguered city. As they neared the harbour the mass of Ottoman vessels rowed out to intercept them.

The following confrontation would become one of the most vividly recalled episodes of the siege. As the European ships approached the mouth of the Bosphorus, the wind suddenly dropped and the four vessels were becalmed. The Ottomans fell upon them. Barbaro claimed the entirety of the enemy fleet was engaged, 'so that the Dardanelles were covered with armed boats, and the water could hardly be seen for the vessels of these evil dogs'. Though vastly outnumbered, the four European vessels were like fortresses to their attackers, whose light culverins were unable to pierce their hulls.

The battle lasted for two to three hours, unfolding in full view of the city, the boats locked together like a great raft. 'Mixed together mothers and children and husbands rush on,' wrote Posculo, who gave the most detailed account of it. 'Some climb upon the walls, others climb upon the roofs of their houses, and others in order to see the battle seek out in a rush the Hippodrome from where they are able to observe the sea far and wide.'

The larger sailing boats depended on the wind for their salvation. When it picked up, they were able to break free of their assailants and make for the chain. Posculo described how, when it dropped again, the crews of the four large boats bound their vessels together with rope 'and all the ships move forward with their cords drawn tight, they remain there jointly like four bound towers.' The Turkish crews fired arrows and hurled javelins and spears at their quarry, and the defenders fired back down on them with crossbows, guns and small mounted artillery pieces.

This siege-at-sea must have had an air of a symbolism about it: the struggle for the city sublimated into a bloody spectacle visible to all sides. 'An indomitable dread exhausts everyone with happiness and fear,' wrote Posculo. Some of the accounts even placed Mehmet himself on the shoreline, riding a horse and screaming orders and encouragement to his men.

Finally, after the wind rose again, the newly arrived ships broke free and reached the chain, and their pursuers, wary of the rest of the Christian fleet, broke off the attack. After nightfall the chain was lowered and the boats towed inside. It was a stirring victory for the defenders, who staged loud celebrations in the city, and a humiliation for the Ottomans, whose entire fleet had failed to subdue the four boats.

One of the very few contemporary Turkish sources on the

siege relates to this incident, and it is an extraordinarily revealing one, telling both how seriously this setback was viewed in the Ottoman camp, and how precarious they believed their own position to be. It is a letter written to Mehmet by Akşamsettin, a prominent Sunni cleric and mentor to the young Sultan who was present at the siege. He wrote:

> The misfortune that befell us as a consequence of the sailors' actions has caused the deepest sorrow and discouragement in our heart. The fact that they failed to avail themselves of this opportunity has resulted in certain contrary developments in this situation: one such development is that the infidel have been encouraged and have staged a raucous demonstration; a second lies in the claim that your noble majesty demonstrated little discernment or ability in having your own orders carried out.

This severe missive goes on to recommend punishment and demotion for those who oversaw the naval engagement, in order to steel the nerves of the army for the coming fight. Akşamsettin continued,

> As you well know, the majority of our forces are, in any case, forced converts, and therefore the number of those who are ready to sacrifice their lives for the love of God is extremely low. But if they saw that they would be able to loot, they would be ready to run up against certain death. I therefore entreat you: Do everything in your power either with actions or orders so that this victory is assured.

Tursun Beg, the main Ottoman chronicler of the siege, agreed with this assessment, saying that the defeat had 'caused despair and disorder in the ranks of the Muslims'. The anxiety revealed here may suggest why Mehmet had not already launched a general attack on the city. Perhaps he feared his men would not have the stomach for it, that they would only fight if they believed victory, and the spoils of it, were almost certain?

———

Faced with the need to shift momentum back in his favour, Mehmet enacted a plan that he had been developing for some time. It seems that close to the outset of the siege he must have ordered the construction of a road running behind the Genoese settlement of Galata on the far side of the Golden Horn, connecting the shore of the Bosphorus with that of the inlet. On 22 April, to the amazement and horror of defenders, teams of oxen began dragging the boats of the Ottoman fleet across this road in cradles mounted on rollers over the lip of land and directly behind the Genoese settlement of Pera and into the Golden Horn. The boats arrived with their crews in them, ready to repel assault, and a battery of cannon had been placed on the shore to deter the Byzantines from approaching. Over the course of the day the Ottomans lowered some seventy ships into the Horn in this way. It was characteristic of Mehmet's daring, resourcefulness and technical ingenuity. At a stroke, it shifted the balance of the siege in favour of the attackers. The Golden Horn was no longer a safe haven, and the allied fleet there now needed to be constantly alert to the threat from the Ottoman ships. More seriously, it forced the defenders to man the sea walls facing the Horn, further thinning their already stretched ranks. In another ominous development, the Ottoman force constructed a pontoon bridge across the harbour to allow them to send troops directly against the sea wall.

A few days later the Byzantines and their allies made a plan to attack this fleet at night and burn it, but the attempt was botched and their ships were raked with Ottoman cannon fire. A boat was sunk, and in the confusion some forty men swam to the enemy shore and were captured. Mehmet had them impaled in full view of the defenders, a method of execution which left its victims painfully alive sometimes for as long as a few days. 'The stakes were planted, and they were left to die in full view of the guards upon the walls,' recorded Tetaldi, the Florentine merchant. The defenders responded to this bloody spectacle with their own atrocity. Taking a number of Turkish captives, and 'slaughtered them cruelly on the walls in full view of their fellows', according to Bishop Leonardo. 'In this way the war was made more savage by a mixture of impiety and cruelty.'

As this was unfolding the fight along the land walls continued. Towards the end of April a major assault by the Ottomans was repelled, with the attackers suffering massive losses. Siege engines were brought against the walls and destroyed. Over time, however, exhaustion began to set in among the defenders. Increasingly they pinned their hopes on the possibility of a relief fleet arriving from the Italian states. Towards the end of May, however, a brigantine sent out to scout the nearby seas returned to port, running the gauntlet of the Ottoman fleet, and bringing terrible news: there was no sign of a relief fleet on the way, nor any rumour of one.

Despair in the Christian ranks seems to have been far from universal, however. Writing to his brother in a state of shock a month after the siege, Angelo Lomellino, the former chief magistrate of Pera, the Genoese colony across the Horn from Constantinople, called the defeat 'unexpected', 'because it seemed to us that our victory was assured'.

Time was not on Mehmet's side. The sultan could not count indefinitely on the cohesion of his huge army, and reports had reached him that the Venetians might be preparing a fleet to relieve the city. He might never have a better chance to attack Constantinople, and failure now could even mean the end of his brief reign. At a war council towards the end of May the old vizier Halil, who had always opposed the undertaking, once again advised him to abandon it. But Mehmet's more hawkish *devşirme* generals urged him on. He ordered another assault, greater and more determined than those that had preceded it and in which his forces would strike from both sea and land at once. Win or lose, it would probably be his final attempt.

Informants in the Ottoman camp made the Byzantines aware of the impending attack through messages fired with arrows into the city. As the defenders worked to strengthen the stockades that had replaced broken sections of the walls, the Ottomans made their own practical and psychological preparations. Mehmet buoyed his troops by promising to grant them the customary three days of plunder, and that the city's riches would be divided fairly between his followers. For three nights before the attack, great fires were lit throughout the Ottoman camp.

'[T]he light from them was so strong that it seemed as if it were day,' wrote Barbaro. '. . . As the pagans made their fires, they shouted in their Turkish fashion, so that it seemed as if the very skies would split apart.' In his account of that moment, the historian Doukas describes the Byzantines rushing to the walls in hope, believing a fire might have broken out in the enemy camp. 'When they saw the Turks dancing and heard their joyous shouts, they foresaw the future . . . The spectacle and din affected the citizens so much that they appeared to be half-dead, unable to breathe either in or out.'

By then there were only around 4,000 defenders left to guard some 12 miles of wall facing sea and land. The sea walls facing the Marmara were largely manned by untrained monks and citizens with only a single trained archer, crossbowman, or gunner for every tower. The bulk of the Byzantine forces were concentrated on the central section of the land walls around the vulnerable Mesoteichion. It was here that Mehmet's cannons had caused the most damage and where he would most press his assault.

The following night the Ottomans again chanted and lit fires. They continued their preparations, stockpiling weapons, arrows, scaling ladders and screening hurdles, and worked feverishly to fill in sections of the moat. As their cannons battered the walls once more, the Byzantines continued to repair breaches in the stockade. Ottoman ships loaded with soldiers began to take up their position all around the sea walls, so that by the time the final night fell and the fires were once again lit, the entire army was in position for its attack.

Barbaro recorded:

> One hour after dark, the Turks in their camp began to light a terrifying number of fires, much greater than they had lit on the two previous nights, but worse than this, it was their shouting which was more than we Christians could bear; and together with their shouting, they fired a great number of cannon and guns, and hurled stones without number, so that to us it seemed to be a very inferno.

Within the city the non-fighting population helped carry stones to the stockade to hurl down on the enemy, and gathered in the churches to pray. For the previous five months, since the rapprochement between Rome and Constantinople, which Constantine had driven through against staunch public opposition, the population had shunned the great basilica of Hagia Sophia, where a new unified liturgy was being read. But on this final night they gathered there nonetheless, with the emperor in attendance, for a service of intercession. Some remained there in prayer throughout the night while others hid themselves in their homes or in the underground cisterns that dotted the city.

The attack began at around 1 a.m. on the morning of 29 May.

Mehmet himself commanded the main assault on the Mesoteichion. He divided his forces into three waves. First were the *azaps*, irregular soldiers who were poorly trained and armed, who had joined his host in hope of plunder, or else Christians levied into service from his vassals. Numerous but of weak morale, their attack was intended principally to exhaust the defenders. '[T]hey tried to raise the ladders up,' wrote Barbaro, 'and at once we threw them to the ground with the men who were raising them, and they were all killed at once, and we threw big stones down on them from the battlements, so that few escaped alive; in fact, anyone who approached beneath the walls was killed.' As each wave of attackers fled, they were cut down by the Ottoman troops waiting behind them, 'so that they had the choice of dying on one side or the other'.

The defenders fired their weapons into the massed ranks, poured hot oil, lime, rocks and logs down onto their attackers. After two hours the retreat was called and the second group came forward, the better-trained regular soldiers of Mehmet's Anatolian armies, Muslims who were motivated by their faith and more eager for combat. They came at the walls 'like lions unchained', wrote Barbaro, but were met with similar slaughter. 'As dawn struggled through the darkness, we began to gain the advantage,' wrote Leonardo, who said there were heavy losses on both sides. 'The firmness of the resistance shown by the Christians caused their ranks to break, yet their cries rose to the heights, and their flags were un-furled still more eagerly. One could only marvel at the brutes: their army was being annihilated, and yet they dared to approach the fosse again and again.'

Finally Mehmet ordered the white-turbaned Janissaries into the attack – 'all soldiers of the Sultan and paid every day, all well-armed men strong in battle'. According to Barbaro they struck 'with such shouting and sounding of castanets that it seemed a thing not of this world, and the shouting was heard

as far away as Anatolia, twelve miles away from their camp.'
Their attack was combined with cannon, so that they could rush
into any breaches as soon as they opened.

Still the defenders resisted, and it was at this moment of
maximum pressure when calamity struck. Giustiniani, who had
led the defence from the beginning, was wounded by a projec-
tile of some kind – a splinter of rock or a culverin shot. The
sources diverge on the nature of his injury, but it precipitated
his departure from the wall, either through a sudden loss of
nerve, as some of the sources claimed, or else with the intention
of seeking treatment and returning. The defenders were fighting
with the inner wall to their backs, its postern locked to prevent
them fleeing, but Giustiniani insisted it be opened to allow him
to depart along with some of his men. His departure shook the
defenders' resolve badly.

'He deserted his position and abandoned the terrified forces,'
wrote Posculo. 'Those who were stationed at the walls of Saint
Romanos, Latins and Greeks began to tremble with fear.'

Further down the wall, in the telling of Doukas, another
postern had been left open by accident – the fateful Gate of the
Xylokerkos – and a detachment of Ottoman soldiers had passed
through it without the defenders' knowledge and mounted one
of the towers, replacing the flag of the Venetians who were
guarding that section with the Ottoman standard. Even though
this group had been contained and the postern closed, the sight
of the enemy's banner on the wall, combined with the departure
of Giustiniani, triggered a panic and general rout among the
defenders. Many tried to flee through the postern he had gone
through, blocking it in a crush of bodies in which many were
killed. Mounting the stockade, the Janissaries now slaughtered
their foes as they were piled against the inner wall before pressing
through the gate and into the city.

It was shortly before daybreak. As Mehmet's soldiers entered they fanned out along the walls, opening each gate as they passed. Elsewhere the defenders fought on, unaware the battle was lost. But as the news of the disaster spread through the city many began to abandon their posts to escape or protect their families. Doukas described how the first bloodied defenders were met with incredulity as they arrived in the heart of the city.

It was early in the morning, still twilight, when some Romans who had managed to flee and reach their houses . . . in order to look after their children and their wives. As they went by the region of the Bull and reached the Column of the Cross, some women who saw them covered in blood asked: 'Well, what has happened?' When they heard that ill-omened shout 'the enemy is inside the walls and is slaughtering the Romans', at first they did not believe it but even cursed and blamed them as if they were the bearers of bad news. But behind them there was another and another, all covered in blood, so they realised that the Lord's cup filled with His wrath had reached their lips.

10

The Cannon Gate

A cold afternoon in February, and the wind was blowing broken clouds across the sky. The drinkers at the Topkapı Gate were scattered across the grass alone or in little groups, hunched in their coats. My friend wished *afiyet olsun* – 'bon appetite' – to a pair sitting beneath the old terebinth as we passed to take our place among them.

'What did you say?' asked a man who surged to his feet and swayed drunkenly towards us. 'What did you say?' he asked again. His companion stood up and held him back. He must have misheard us. We sat there uneasily, pretending to ignore him.

'He didn't do anything,' said his friend as he struggled to restrain him. 'He said *afiyet olsun!* You're the one insulting him.' The man threatening us was young, massive – as tall as me but broad and barrel-chested. Eventually his friend convinced him to sit down but he continued to glare at us. We moved a little further away.

The pair continued to argue, and now and then the young man got to his feet and lurched towards us, his friend holding him back, planting his hand on his chest. 'You've been trouble since you were a kid,' said the older man. We thought they might be brothers. Another guy sitting near us looked on impassively, munching a sandwich of bread and cheese and drinking wine from a paper cup. He wore a heavy parka with 'private security' written on the back in reflective lettering.

'Ignore him,' he said. 'If he starts anything, break a bottle over his head.' I told my friend we should probably leave but he thought the guy would follow us. Better to stand our ground. I shivered beneath my coat. It was a fickle day, by turns threatening and enticing; sometimes a light rain spat and felt like it would set in, but then it would lull and the sun would light up the grass with brief ferocity and for a moment it felt like summer.

The drunk man approached again to where we were sitting. There was something faintly comical about him. He was so big he seemed to be bursting out of his clothes, his hair was thickly gelled into a side parting and he had a tenuous, wispy beard. He bobbed over like a helium balloon, shiny and pink with booze. His friend, or brother, had finally convinced him that we meant no offence and he'd come to beg our forgiveness.

'Kusura bakmayın,' he said gravely to both of us in turn, kneeling to be at eye level, 'kusura bakmayın'; and we replied 'estağfirullah, estağfirullah'. He placed a great meaty hand on the back of my head and I tensed for a moment, fearing he would smash my face into his knee, but he just tapped each side of his forehead on mine and then did the same to my companion. An ultranationalist thing, I'd always been told, though it was fairly mainstream; the intimacy of this allegedly fascist greeting had never stopped seeming weird to me.

'There was some trouble last night,' he slurred, gesturing to a smear of blood on his knuckle. It looked quite fresh and judging from the state he was in, I thought it was more likely to be his own than anyone else's. He told us he worked as a doorman at a hotel, and invited us to come by sometime and drink tea with him. Then he asked for a cigarette, and we gave him one, and he took my friend's lighter and cupped his hand around it. After a few tries it wouldn't light and for a moment he looked up at us again with an expression of pure fury, as if our broken lighter was another slap in the face, but then his companion called him back, frantically waving his own lighter, and finally he left us in peace.

It was a while before the absurdity of the exchange sank in: the profuse apology, the invitation to tea, the lingering threat of violence. It epitomised something I had come to notice in Turkey: an odd juxtaposition of civility and savagery, pressed together and drawn to extremes. Perhaps you could put it down to the ornateness of Turkish etiquette, which put a fine veneer over even the coarsest of interactions. The language was so well tailored for everyday courtesies, the phrases so varied and specific, that it made English seem impoverished by comparison. It made me feel like Busbecq marvelling at the attire of the Ottomans, suddenly aware of his own ill-fitting garb. Everyday phrases had a wonderful decorousness and musicality to them: *kusura bakmayın* – 'look not at the fault'; *estağfirullah (es-TAH-froo-la)*, an Arabic loan used to admonish someone for being too hard on themselves. *Afiyet olsun* – 'may there be health', when presenting a meal, and the reply, *elinize sağlik*, 'health to your hands'. To someone travelling: *yolunuz açık olsun*, 'may your road be clear'; to someone mourning, *başınız sağolsun*, 'may your head be sound'.

Returning to Turkey after an absence, I found these exchanges of everyday expressions to be grounding, and when I was in England I found it hard to do without them: *geçmiş olsun* ('may it be in the past'), the usual reply to someone who has just disclosed some illness or misfortune – was particularly useful, its nearest English equivalents seemed either overly grave or else awkwardly insufficient. It was something I always appreciated about Turkey: the care taken over everyday interactions, the awareness that perhaps they held more power than their triviality suggested.

At this point I had begun to split my life between England and Turkey, and was becoming more prone to these kinds of comparative observations. I felt ambivalent about them; I feared they were a symptom of estrangement, the superficial impressions of someone no longer close enough to the culture to see its deeper dimensions. Friends assured me that distance brought perspective, but I wondered if 'perspective' didn't just mean complacency. An old cliché often repeated about Turkey was that the more time you spent there the less you understood it; it was presumably intended for the benefit of people like me, foreign journalists who arrived, usually with more confidence than knowledge, in order to report on and interpret its current affairs for outsiders. In my case, it wasn't just that I realised over time how complicated Turkey and its politics were (I'd have been a fool to think otherwise), but that the continual shifting of my understanding led me to look askance at the insights I felt I'd gleaned.

But this feeling of estrangement was about more than my own shifting perspective; it came from witnessing a society undergoing rapid change. There was the physical transformation of the city: the levelling of old neighbourhoods, the new mosques and highways, the gargantuan new airport you arrived at. The weather was changing too. The summer heat had become even more stifling and humid; friends recounted hurricane-force winds, storms that turned streets into rivers, hailstones so big they dented cars.

Then there was the steady economic decline – shops, bars and restaurants closing, the places I'd habitually visited dwindling until the few that remained seemed on borrowed time. Each time I was in the city more friends had left, escaping to find better opportunities elsewhere. It wasn't a decision that required explanation or discussion. Those who had the means to leave but decided to stay were the ones who were asked to explain themselves. The profile of the kind of Westerner who lived in the city had changed; they used to work in any kind of industry – fashion, law, finance, art – as you might expect of any global metropolis, but those kinds of people had mainly left, to be replaced by aid workers and journalists drawn by the proliferating conflicts on Turkey's borders.

Then there was the constant ratcheting up of oppression and paranoia. When I'd lived in Turkey I'd become used to it, but now my periodic absences made it seem more jarring. I'd switch on the car radio and feel like I was eavesdropping on an alternative reality. News items had become little more than statistics of the latest arrests, reeled off without explanation or context or any hint of criticism: thirty-five people detained in Istanbul for membership of the FETÖ terrorist group, twenty-four committee members of the People's Democratic Party held across four cities, twenty-two insurgents 'liquidated' in northern Iraq, and so on. The impact of the brewing economic crisis was conveyed only in oblique hints: rising food prices were made to seem as natural and inevitable as winter snow, and no more worthy of explanation. On the television there was grainy drone footage of Turkish forces striking against targets in one or other of the proliferating foreign wars the country was becoming embroiled in – Libya, or Iraq or Syria. This was all shot through with the pain of familiarity, all the things that remained the same and which were somehow harder to bear than the changes.

Strangest of all perhaps was the way in which my own relationship to the city had contracted down to the walls and their environs, this strange world that felt so distant from the one I'd inhabited when I lived in the city.

The man sitting near us in the private security jacket was called Ahmet. He was in his fifties, thick jet eyebrows and grey moustache under a wide nose. He'd recently finished his shift and had been coming to drink at Topkapı for about ten years.

'Things like that never happen here,' he said, nodding at the drunk who'd accosted us. '*Afiyet olsun*, you said, *afiyet olsun*! What's the problem? If there had been more people around, they would have beaten him up.' The wind was blowing hard now, and he stood up and wrapped his coat around himself, pulling the hood over his head. He told us he was exhausted but after a few minutes his desire for company overcame his tiredness and he suggested we repair to a nearby café where it was warmer, and once we'd had a cup of tea there, he suggested a nearby bar. Soon after that he wanted us to go to Tarlabaşı, a seedy neighbourhood on the other side of the Golden Horn. 'There's a club there,' he said, 'they have all kinds of people: blacks, Germans, transsexuals.'

He told us he was a baker and had worked in bakeries since he was a child, making *simit*, but for the last few years he'd become a security guard in a car showroom. He hated the job and missed his old profession, but it offered a pension and he could one day hope to retire. He had a wife and grown-up children, but he didn't talk about them much. His stories mainly revolved around baking, drinking and money. He told us about the six months he'd spent working on a building site in Kerbala, in Iraq, in 2014, a story that combined all three of these themes. His job had been to operate the site bakery. He had spent his spare time fruitlessly searching for booze, and had saved a huge chunk of his salary through his inability to find it. The workers ate and slept on site. Ahmet recounted his few brushes with Iraqi culture: the time he tried to buy dates from a market, not realising that the Turkish word for 'date' sounded like the Arabic word for 'girl', the time he went to an Iraqi restaurant and found the food horrible and greasy, and finally the time when the Islamic State seized Mosul and he had to be evacuated.

Kerbala was far from Mosul, but in that uncertain moment, when the Iraqi army crumbled in the face of the ISIS insurgents and some fifty Turkish consular workers were taken hostage, Turkish companies evacuated their sites across the country. Ahmet and his colleagues were given six hours' notice before being taken by minibus and deposited at Baghdad airport. However, they had to wait a whole day for their flight, and security wouldn't let them into the terminal until it was due, so Ahmet and a friend of his headed into the city to find a hotel. Once they'd found somewhere, Ahmet headed out in search of booze.

'My friend was the praying type, so he wouldn't drink,' he told us, 'but I had to find some. I hadn't had a beer in six months and fifteen days.' Alcohol wasn't technically illegal in Iraq at that time, but it was hard to obtain in many parts of town and not sold openly. Eventually he came across a black-painted iron door with a hatch in it. 'Cars were stopping, a black plastic bag – just like the ones we use here – they were walking fast and jumping into a car and – *yallah!* – I got suspicious and waited a bit more. Another car stopped and I told myself to follow it. I took out ten dinar, that makes it around fifteen lira. I heard it was cheap so I thought it would be enough for three beers. The man got his bag and the window was just about to close and I jumped in. The guy was young, around twenty-four, twenty-five years old. He looked at my face and understood from my complexion that I was Turkish.

He said, "Turko!" and I said, "Beer!" He asked which one and I said it didn't matter. I gave him the ten dinar and he said OK and gave me a such a big bag, I could hardly lift it. A beer was one dinar apparently, and I thought, "You idiot, why didn't you buy whisky?"'

The job had been well paid and he was disappointed when it was cut short. After he'd come back from Iraq he'd tried to set up his own bakery but had lost money, and in the years since his financial situation had got worse and eventually led to a family rift.

'When my financial situation got shaky my wife and children's attitude changed, and I resented it. It meant everything was about money.' He'd moved out of his home for a few days and slept in a friend's bakery on the Anatolian side; eventually his children found him and begged him to come home.

When I asked Ahmet if he lived on credit he laughed.

'Of course I do! Everyone does!' He showed us messages from his bank on his phone. A 3,000 lira debt had now grown to 7,000 lira; soon it would be 10,000 lira. 'They are constantly messaging me but I can't respond,' he told us. 'The messages say, let's find a solution. I understand that, but I don't have the money, so how can I?'

He was currently earning around minimum wage from his job – then about 2,300 lira a month, or £270. He supplemented this by working at a bakery one day a week. 'I go there and help them on Fridays. They give me a hundred lira. Pocket money. There are twenty days until my paycheque arrives, until then I'll be on edge. I am calculating how I can survive in the next few days.

'It goes on rent. We pay 1,050 lira. You close your eyes and open them again, and there it is: rent due. Sometimes the landlord gives me a call. He owns a shop. Every month he asks if I left the rent money in the shop. I say no. He asks when I will do it. I leave it there and then he goes and takes it. I paid 200 lira less this month. I will pay 1,250 lira next month. I'm struggling again. There's no cash flow.'

Turkey's consumption boom of the preceding years had been fuelled in large part by cheap credit. People had been encouraged to get credit cards and buy goods using instalment purchase plans. Now, with the economy tanking and inflation rising, millions of people like Ahmet were treading water. He was worried about the way the country was heading, and saw a disconnect between the apparent confidence Turkey was projecting as a regional military power and the worsening economic situation at home.

'Why are they doing this operation in northern Iraq, in Syria?' he demanded, 'and doing it with what? Where does the money come from? They get all this money off the backs of the people. Price hikes in everything, price hikes in public transport, price hikes in food. How are people going to get by? There needs to be at least three people working in every household so you can have a breather. Otherwise it's futile. Men are finishing college and working as security guards.'

On another, sunnier day at Topkapı I met a man named Yaşar, who was sitting alone, tanned and neatly turned out in jeans and a polo shirt, with a beer and a bag of dried chickpeas, short-cropped hair and a gold watch on his wrist. He worked in the leather industry. His wife and son were away at his wife's home village, he was missing them and had come here to pass the time. His office was in the old city and he regularly passed through the Topkapı gate on his commute, and had noticed the men drinking here.

'The first day I came here I smelled the scent of the grass and

I just fell in love with it,' he said. 'I saw that this was a place where nobody bothers you, where you can sit quietly and relax . . . I love nature, even just this little bit of green. I can get away from my daily concerns here.'

When I asked him about those concerns, he complained about Syrian refugees, rising rent, and the falling value of the lira, which was hitting his business, which relied on importing materials from India. But he stressed he was happy with his life in general, though. When I asked him how he felt about the political situation in the country, he told me with sudden vehemence that he wouldn't discuss politics: 'In politics you end up in a situation where I think one thing and you think another, and I don't want to get involved in that. Politics is based on lies. I don't get involved in this subject.'

'I'm a nationalist,' he told me abruptly, immediately diving into the subject he'd vowed not to discuss, as if I'd reminded him of an itch he couldn't resist scratching. He said he'd grown up in Ağrı Province, in the east of Turkey. I had passed through there once and remembered it as a barren place of stony hills, poplars and huge skies dominated by the distant cone of Mount Ararat. Ağrı itself was mainly Kurdish, and during the early 1990s when Yaşar was growing up the area was in the grip of the PKK insurgency and the whole of the south-east was in a state of emergency.

'It was a dangerous time in our region,' he said. In Turkey there are several different words for nationalism, each with subtly different political connotations. Yaşar was an ülkücü – a word that literally means 'idealist' and is the preferred label of a brand of Turkish ultra-nationalists aligned with the far-right National Action Party, or MHP.

'In high school I worked in a teahouse,' he told me. 'I was very excited about the ülkücüs and the MHP. I found out that there was an ülkücü gathering in Ağri where they would all meet and I wanted to go but I had to ask permission from my boss. You had to pay to go and I needed his help as well – he was an MHP supporter. He said he would put the money I needed in the money belt I wore when I was working at the tea shop. But he said: "You're young, and you have a bright future, and you don't want to ruin it. You don't know who'll be there, you don't know if anyone will take pictures." I thought about it, and I decided not to go. I kissed his hand, and I thanked him, and that was one of the biggest lessons I ever received . . . That's why I don't get into politics.'

'I'll tell you a story,' he said, after hesitating for a moment. 'At the time I finished high school, because it was the nineties, and the PKK was very strong at that time, the teachers appointed to Ağrı wouldn't come, so the state devised a system where you could pass an exam and go to teach straight out of high school. I was teaching for a couple of years when I was eighteen, nineteen.' The PKK had a policy of targeting functionaries of the Turkish state, including state school teachers, who were among the most vulnerable of these, being sent out all across the country, sometimes to isolated village primary schools where there was little to protect them. It was so dangerous that many refused to take up their positions at all.

'I had a friend,' said Yaşar, 'later he was martyred during his military service – he was teaching too, and I was staying in his house one evening, and we heard some noises right outside. My friend had a dog that could open doors. It was that clever. We heard doors opening and we assumed it was the dog. The next morning we went outside and right by the door there was a note and it said: "Leave the school or this house will burn and you will burn with it."

'We went to the *muhtar*, who was Kurdish, and told him what had happened and asked him what we should do. He told us that he couldn't help us. He told us he wouldn't even be able to protect his own children in this situation. He said we should go through the official channels and try to get protection that way. In the end we had to quit.'

'A few weeks later two other teachers were kidnapped in Ağrı, and the PKK demanded 600,000 lira ransom for them – a huge amount of money. The whole community came together and we collected and paid a sum that was very close to what was being asked for, and we got the teachers back.'

Now, as if finally arriving at his point, he turned to face me full on and said, 'If you can sit down and look into a person's eyes and understand each other then things are OK, but on the other hand, if someone is a traitor to this country their throat should be cut. *Cut!*' he repeated, drawing his finger across his throat. '*Cut!* You say you're writing about the walls but then you lead me on to these political topics. I don't know what you're really doing. I don't care who anyone is, there could be secret police anywhere. There are plainclothes police all around here,' he said, gesturing about us. 'I have nothing to hide!'

11

The Gate of the Spring

The gate of Silivrikapı was named after Silivri – ancient Selymbria – the town on the Marmara coast to which its road had led, now known chiefly for its huge court and prison complex at which numerous politically-driven mass trials were conducted. In Byzantine times it had been known as the Gate of the Spring, on account of the holy waters of the Balıklı monastery that lay nearby outside the walls. My first visit there had ended in disappointment.

I'd gone to the monastery, one of the most important sites of the Greek Orthodox community in Istanbul – the 'Rum', or Romans, as they were still known, in the hope of getting in touch with those who remained living around the walls. The existing monastery had been built in the mid-nineteenth century but the history of the place was far older. Its legend dated to the Byzantine Emperor Leo I, who ruled from AD 457. When he had been a soldier, he was said to have encountered a blind man outside the city who asked him for water; he heard the voice of the Virgin, who commanded him to wet the man's eyes from a nearby spring. He did so and the man regained his sight. After his accession, Leo erected a church there and that, so it was believed, was how the Monastery of the Life-Giving Spring came into being. For centuries it played a role in the coronation ceremony of the emperors and in royal weddings. It was apparently destroyed either at the time of Murat's siege in 1422 or during Mehmet's siege, but remained a site of pilgrimage.

In its latest incarnation it was the place where the patriarchs of Constantinople were buried. In 1955, when a devastating pogrom was launched against Istanbul's Greeks, the monastery was attacked and ravaged by a mob, its abbot severely beaten, and the tombs of the patriarchs opened up and their contents scattered. In similar attacks across Istanbul, armed mobs encouraged by the state destroyed some 3,000 buildings, attacking both businesses and homes owned by Greeks, but also Armenians and Jews, striking a massive blow to Istanbul's Rum community. Before 1955, the population had been about 120,000; after the pogrom, tens of thousands emigrated to Greece. Sixty years later the population stood at less than 1,800, mainly concentrated in the neighbourhood of Kurtuluş across the Golden Horn.

I went to the monastery and spoke to the priest there who, after I had explained my project, politely but firmly deflected me. When I asked him if there were any Greeks still living around the walls, he said he didn't think so, then added, almost as an afterthought, that he himself had grown up in Yedikule, just down the road.

'Could I interview you?' I asked.

'Of course not, I'm a priest,' he told me with finality.

Later I went to meet Mihail Vasiliadis, the editor of Istanbul's tiny Rum community newspaper; a rumpled-looking man in his mid-seventies with a receding hairline and greying ponytail. He confirmed that to his knowledge the Greek population had left the area around the walls entirely. He said that the 1955 looting had mainly targeted businesses in the richer areas, but since the communities around the walls were poor, there the attackers had focused on people's homes; more rapes and physical attacks took place and the destruction and fear they seeded was more intense. Those who didn't leave the country entirely moved into the newly vacated houses of Greeks who had left the wealthier areas.

When I asked him what meaning the walls had for him, he gave the kind of reply that made me feel silly for having asked: 'Everything that harbours history in it is important to me,' he said. 'I'm sad to see it's become a shelter for junkies and forgers to print counterfeit money. It has to be protected. Sadly, there is this weird mentality: some people think Istanbul was built in 1923, some in 1453. Others in 333. Some others think it was during the period of Midas in 400 BC . . . That's wrong too. Istanbul's history began five thousand years ago.'

He mentioned the recent discovery of footprints thousands of years old that had been found by archaeologists during excavations accompanying the construction of a new tunnel under the Bosphorus. 'I'm still thinking about that five-thousand-year-old footprint. When I saw that, I said to myself we are all descendants of those men. If those men could see us from somewhere, and see that we can't get on with someone called Ahmet, or Mihail, or Simon, he would be banging his head and saying what did we do wrong? Look at our grandchildren all against one another.'

I told him of the priest at Balıklı and his unwillingness to talk to me.

'I wish he had. It would give me less work to do,' he laughed. 'It would have been good if others started talking too, but the silence has a meaning, you know.'

When I returned much later to Silivrikapı it was to meet with members of a different minority community, a group of Kurdish activists affiliated with the People's Democracy Party, or HDP, the main legal pro-Kurdish party. Among the group who gathered in a small teahouse one evening was a wiry, dark-skinned man named Tarık. He was a father of four in his mid-thirties but looked far younger. His family had come to Silivrikapı when he was six years old. Just as the Greeks had fled from the areas around the walls, so his family had fled to them in search of refuge from the oppression and bloodshed that was gripping the south-east during the mid-1990s as a result of the war between the Turkish state and the Kurdish separatist PKK.

Tarık had a job as a baggage security checker at Istanbul's airport; he told me the story of how he came to lose it. His problems had started in early 2018 when he had begun to experience dizzy spells and pins-and-needles in his limbs, which gradually worsened into balance problems, headaches and a dull pain in his arms that grew more intense over time. He was his family's sole breadwinner; the job was a good one even though it was physically demanding – sometimes he had as little as eight hours' break between shifts, and his health issues meant he increasingly found himself exhausted. Doctors couldn't work out what was wrong: his heart seemed fine, and he seemed to have no back or spinal issues that might normally cause these symptoms.

After this had been going on for more than a year his work took an even more stressful turn. He had been based at Atatürk Airport, the city's main air hub and a twenty-minute ride from his home in Silivrikapı. But Atatürk was in the process of closing, and all the flights were being moved to a vast new airport which had just been built out near the Black Sea. In theory it was only a forty-minute trip away on a new highway cut through the forests north of the city, but the traffic was often terrible and the bus that picked up the airport employees sometimes took well over an hour each way, greatly extending his working day for no additional pay.

The scale of the new airport itself was a challenge. It took half an hour just to walk from the temporary building that accommodated the staff locker rooms to the baggage areas. Standing on the tarmac while loading planes, a great expanse of flat asphalt stretched away in all directions. Its single huge terminal – the world's largest under one roof – was the size of 200 football pitches. The place had been opened in a hurry, which only made things more stressful. Sinkholes kept opening up in the runways, causing flight cancellations while repairs were made, and sometimes parts of the runways flooded during heavy rain. At one point the roof of a temporary building where Tarık was working collapsed. Thankfully no one was injured. He also noticed a lot of animals, including huge rats, which he'd see scurrying about when he was loading bags onto planes. It seemed odd that they were there: the areas where food was served and stored were on the higher floors.

Not long after he started at the new airport he discovered the cause of his worsening symptoms. A brain scan revealed a malformation in his cerebellum: it had probably been with him since birth, but its symptoms only now began to develop as the abnormality was putting pressure on his spinal cord. The problem would require immediate operation to prevent his symptoms worsening and to avoid the risk of permanent disability. The recovery would take months.

After he left work to undergo brain surgery, his memories of that time were quickly subsumed by the worries and pressures that would come to dominate his life. His employer paid him 2,000 lira sick pay a month, but it was not enough to support his whole family. He'd also been supplementing his income with waiting tables but had to stop that too.

But an incident from that final week at the new airport did

stick with him. One day he and his colleagues discovered a swarm of bees had made a hive in the cavity above one of the legs of a boarding bridge. Instead of bringing in professionals to remove and relocate them, the managers called the fire brigade, who tried to suck the bees up with a kind of large vacuum cleaner. When this didn't work, they instead sprayed them with the chemical foam they used to put out fires and this eventually killed them. It was an incident that stuck in Tarık's mind: he had visited the site of the airport with friends before its construction and remembered the area as a beautiful place of lakes and trees. The fate of the bees seemed to epitomise the callousness that lay behind its construction.

'Bees are creatures that sustain our planet – they make honey, they pollinate flowers. The cycle of life turns with them . . . There was no team called from the Ministry of Agriculture or anything. They just called the fire department. The bees must have thought it was a tree. Maybe that place used to be their home. There is no contemplation, no questioning. No one asks why they did it. It was just enough for them to get the job done.'

The new Istanbul Airport was the government's effort to turn the city into a regional air hub to compete with Amsterdam, Frankfurt and Dubai. It had been built at speed in just over four years amid persistent controversy. It covered a total area of nearly 19,000 acres, more than three times the size of London Heathrow. Although initially two runways were opened, it was eventually projected to have six with a capacity to handle up to 200 million passengers a year. The landscape on which it was built was almost entirely undeveloped; although it did include former quarries and lakes left behind by old mining operations, it was mainly forest, farmland and meadow, and covered part of the catchment of two of Istanbul's largest reservoirs. It lay within the Northern Forests – the 'lungs of the city', and home to extraordinary biodiversity; the province of Istanbul alone contained fifty-eight plant species endemic to Turkey, more than the total number of endemic plant species in the British Isles.

This region had long been a target for Turkey's construction industry, which saw it as a bonanza of untapped development land that would extend the city up to the Black Sea coast. The airport was one in a trio of infrastructure projects designed to unlock its potential, the others being the third Bosphorus Bridge, which had already opened in 2016, and Erdoğan's 'crazy project' of a canal linking the Marmara and Black Seas. The government forecast that the airport's construction would involve felling 2.5 million trees and that there would be a 'massive loss of biomass and flora' (its own ecological assessment), before concluding there was no alternative site.

Its critics disagreed, arguing that Istanbul could just as easily compete as a major air hub by investing the airport's $12bn price tag in modernising the city's existing main airport, Atatürk, and expanding the airport on the Anatolian side – Sabiha Gökçen. Other than the environmental costs, they also pointed out that the land where the runway was built was potentially unstable, that frequent inclement weather on the Black Sea coast might affect flights, and that the proposed new airport was on a major bird migration route, potentially endangering aircraft and causing further ecological harm.

A different controversy revolved around the funding of the project and the consortium behind it. A tender for its construction had been awarded to a group of five firms all with close ties to the AK Party. One of the corruption probes that had been launched into the government by Gülenist prosecutors had included extensive wiretaps that seemed to show Erdoğan was offering a stake in the airport project to one firm in return for buying a large, loss-making media conglomerate that was up for sale, in order to keep it under government influence and stop it from falling into foreign ownership. This alleged backroom deal was one of the clearest examples of Erdoğan's use of public contracts as a way of cementing his grip over Turkish society and politics. Such infrastructure projects were highly lucrative to the firms that won the tenders, but often damaging to the public purse, since they involved the Turkish taxpayer guaranteeing a certain level of revenue for the companies involved. These promised returns often proved to be far in excess of reality. In the case of the airport, the operating consortium had been guaranteed €6.3bn over the first twelve years of operation. Critics said it was a way of siphoning public funds into the coffers of AK Party allies.

It was also a matter of prestige for Erdoğan: another demonstration of the relentless modernising drive that lay at the heart of his political message. The government applied enormous pressure to ensure its swift construction. In 2014, a court had ordered that its plans be frozen pending an environmental impact assessment. But work began anyway and progressed at a blistering pace. There were claims of large numbers of deaths within the 31,000-strong workforce on site, as well as human rights violations, illegally long shifts, a lack of running water, rotten food, and bedbugs in the workers' accommodation. Workers claimed they were forced to sign documents agreeing they had been given health and safety training even though there was none. When workers on the site staged a protest in 2018, shortly before its official opening, gendarmerie officers violently suppressed it, with some five hundred of its participants detained.

Nonetheless, its official opening took place as promised on 29 October 2018, to coincide with the ninety-fifth anniversary of the founding of the Turkish Republic, presided over by

Erdoğan himself, who had described it as 'not just an airport, but a victory monument'.

'Generating its own energy, this nature-friendly, environmentally-friendly, and disabled-friendly airport will create 120,000 jobs,' he proclaimed. '. . . With the opening of Istanbul Airport, European airspace will have to be restructured. Since Istanbul will now be the most important transfer point, the routes of intercontinental flights will also change to a great extent. It is no coincidence that this work, whose position and qualities will leave a mark on history, was built in our country.'

———

Tarık had been six years old when his family moved from their village in Van province in the far east of Turkey. They fled suddenly, leaving in the night and packing only what they could carry, abandoning their home and livestock. It was the early nineties and they were among tens of thousands of Kurds making similar journeys. The war between the PKK and the Turkish state had become a bloody rural insurgency fought in the mountains of the south-east. The region existed in a permanently militarised state of emergency, with checkpoints restricting movement and shadowy state security forces torturing and 'disappearing' suspected PKK supporters.

The rebels relied on rural communities to be their eyes and ears, and to provide shelter and logistical support. Turkish forces responded by burning down villages in the areas where the rebels operated, hoping to starve the PKK out by forcing the local populations to flee. In the rest of Turkey life continued normally, such that the reality in the Kurdish south-east was filtered through the distorting and dehumanising language of a 'war on terror' in which the enemy combatants being 'liquidated' were not fellow citizens with possible grievances but an evil force with which there was no reasoning or possibility of dialogue. But the war was warping Turkish society; the brutal and repressive state apparatus set up in the south-east could be employed to suppress internal enemies elsewhere in the country if the need arose; meanwhile, thousands of young men were sent away each year on military service – like Cem – then returned traumatised by what they had experienced. A whole generation of Kurds were growing up in the shadow of the persecution and brutality visited on them and their families by the state. Driven from their homes, hundreds of thousands moved to the west of Turkey in the hope of a peaceful and secure life.

In Tarık's village, most of the men had joined the state-backed militia, the 'village guards'. His father was among the few who refused, marking him out as a PKK sympathiser in the eyes of the authorities. He was arrested and held for a year, released for a short time and then arrested again. His father's stance made Tarık's childhood one of constant fear and persecution. Among his earliest memories was an encounter with a Turkish soldier at an event during which the whole community had been gathered together at the village school. He couldn't remember what the occasion was – it may have been a military raid or else an election.

He spoke in Kurdish to one of the soldiers: 'I was asking something and the soldier was holding a gun. I don't remember what was said – it's like a dream actually . . . He pointed the gun at me. When he made a gunshot sound from his mouth, I collapsed to the ground with fear. I really thought he'd shot me.'

It would take years for him to shake off the terror instilled by that experience. During that time, when his father was in prison, the military would come to his family's house and search it for Kurdish music or books – anything that might indicate separatist sentiments – and each time Tarık feared they would kill him or his family. Eventually the pressure of life in the village became intolerable. One night, when his father had been released from prison, they made a snap decision to flee.

That was how they arrived in Silivrikapı. Tarık's father had worked in the old city before and had connections in the textile industry. They rented a cheap fourth-floor apartment that was near to where he could find work, but it was an unwelcoming place for Kurds. Silivrikapı was mainly populated by Turkish migrants from the Black Sea region, an area known for its staunch nationalist sentiments. Tarık's family spoke little Turkish, and he knew none at all. They were often harassed in the street.

'I knew as much Turkish as I did English,' he recalled. 'I could just say "Hello, my name is Tarık." People would shout at me and insult me in the street and I would just stare at them.' The local primary school refused to take him because his Turkish was insufficient, and he was ten years old when he was finally admitted, after his Turkish had improved and a neighbour who was a teacher pleaded his case. It was about a year later when he began to get involved in politics with his older brother. The two of them would distribute a banned Kurdish-language newspaper at political rallies for the pro-Kurdish party of the time. They were frequently stopped and searched by police.

'I thought that if I am being persecuted and criticised because of my identity then I should be conscious of it,' he recalled. For young people like Tarık, awakening to Kurdishness was like a switch tripping in their heads: it offered an understanding of the society in which he lived that, once encountered, could not be unseen. Oppression on the basis of his ethnicity had marked his life at every possible turn: embracing Kurdish politics would redouble this oppression. Even ostensibly innocuous symbols of Kurdish identity had become bound up with the idea of separatism and, by extension, terrorism. It was a situation enforced from two sides: on the one hand the state's repression made any embrace of Kurdish identity a potentially criminal act, and on the other hand the PKK aggressively sought to claim and co-opt all expressions of Kurdishness to its own cause. Kurdish political parties existed under the aegis of the PKK's influence, and if any Kurdish political movement sought to step out of the PKK's shadow and gain legitimacy in Turkish society at large, the Turkish authorities tried all the harder to suppress it and tar it with the label of 'terrorism'.

By the time Tarık was working at the airport he had become long acquainted with the injustices inflicted on Kurds in Turkish society. He had been forced to drop out of high school due to an investigation against him for his activism and had to complete his studies at home. Later he took the state exams for entry into the civil service, and although he got a qualifying mark, when he applied to enter he was rejected on the grounds that two of his family members were under investigation as part of a mass trial targeting the alleged civilian wing of the PKK. He had seen colleagues at the airport suffer for similar reasons. One woman he worked with was fired after a senior manager saw her wearing a wristband with the Kurdish national colours of red, green and yellow.

When he had recovered from his operation – it ended up taking two years, during which he was paid a share of his normal salary – Tarık was eager to reclaim his job. His convalescence had been difficult. The loss of income meant he had been forced to take out a 75,000-lira loan and had eventually sold the apartment he and his family owned, in order to pay off his debts before buying a cheaper one.

However, when he went back to the airport he was instead offered a meagre severance package and told there was no job

The Golden Gate, the largest of the land walls, which may have been originally constructed as a free-standing triumphal arch at the height of Byzantium's power

Bust of Emperor Theodosius II, during whose reign, from AD 402 to 450, Constantinople's land walls were constructed

(*Opposite*) A painting of the siege of Constantinople composed in 1455, depicting many of the key events

Erdoğan delivers a speech to the nation via mobile phone during the coup attempt of July 2016

A demonstrator uses his belt to whip disarmed soldiers on the Bosphorus Bridge following the failed coup attempt

Rioters destroy Greek businesses in Istanbul during the pogrom of
6–7 September, 1955

Kurds displaying nationalist symbols celebrate the Persian new year festival
of Newroz in Diyarbakir, March 2011

Newly constructed highways cut through the city's northern forests

Land allocated for the development of Istanbul's new airport, slated to be the world's largest, before work began in 2014

The airport under construction. Its site covers a total area of nearly 19,000 acres

Bostan market gardens lying in front of the restored Belgradkapı gate

Destroyed buildings in Kahramanmaraş following the earthquake of
14 February, 2023

Municipal vessels attempt to clean and contain the tide of mucilage –
'sea snot' – that afflicted the Sea of Marmara in the summer of 2021

The Hagia Sophia, overlooking the mouth of the Bosphorus

Erdoğan attends the first official prayers at the Hagia Sophia, newly reopened as a mosque in July 2020

for him any more. Since he was an existing employee who had developed a disability, his employer had a legal responsibility to find a role for him that fitted his condition, but when he threatened to involve a lawyer, his bosses threw his Kurdish politics at him, threatening to counter his civil litigation with criminal prosecution: 'They told me that if I came at them with a lawyer, they would come at me with the state.'

The pressure of his economic situation was compounded by his political activism. In the early summer of 2022, a court case was opened against him for 'illegal organisational activity' based on his activism for the pro-Kurdish party. He was called into a police station in the centre of the old city, taken to the top of the building to what seemed to him to be a kind of hidden interrogation room and questioned for two hours. The police pored over his phone, taking as potential evidence against him articles and pictures he had shared on Twitter relating to Kurdish politics, an image of the flag of the northern Iraqi Kurdistan region, and the banner of Amedspor, the football club of the Kurdish-majority city of Diyarbakır. 'They said that I was a member of HDP [the pro-Kurdish party], and I stated that I was a member of a legal party . . . I denied the accusations, but we know how these kind of things end with prison in Turkey,' he said.

The situation for the country's Kurdish movement had become increasingly grim since the coup attempt. Abuse of detainees in custody had become widespread, especially in the south-east. Among the cases of those imprisoned was that of twenty-eight-year-old Garibe Gezer, who was found hanged in her cell after she had claimed that prison guards had stripped, beaten and sexually assaulted her. She had reported her abuse and had attempted suicide on previous occasions, which her family claimed had only led to worse treatment. Many members of the Kurdish party's senior political leadership remained in prison, including the charismatic former co-chairman Selahattin Demirtaş, who had been arrested in November 2016 and would still remain behind bars seven years later. Others included a former member of parliament, Aysel Tuğluk, who was forced to attend court hearings despite suffering from early onset dementia.

Reports of abuses in the south-east began to escalate in a way reminiscent of the dark days of the 1990s. In one notorious incident, two Kurdish farmers were beaten by soldiers and thrown from a military helicopter in the south-eastern Van province from which Tarık himself hailed. One died from his injuries, the other, Osman Şiban, who was fifty, survived his injuries but was left deeply traumatised. 'He is absolutely terrified. He's lost his sense of time and place. When he speaks, it's childlike blubbering,' a lawyer representing him told a Turkish news website soon afterwards. He was later prosecuted as a member of a terrorist organisation for allegedly providing logistical aid to the rebels.

A few weeks before the investigation was opened against him, Tarık's brother was detained by the police and held for two days for distributing flyers. Tarık was so worried about his own situation that he couldn't bring himself to tell his family. He began looking for a means to leave Turkey.

He acknowledged that there were ways he could have got by as a Kurd in Turkey: by professing allegiance to notions of Turkishness or Islam, for example. 'I can say that I am Turkish of Kurdish origin: that would not be a problem,' he said. 'Or I can say my parents were Kurdish, but I am Turkish. Around conservative people I can say the following: "We are all [part of the] *ummah*" – that doesn't create a problem then, either. It's OK if I say: "We are all brothers, we founded the Republic together, we kept it alive together. I am also a patriot, a nationalist, I would die for this flag", and I can say: "The prayers will never end, the flags will never fall." Nothing will happen if I say these things.'

What made this impossible was the daily small indignities he was subjected to because of his accent and his dark skin colour, which marked him out as a Kurd – the needling, casually racist comments. There was the neighbour who told him, 'You look like a Kurd, *god forbid*'; there was the old woman who, when he said he was from Van, had said, as if paying a compliment, 'Oh, you don't look like you're from Van'; there was the surprise many Turks would show when they learned his daughter's name was Sevilya, after the Spanish city of Seville. '"Oh, how can that be?" they say . . . They approach us as if we are cave-dwelling, obtuse people who still communicate in sign language.'

Beyond that, there was his awareness of the long history of oppression Kurds had faced in Turkey, which far predated the rise of the PKK: 'My grandfather, my great-grandfather and his brothers were suppressed only because they raised their voices against the thefts committed by the district governor and the state bureaucrats at that time,' he said. 'This is not something that is limited to one thing: there is still a political genocide in our country . . . If we were a conscious society with a sense of belonging, we would be in a very different place today. But, unfortunately, there is no sense of belonging, no common life, no common space, nothing in common. If I put aside my political stance today, I would erase everything that has been done so far. It would justify the injustices that were done. My ethnic and political identities are one because this didn't start today. It is a fight that will not end, but will always continue because this is not a goodbye, not a confrontation. It is clearly a matter of empathy: it's your ability to put yourself in my place.'

When I last spoke to Tarık, he had fled Turkey and travelled to the United States, climbing over a seven-metre-high wall dividing Mexico from California, where he had claimed political asylum and was now living in Los Angeles. He had left because he had heard a rumour that he was about to be arrested. The police, he said, had been trying to pressurise him to become an informer against fellow HDP activists, and he'd refused to do so. His wife and children remained in Istanbul and he was hoping they would soon join him. He was worried about them; the police had been round to the house asking where he was, and since he had made the journey to the US, border security had tightened and they would likely have to go via a more difficult route through Texas, where they could expect worse treatment, if and when they did arrive. They had sold their last remaining asset – their apartment – to pay for the illegal journey.

The new Istanbul Airport would be judged a broad success. Within three years of opening it had become Europe's largest air hub, serving 64 million passengers in 2022. People sometimes complained about the long walks between gates and baggage carousels, but it received positive reviews for its customer service and the quality of its entertainment amenities along with a raft of awards. Fears of flight cancellations due to migrating birds, inclement weather, or collapsing runways were generally not borne out: its rate of cancellations were similar to other European airports.

The controversies over its construction would largely remain unknown to the millions of people passing through its vast halls each year. It remained unclear whether the airport would entail a cost to the public purse: after exceeding its revenue guarantee in 2019, the airport missed them during the pandemic and post-pandemic figures have not been released. An investigation by the *Architects' Journal* and *Construction News* would reveal that a minimum of 55 people were killed during its construction, with claims among the workers that the true level could be as high as 400. Meanwhile, analysis of satellite imagery by Northern Forests Defence, a Turkish environmental group, suggested that the true number of trees felled was not the 2.5 million the government had claimed but was in fact closer to 13 million.

The Rebuilt Gate

Until the mid-1980s the gate of Belgradkapı had been one of the most decrepit of all those along the walls. Severely damaged in an earthquake in 1894, its main arch had caved in and one of its flanking towers had almost completely collapsed. It was a hulking ruin amid a makeshift urban geography of dusty roads and clapped-together houses of wood and corrugated iron. This was the Gate of Xylokerkos – the 'Wooden Circus' – through which the Byzantines had feared the city's doom would come.

But in 1987 change came to Belgradkapı. Istanbul's mayor, Bedrettin Dalan, the same man who cleansed the Golden Horn and swept away the industry around it, turned his gaze to the city walls. Turkey had just joined UNESCO and the walls had been listed as a World Heritage Site. Dalan vowed to repair them 'from Yedikule to Ayvansaray' as part of a programme intended to 'maintain our national nobility'. Belgradkapı was chosen as the starting point. Works commenced, but when the first restored section was unveiled about a year and a half later, the city's architectural and archaeological community recoiled in horror. The existing structure had been rebuilt entirely using cement and industrially produced bricks. It was not just the poor quality of the work that caused a storm of complaints, but the whole approach. The gate had been reconstructed as an approximation of the fifth-century original, erasing centuries of alterations and additions. One American professor of Byzantine Art accused the municipality of turning it into a 'Universal film set'.

Belgradkapı was a place that instilled sadness whenever I passed it. Time had only accentuated the damage done by the municipality; it had the air of a shuttered theme park whose attractions have begun to fall apart. The metal railings put in to restrict access here and there had begun to rust and stain the masonry. The cement had turned a shade of grey that was different from the pinkish mortar elsewhere on the walls, and the brick tiles that capped the new crenellations had begun to fall off. Dishevelled as the rest of the walls were, the dilapidation at least had a vibrancy about it; Belgradkapı looked cheap and dead. Only the thick fingers of ailanthus saplings pushing through the concrete lent it an air of life, their rippling trunks swelling through the tiniest cracks. Ailanthus had a relentless, faintly antagonistic vitality about it, bursting on the stage impatient for our departure. I used to think that if Istanbul was ever truly abandoned, it would be that unloved pioneer from China – known there as 'The Tree of Heaven' for its curative abilities but in Turkey as *kokar ağaç*, the 'rotten tree', for its foul-smelling foliage – that would do the heavy work of breaking up the city's streets and roads and returning it to nature.

Dalan had not intended to ruin Belgradkapı. The works had been overseen by one of Turkey's top professors of archaeology, who was also a restoration architect. To its credit the municipality took on board the criticism and subsequent repairs elsewhere were handled more sensitively. But the model of renovation inflicted on Belgradkapı would come back with a vengeance in Erdoğan's Turkey. In the first two decades of the twenty-first century, a growing list of the city's most precious monuments were subjected to total renovation that went far beyond stabilising them in their existing state, often with total disregard for the history of the building's development over its eras of existence.

The worst cases tended to be lesser-known monuments. One two thousand-year-old tower near the town of Şile just outside Istanbul was rebuilt so completely as to be unrecognisable, a single window in each face replaced with a pair topped with strange eyebrow-like lunettes that gave it a cartoonish appearance. Monuments with greater significance, such as former Byzantine churches that were later converted to mosques, tended to be approached with slightly more sensitivity, but here too the renovators tended to remake them firmly in their Ottoman guise, the era from which the AK Party drew its ideological inspiration. Frequently the firms commissioned to carry out such work were better known for their close ties to the government than for their credentials for restoration. Examples included the Palace of the Porphyrogenitus, or Tekfur Sarayı, the best preserved of Istanbul's Byzantine royal palaces, which stood atop the walls north of Edirnekapı. The formerly roofless structure was completely renewed and turned into a museum primarily devoted to Ottoman-era ceramics, tiles and glassworks. It was given a new red-tiled roof and wooden windows, with some surviving features of the previously ruined buildings completely removed or rebuilt from scratch with new materials and accents of seventeenth-century Ottoman style.

As in Dalan's time, a debate swirled around these works though in this instance the authorities showed no sign of being chastened by the criticism. Supporters argued that they were being given new life and purpose that would carry them forward for a generation, but critics accused the authorities not just of indifference to the city's Christian Byzantine heritage, but the same hostility that often characterised earlier eras of Turkey's past.

And so it was with a mixture of apprehension and curiosity that I regarded the striking lattice of bright yellow scaffolding that spread across sections of the walls between Belgradkapı and Yedikule at the beginning of 2021. It would mark the start of what promised to be the most extensive repairs carried out on the land walls since Dalan's time, and once again it was the Istanbul municipality undertaking them. In the intervening years, numerous mayors had vowed to restore the walls and realise their tourism potential, and in doing so transform the drug and crime-blighted neighbourhoods around them. None of these projects ever got anywhere.

Over the past two years, however, change had been afoot in the city's politics. In March 2019, municipal elections had yielded a shock defeat for the AK Party, which had controlled the municipality in one guise or another ever since Erdoğan himself had won the mayorship a quarter of a century earlier. The opposition candidate for the CHP, the ambitious, youthful and savvy Ekrem İmamoğlu had eked out a narrow victory by successfully appealing to some conservatives and nationalists while also winning over the Kurdish vote, a small but crucial slice of the city's electorate. Other opposition candidates had agreed not to stand and to put their weight behind him, making it a two-horse race between himself and former prime minister Binali Yıldırım, a steadfast if uninspiring lieutenant of Erdoğan's. İmamoğlu won by a hair's breadth: about 14,000 votes or a fifth of a percentage point, but the implications were potentially enormous.

Istanbul was a massive economic and political prize, home to a fifth of Turkey's population and making up nearly a third of its GDP. The municipality, including its transportation and water distribution arms, controlled a budget of $6.2bn in 2019, as well as twenty-eight affiliated companies with an annual turnover of $4.2bn. With the power to award valuable development contracts, it had long been a centrepiece in the network of patronage and graft which underpinned the AK Party's grip on power. It provided the biggest stage on which an aspiring national leader might audition for the role. Erdoğan's own victory had marked a turning point in Turkish political history and his springboard to national power. Now he responded to this clear threat by pressuring the country's supreme electoral board to force a repeat of the election, ignoring his own candidate's lack of appetite for such a gambit. In the event this obvious attempt to force a different result backfired, angering and galvanising voters; İmamoğlu once again defeated Yıldırım but this time by a nine-point margin and on a higher turnout, leaving Erdoğan with no choice but to accept defeat.

However, the government still had many levers with which to pressure the new mayor's administration. It started by stripping municipalities of powers that had once offered lucrative opportunities for political patronage, for example by passing regulations allowing the Ministry of Environment and Urbanization to intervene in urban development projects, and another preventing mayors from choosing the officials who ran companies affiliated with the municipality. Other kinds of softer pressure also came into play. Turkey's state banks, for example, became reluctant to lend to the opposition-run municipality. İmamoğlu responded by successfully tapping international financial markets to raise the money to build four new Metro lines.

The municipality's heritage department was a minnow compared to some of the larger directorates for transport or urban planning, but it controlled some of the city's most iconic monuments, including the Basilica Cistern, the cavernous underwater reservoir that was one of its top tourist draws. Responsibility for the land walls was divided between a confusing and sometimes overlapping mosaic of different agencies and foundations, but there too the municipality was the principal stakeholder. Under its long tenure, the AK Party had often announced repair projects for the walls and other monuments under its control, but when these did not involve buildings that were former or potential mosques, or where there was no clear financial incentive, there seemed to be a lack of political will to push them through. But now İmamoğlu, like many before him, had vowed to rejuvenate the walls and open them up to tourism.

———

I met Ayşen Kaya, the project's deputy director, at the site office of the works south of Belgradkapı. A longtime municipal employee, she was careful not to be drawn on the politics surrounding the restoration, but she was quite clear in distinguishing their work at Belgradkapı from various projects overseen by the government.

'Our basic restoration approach is to freeze the ruin as it exists with minimal intervention,' she said. 'We do not adopt reconstruction as a preservation method except in exceptional circumstances.' She said the mortar they used had been created by analysing and matching samples of the mortar from the original parts of the wall; the stone masonry couldn't be perfectly matched to the original because the quarries from which that came were long closed, but samples were obtained from various similar quarries so that as close an equivalent as possible could be found. She mentioned that among the advisors was Dr Zeynep Ahunbay, one of Turkey's foremost architectural historians, who had been a critical voice regarding past restoration projects such as Dalan's.

The immediate remit was simple: stabilise the most heavily damaged towers on the walls so that they would survive the coming earthquake. The funds assigned were minuscule in municipal terms: just 14 million Turkish lira, with an option under the terms of the tender to increase this by half – 'which we will definitely do,' she added. For now, in the area around Belgradkapı they were working on five of the ninety-six bastions that ran the length of the inner wall. This was the first stage of the project. Work was beginning on another three, and there was an expectation that further funds would be available to eventually repair twenty in total, and perhaps more after that if the situation allowed.

As we walked across the worksite piles of dusty white boulders lay waiting to be cut into blocks. Ascending the scaffolding and crossing the walls, Kaya showed me the towers that were in the process of repair. Each had been deliberated over by the committee of advisors for several months before an approach was chosen, she said. The difficulty was balancing this 'freezing principle' of preservation with the paramount need to stabilise the towers in the face of the coming quake. Most striking were a series of round steel support plates, several of which dotted the surface of the repaired towers, supporting hidden braces that had been drilled through the structure to stabilise it. Beyond this, however, the works indeed appeared to be light touch. On the walls themselves, the irregular courses of the new bricks and masonry blended so perfectly with the old that only the weathering distinguished them. Most strikingly, Kaya said the team intended to leave the crowns of foliage that stood out on top of them.

We arrived at the latest tower where work was beginning. It was very familiar to me: one side had slid away, to reveal the two-storey domed structure within, neat as an architectural cross-section. This partial collapse had occurred during the 1999 Marmara earthquake, and Kaya said the rest of it would certainly go in the next one. Lying in front of it was a huge chunk of the fallen masonry, which according to Kaya weighed 130 tonnes. They had discussed lifting and repositioning it, and although they could find a crane that could do it, the operation would have swallowed most of their budget, and the piece may have fallen apart anyway. Salvaged and new masonry would be built up to a point where the edifice was once again stable. She pointed out how the block had fallen from the wall: not cleanly but at a twisted angle. This was a result of the complex nature of the fault lines around Istanbul, which during earthquakes generate movement in multiple directions.

'The Istanbul earthquake will not be a one-way earthquake,' she said. 'With this building, the parts here fell by rotating. They don't fall where they are . . . It's a tough job. It's a job that gives you sleepless nights.'

It was unnerving to hear Kaya discuss the disaster facing the city in such precise and inevitable terms. It was also inspiring: this seemed to be earthquake preparation as a public service, pure and simple, not undercut by any extractive profit motive or warping ideological agenda. It was the kind of disaster planning you rarely saw in the city, and I suddenly thought how strange it was that it could be done here, in these uninhabited ruins, but not in the millions of inhabited homes throughout the city.

There was also a larger plan behind the works. Along the course of the walls several visitor centres and museums dedicated to the fortifications and their history were being built in disused historic buildings 'in the form of parts attached to a backbone,' as Kaya described it. The idea was that eventually a visitor could walk from the Sea of Marmara to the Golden Horn, taking in the most important sites along the way. The first element of this, an old Ottoman police station at the corner of Mevlanakapı – would shortly be opened as a visitor centre. Meanwhile, a museum devoted to the walls was being built in an old disused gasworks in Silivrikapı.

A few months later İmamoğlu himself would inaugurate the visitor centre. He, like Dalan and others before him, promised to transform the walls and through them the lives of the people around them. 'You will see that we will create a pathway here along which tens of thousands of tourists will pass at any moment,' he told a crowd of mainly young people who had gathered from the neighbourhood. 'These kinds of places are the very places that enrich our lives . . . [Right now] the number of tourists is just under seventeen million. Together we will see and experience thirty million tourists, in an Istanbul that reflects our enlightened understanding of life, in which people exist and lead their urban lives in a democratic environment . . . You will earn money by gaining professions, especially in the environment created by the tourism sector and the service sector . . . This is what the improvement of these derelict, neglected areas gives us.'

Just beyond the municipality's restoration area stood a wide expanse of rubble. It looked like a construction site waiting to be developed and had lain in that state for several years. It was the grave of one of the last areas of *bostans* – the city's ancient market gardens – that had existed inside the walls. In the summer of 2013, Fatih Municipality had swept in and destroyed the vegetable plots with bulldozers by bringing in truckloads of rubble and stone which were spread on top of the soil. The municipality had acquired the land in 2010, and the rumoured reason for the demolition was an objection by the owners of the adjacent block of luxury apartments, who claimed the presence of the gardens drove down their house prices.

It was Ramadan when the bulldozers arrived, and Recep Kayhan was there with his family enjoying *iftar* – the evening meal at which the daily fast was broken – at the *bostan* farmed by his cousin Mustafa. They were all on edge after fasting through the hot summers' day, and Recep's wife was so furious at the destruction unfolding in front of them that she began pelting rocks at one of the bulldozers. It was in vain though. Within little more than a day the gardens were gone.

The *bostancıs* – the city gardeners – were not a powerful, unified, or politically connected group. But the destruction took place in the immediate aftermath of the Gezi protests, and amid an atmosphere of heightened sensitivity over the city's dwindling green space, their plight caused a storm of anger that went far beyond the gardens themselves. The *bostans* had existed for at least as long as the city walls – the first written record of their existence dated from Theodosius II's construction of the fortifications – and they were probably for far older. At one point the gardens were so extensive that they could feed much of the city, but as Istanbul's population increased and urban space became more valuable, the bostans had dwindled until it was only these areas in the immediate environs of the walls that survived. They had changed hands many times over the years, from Greeks and Armenians to Bulgarians and Albanians, and now to Turks from the Black Sea coast – usually members of recent immigrant communities looking to make their way. One nearby *bostan*, Recep told me, was now run by an Afghan family. But suddenly their preservation appealed not only to their immediate tenants and to academics concerned about the erosion of a traditional urban landscape, but to ecologists who had already been advocating the creation of new urban gardens as a way of addressing some of the environmental threats facing humanity.

For Recep, however, it had just been a hobby. Part of his cousin's land had been spared by the bulldozers, but what remained was only about five acres – too small to be commercially viable – and so a few months later he handed over stewardship of it to Recep. It was a little ironic, Recep reflected, because he had left behind a farming life in his home village of Kastamonu on the Black Sea coast only fifteen years earlier due to the lack of economic opportunities. He now worked a day job as a caretaker in a hospital, and would come to the *bostan* after work and on weekends, sometimes staying past midnight in the summer, growing tomatoes, peppers, potatoes, cress, mint, parsley, radishes and onions.

'If the flies didn't bother me, I wouldn't actually go home. I'd sleep here,' he said. We sat on the small veranda amid his plot of land. I had visited other bostans – those hidden between the inner and outer walls or in the old moat – which felt like their own humid secret worlds, gardened jungle valleys. Recep's was not quite so idyllic as those. Only a few metres from the small veranda he had built onto his hut was the expanse of rubble that stretched off towards the walls, which now served as a makeshift carpark. Nonetheless, what little space he still controlled was bursting with manicured greenery. In one corner he showed me a huge well dating from Ottoman times – it was at least twenty feet across – from which he and the neighbouring bostans drew their water.

It didn't bring in significant money, but amid the surging inflation facing the country it helped a little to be able to grow his own food. People from the neighbourhood came to buy directly from them, and the rest his wife sold at local markets. One of the greatest joys of the place, he said, were the celebrations they would have at *Kurban Bayramı*, the holiday to mark the end of Ramadan. Sometimes sixty or seventy of their friends and relatives would come to join them and they would sacrifice five or six cows to mark the celebratory feast.

After the outrage following the destruction of the bostans in
2013, Fatih Municipality had backtracked, pledging to respect
the existence of the remaining bostans and to work with and
consult the gardeners on future plans, but they refused to rein-
state those they had destroyed. Recep was still unsure what the
future would hold for them. Part of the problem was that the
ownership of the bostans themselves was incredibly complicated.
Often an individual plot could have several owners, ranging
from private individuals, the neighbourhood or city municipality,
charitable foundations, or the state treasury. The tenancies for
them often rested on little more than private agreement or
tradition. While the gardeners had made many allies, within the
neighbourhoods around the walls themselves, he felt that support
for them was more ambivalent.

'No one cares about buying everything fresh from here. They
want a park, the women are looking for a place to sit and eat
sunflower seeds. There has been a tense conflict here about
whether people wanted a park or a *bostan*.'

Ayşen Kaya, the Istanbul municipal official involved in the
walls restoration project, had been notably vague when I'd
asked her what place the bostans might have in their future
plans: 'It is necessary to come together with *bostancıs* and create
a long-term plan for this use because these are public spaces.
Allocating it for use by a single person creates various handi-
caps in relation to public use. A solution that will satisfy
everyone needs to be agreed upon, but the restoration process
needs to be completed; then a consensus must be reached with
the interlocutors in this area.'

Recep reckoned they would not be allowed to remain. 'Once
they have renovated these walls, they probably won't leave this
here afterwards,' he said. In the meantime, he had pressed on
anyway, claiming back a tiny portion of the land destroyed in
2013 in the hope of making his plot more viable in the long

term. He showed it to me: no more than about twenty or thirty square metres in which they had cleared away the rubble and was now once again tilled and planted with crops. They hired a digger to remove it, and brought in new soil, but the cost didn't really justify it, and someone from the neighbourhood municipality that had carried out the original destruction warned him against going further.

He was still thinking about expanding a little further, he said, as he pointed to another small area of wasteland abutting his crops. 'There's a lot of rubble here,' he said. 'To do the lower part from here, I'll have to clean that mess with the digger, I'll have to put in the soil again. I'll have to make a new bostan.'

13

The Crooked Gate

I returned to Tokludede after a long absence to see how the development had progressed. I'd phoned Mahinur to ask after İsmet and she'd said he was too sick to receive visitors, so I met Mustafa – the pious, genial friend of Salih's – at the teahouse and we walked around the new neighbourhood. The houses were more or less finished now and the place was nearly ready to receive its future inhabitants, whoever they might be. The hotel was due to open soon. Mustafa showed me his own house, which was attached to the side of it. To me, the whole project looked like a Disneyfied version of what had gone before, but he took evident pride in it. I tried to see it from his side: the new homes were no doubt better insulated and more comfortable than their predecessors; the picturesque shabbiness of the old neighbourhood might be fine for a nostalgic stroll, but not to live in. But I still thought there was a certain absurdity to the whole: a real old neighbourhood knocked down in order to make way for a fake one for people who wanted to live somewhere steeped in history.

İsmet's house was in the final stages of completion, and it looked more or less like the original I had first seen several years earlier: a link to the past forged by his own tenacity. Mustafa suggested we visit him and when I said that Mahinur had told me I shouldn't, he dismissed my objections, so we went anyway. Mahinur welcomed us in politely, and I tried to apologise to her as Mustafa swept us into the little room where İsmet lay just as I had last seen him before, his temples sunken and the globes of his eyes visible under darkened lids. He took in the sight of us, lifted his hand in a gesture either of greeting or self-defence, then turned his face away and began weeping uncontrollably.

'You're in our prayers . . . you're getting better,' Mustafa repeated awkwardly as we retreated from the room, half-stunned, and said our goodbyes to Mahinur.

Later on, I met up with Salih. It was a fine day, and we went out on the Golden Horn with a friend of his who kept a small boat. I told him what had happened with İsmet, and somehow we got talking about his suicide attempt.

'He didn't really try to commit suicide, you know,' Salih told me. 'He was mixing weedkiller in his basement – the fumes overcame him and he passed out. His son took him to hospital. He wrote the suicide note later because he thought it might help draw attention to his case.'

Crazy, crafty old İsmet. Something had always seemed off, I told myself: drinking pesticide was an odd way to try to kill yourself, and he'd never struck me as broken or defeated, even in his sick state. I thought also about the theatricality of his suicide note, addressed to the prosecutor and fingering everyone up to Erdoğan himself. I remembered his triumphant words – 'I am an eagle in this neighbourhood' – and felt admiration at the audacity of what he'd done.

'He was a smart man . . .' said Salih. 'I told the developers myself that they had to give at least three to five people permits to develop their own homes. The strongest candidate was İsmet. He practically had a sign . . . He had his picture taken with all the journalists. There were a couple of others. Mustafa, because he's one of the elites of the neighbourhood, somehow he had the connections. Of course we said we'd do it too, but even coming together – my mother, my three uncles and I – we couldn't succeed.'

As we talked, Salih's friend took the boat over to the opposite shore, where we bought some beers and sat drinking them beyond the shadow of the Golden Horn Bridge. We talked more about neighbourhood culture, and its decline, and I asked him about what he thought this meant for the next generation.

'I don't want my children to be like me, I never wanted that,' he said. 'When I talk about all this swaggering and bragging and so on, I'm describing a period long buried in our imagination. Our generation were the children of [that] era . . . My elder son plays the violin. The younger one plays the guitar. They both have great English, they both swim well, the younger one does skating.' He showed me photos and videos of his sons. There was one picture of them sat together at home, playing a traditional Turkish song on the guitar. He had long blond hair. He also wrote and performed plays at his university, Salih said, and he showed me another video of him acting onstage. 'I wanted to raise them differently from how I was raised . . . I didn't want them to be geographically insular, to learn the ways of Ayvansaray and say, "We're Ayvansaray kids." I want them to say, "We're children of the world," because we – the older generation – experienced the torment of not being that.'

When he was young, Salih continued, he'd been approached by Vakko, one of Turkey's biggest clothing brands, and offered a job as a model. 'I would have done it, but then I would have come to the neighbourhood and all my friends would have said, "We saw you on TV last night shaking your arse, faggot." So it was impossible. The man says to me, "Boy, are you crazy? Your salary is 12,000TL. You could earn 36,000TL and you wouldn't even have to work full-time." But I had to refuse. Can you imagine it? I don't want my children to go through that. When we go out into the world from our own community, we look good – handsome, tall, and so on – and we are appreciated. But then you start to think what's going on here, is this guy a faggot? Is he flirting with me? The thing is, it's not true, but you start to think like this in your own head and you do it to yourself and I didn't want my kids to think this way.'

He then showed me a video of his younger son, then eleven years old, standing on a podium at a town hall in Norwich in England, delivering a speech in faultless English in front of a room full of war veterans. It was part of an exchange his school had done, and because his son was giving the speech Salih had travelled with him to attend it. 'We are a generation who are the future's global citizens, and we are a generation who know the future we dream of can only be shaped by peace,' he said. Salih said it was one of the proudest moments of his life.

───

I had met Ömer the first time I entered the Ayvansaray Sports Club. When I said I was writing about the walls, a man had jumped to his feet, walked over to another table, and clapped one of the men on the shoulder.

'Talk to this guy! His girlfriend killed herself: threw herself off the walls!'

The man glanced up silently from his game of *okey*. He had wet, bloodhound eyes and a long face crowned with a comb-over of greying hair. There was a nakedly mournful look about him that made the other man's casual mention of this tragedy seem cruel, and after an awkward moment I left him alone and went to speak to other people. Later when he was having a cigarette outside I approached and asked if he would talk to me. He said yes, but not at the café, and so we arranged to meet up a couple of days later and spent some hours wandering around Ayvansaray.

For a while we talked about his family. His grandfather had been the imam in a village on the Black Sea coast; his father was the youngest of four brothers. Two lost their lives in the First World War, one at Gallipoli and the other at the disastrous Battle of Sarıkamış, where a hastily assembled and under-equipped Ottoman force was hurled against the Russians. Seventy thousand of them died, mainly from exposure to the bitter winter cold. Ömer's third uncle was also believed dead, but twelve years after the war he reappeared in his home village, starving and in rags, having escaped on foot from a Soviet labour camp in Batumi. He died in 1946, two years before Ömer's birth.

Ömer's father was among many from the Black Sea region who migrated to Istanbul in the early years of the Republic. He started up a haulage business and grew rich, and in Ayvansaray became what was called a *patron*: a neighbourhood big man, wealthy and respected, a supporter of local causes who was sometimes called on to resolve communal disputes. He got involved in politics, met Atatürk, and was a notable member of the Republican People's Party, which governed Turkey until the first democratic elections in 1950.

Ömer said that his father was guided by a strong sense of duty to family and community. Throughout his life he continued to support not just the widows and children of his brothers, but more distant family members and friends from his old village. 'If someone arrived from the village, he would tell them to come and stay,' he said. 'If help was needed, he would give it. I don't want to boast, but my father was taking care of all of Ayvansaray.'

Ömer was the third youngest of ten siblings: six girls and four boys. The home where he grew up on the edge of Tokludede looked onto the local mosque. As a child he remembered seeing a ghostly figure kneeling in the graveyard, praying among the tombs. He had pointed it out to his sisters, but they couldn't see it. He still lived in the same house, in a first-floor apartment above a café that looked onto the development.

Ayvansaray had been a diverse place, he recalled; besides Turks, there were Greeks, Armenians and Jews. 'The Jews had the money,' he said, 'the Armenians were craftsmen, the Greeks ran entertainment houses.' He was about seven years old on the night of 6 September 1955, when the pogrom had been launched against the Greeks. He said the rioters who ransacked Greek shops and homes were outsiders and not from the neighbourhood. 'The locals didn't do anything. We all lived here together and everybody knew each other. But they were afraid as well so they hid in their homes.' His parents made their children stay inside. Ömer's father went out with a Turkish flag and stood in the gateway to the local Greek church, the Church of the Blakhernai, waving it to warn away the looters, and in doing so saved the church's property. Turkey's non-Muslim minorities were already dwindling by that point, driven away by punitive wealth taxes levied against them. For the Greeks, however, the 1955 pogrom was the last straw. Many of those in Ayvansaray left within a few weeks of the riots.

After first walking along the streets of Lonca, a run-down Roma neighbourhood, we turned back on ourselves until we came to the charming gate of Eğrikapı – the 'Crooked Gate' – nestled next to a tower and so-called because the road leading out from it veers to the left to skirt around the tomb of a saint. In Byzantine times it had been known as the Gate of Caligaria – named after the *caliga*, the military sandals that were manufactured nearby. Here there was only a single wall, high and strongly built but without a moat, and constructed later than the main fortifications, during the reign of Emperor Manuel I Comnenus in the twelfth century.

Passing through it, we walked along the narrow pavement beside the highway. It was a cold and windy afternoon; a light drizzle had begun to fall, scarcely more than mist, but it soaked our hair and faces. To our left the traffic of the highway screamed past towards the Golden Horn Bridge.

'That's where she did it,' he said abruptly, pointing towards a tower projecting from the walls. It was a square edifice with three arched windows rising from the walls of the Anemas dungeon: the Tower of Isaac Angelus, built by that emperor in the twelfth century. He was later overthrown, imprisoned in the Anemas, and blinded: a not unusual fate for Byzantine emperors.

In his early twenties, Ömer used to make money driving a taxi that belonged to his father. One evening he was going along the outside of the walls when he picked up two teenage girls, who asked him to take them to Ayvansaray. After driving in silence for a few minutes they began to ask him questions: What was his name? Where was he from? He didn't know these girls, and in that time and place in Turkey this kind of casual conversation between opposite sexes carried a thrill of risk. He became shy, clammed up, and their questions petered out into silence well before he dropped them off at their destination.

A few days later he was out in the taxi again, stuck in traffic, and the same girls passed by him. It was a hot day and one of them had a bottle of water, which she splashed on him. They laughed, pretending it was an accident, and jokingly offered to get him a towel.

A few days later he saw them again, this time as he was queuing at the taxi rank waiting for a fare, and they got into the back of his cab.

'It's not my turn yet,' he told them. 'You have to get in the taxi at the front of the queue.'

'We don't mind, we'll wait,' one of the girls replied. And so they sat in the back of his cab until those in front had gone and it was Ömer's turn to take a fare. He asked them where to and they said Sarayburnu – the promontory at the tip of the old city, where a collection of teahouses and bars overlooked the water.

'Why would you girls want to go to Sarayburnu?' he asked.

'We want to drink a glass of tea with you,' one of them replied.

So Ömer went for tea with them. They made awkward conversation about day-to-day stuff; the two girls were nervous and kept whispering to each other. When one of them went to the toilet, the other leaned in and confided to Ömer that it was her friend, Emine, who had engineered this outing. She liked him.

Ömer was vague in his description of Emine, but he later showed me a black-and-white portrait photo of her from around that time. Her hair is cut into a short wavy bob that makes her look older than her sixteen years; her heavy-lidded eyes gaze into the middle distance with an almost drugged languor, but there is something determined or defiant in her expression, the hint of a set jaw and pursed lips. You could imagine her as the kind of girl who would chase a crush four years her senior. And Ömer himself was strikingly handsome in a wholesome, teenage pin-up kind of way. When he showed me a photograph of himself from that time, my first thought was that it looked more like the actor who would have played him in the movie version of the story.

After they'd finished their tea, he asked the girls if they'd like to go anywhere else.

'Maybe next time.'

There followed a blissful few weeks. Emine would come to the taxi rank, sometimes with her friend, sometimes alone, and Ömer would take her places. After a while he gave her his home phone number and she would call him from a payphone across the street. And so they began to go all over Istanbul: beauty spots along the Bosphorus and picnic areas in the Belgrade Forest north of the city.

She used to tease him, saying: 'What kind of a person are you? You skip your job and spend all your time taking me out to these places.' Ömer offered to take her to any restaurant, but in general she only wanted to go to her favourite İskender kebab place in Balat, just down the road from Ayvansaray. She had started smoking, and even though he disapproved, Ömer would always make sure he had a packet on him, because he didn't want her to beg a cigarette from anyone else. Their happiest moments, he said, were when they would sit and watch the sunset together, either at the rocks looking over the Bosphorus at Sarayburnu, or the big hill at Çamlıca on the Anatolian shore.

Their relationship remained chaste. Emine came from a poor conservative family that had moved to the city a few years earlier from Kastamonu, another region on the Black Sea coast. Her parents had divorced, and she lived with her mother and sister in Ayvansaray, while her father had remarried and lived elsewhere. Her culture was a little uncouth, Ömer said, but she'd begun to pick up city ways and fashions. He described her as fragile, easily upset at things she saw, and she would sometimes make odd cryptic comments. 'I'm the cloud behind the darkness,' she'd said one time as they were watching the sun set. When Ömer asked her what she meant, she went quiet.

They tried to keep their meetings a secret, but in the claustrophobic atmosphere of the neighbourhood it was inevitable that people would find out. After about three months, Ömer's father confronted him and demanded he explain what was going on. When he told him, he said he would not tolerate this kind of relationship, and that if it was serious they should ask Emine's family for her hand in marriage. Ömer said it was serious, and so his father went to Emine's parents, both of whom consented to the match.

After this point, the details of Ömer's story became confusing. Apparently planning began for the *nişanlık*, the traditional engagement party. Ömer and Emine continued to see one another. She seemed happy and excited about the engagement; he introduced her to his mother, who liked her very much. But soon he began to notice a change in her behaviour. She became tearful and withdrawn. When he asked her what the matter was, she would cry, and say, 'I can't tell you.'

Ömer didn't know it at the time, but apparently Emine's father had changed his mind about the match and was planning to marry her to a relative of her stepmother. Ömer's own father began to suspect something was wrong, and after a month or so he offered to prepare a car so that Ömer and Emine could run away together to his family's village on the Black Sea coast, where they could wait till she turned eighteen, and then legally marry without her parents' consent.

He shared the plan with Emine, and their departure was set for a Monday in April. The previous day counting took place for a national census, and Ömer worked on it with a friend. One of the homes on their list was Emine's house, and when they reached it, Ömer said that he should stay outside and his friend go in alone. When the friend came out he said that he had not seen Emine there but had heard crying from a locked room. They were still working a few hours later when he heard a commotion down the street and several of Ömer's siblings came rushing towards him, crying, shouting and hugging him. They told him that Emine had thrown herself from the tower of the Anemas dungeon that lay just a few metres from her home.

She had been taken to hospital, and when Ömer went there and explained who he was the doctor gave him a visiting pass but warned him only to come in the evenings, outside of regular visiting hours. Her injuries were severe but not fatal. She had broken both her legs, one of her arms, and several ribs. For two weeks she was unable to speak. Every evening Ömer brought flowers for her and sat by her bedside. Their two mothers spoke to one another, and it was in that way that he learned about the plan to marry her to another man.

For a few days both families hovered around the stricken girl, and after a while tensions boiled over. Ömer's father had told Emine's that he would pay for her medical expenses. Emine's father said he didn't want the help, and that if he ever saw Ömer at the hospital again, he would shoot him.

'You think it's easy to shoot someone?' Ömer's father had said. He owned a revolver, and went and summoned Ömer and then offered Emine's father the gun, saying, 'Here, shoot him if you can, because if you don't let him marry your daughter, you'll be killing him anyway. And if you don't have the guts to kill him, then I'll kill you.'

It was bravado. Neither man followed through on his threat, and Ömer continued visiting, but Emine's father wouldn't back down, and he refused to consent to the marriage. Emine spent six months convalescing in hospital until one day she disappeared and he never saw her again. A while later he learned that she had been taken off to her stepmother's village and married there.

That was the end of it. Ömer carried on working in Ayvansaray; he had a comfortable life due to his father's wealth and connections, and took a job running a factory that made knitting looms, but he felt sick and disgusted by everything around him. His family tried to organise other matches – various distant relatives from either side of the family. He refused them all. His father died not long afterwards; the crowd at his funeral at Eyüp Sultan stretched all the way back to Ayvansaray. The prime minister, Bülent Ecevit, was among the mourners.

Soon afterwards a job opportunity arose to work abroad as a long-distance truck driver; it was a step down, but it offered an escape. He spent the next three years driving a lorry around North Africa, until his mother had a stroke and he returned to Ayvansaray to care for her. She was paralysed and bedridden, and he lived with her in their old family house by the now-ruined mosque for the next twelve years before she died. In all that time she continued to try to find a match for him but he kept putting her off. He had decided he would never marry.

When his mother died, he carried on living in the family house. At some point the building was split up and the ground floor became a bakery. Ömer lived in one of the apartments above; the old mosque and cemetery had disappeared and it now looked onto the new Tokludede development.

He kept songbirds and fishes, he told me. Every morning he would get up at 8 a.m. to tend to his animals and then head to the teahouse. 'I used to be a very romantic man,' he told me. 'I wrote down all my feelings, I expressed them. I've lost everything now: no feelings.' Two of his brothers had died, and he had decided to devote his remaining years to supporting their four sons through university. The last of them was due to graduate in a year's time.

'After that I can die,' he said.

I asked him if he ever saw Emine again, and he said that he did, once, about six years after her suicide attempt. Her younger sister, who still lived in the neighbourhood, was bitten by a street dog and Ömer happened to be on hand to take her to hospital. On the way there she started crying and told him how sad she was about what had happened. A few days later she approached him and said Emine was living in the city now and wanted to meet him. At first he refused, but she insisted, and so a meeting was arranged at a cake shop in Merter, a neighbourhood beyond the walls. Emine came with her sister.

'Everyone was looking at us and I couldn't control myself,' he said. 'She was crying and I started crying too.' They were too overwhelmed to talk to each other. People started asking what had happened, and her sister explained the situation.

Someone sent an order of *muhallebi* – milk pudding – over to their table. Someone else sent a cake.

'She had her own family and children; there was nothing to say . . . Afterwards I came back here and wandered around like a fool. With time I got used to it and my sisters consoled me, told me I should move on with my life. We never saw each other again.'

Our wanderings had taken us to the fringe of Eyüp, where we had stopped for tea in a café, and now we headed back towards the place from where we'd set out. By this time the drizzle had abated. We passed beneath the Golden Horn Bridge, its great concrete legs rose above us and the sound of the traffic reverberated down. Just beneath it we passed the old shrine of another saint that had been preserved beneath the footings of the bridge, pinned like a brooch on the shifting fabric of the city. One small detail Ömer had mentioned would stay lodged in my mind: he said that when he was a child camels were still stabled at the place where the bridge now stands; they were used to bring food from Kemerburgaz, a village a few miles away.

Much later I looked up when the bridge was built, and discovered that its construction coincided with the time of Ömer and Emine's romance. As she looked out from the Tower of Isaac Angelus, preparing to end her life, she would have seen the mass of earthworks stretching out before her on the scarred ground of the former market gardens. Did she really want to marry Ömer? Did she even have a say in the matter? Why did she try to kill herself the day before they were due to run away? Ömer said he didn't know. Perhaps her family knew of the plan and hoped to take her away imminently, but perhaps not. I thought of her lying in the hospital ward, still and silent as the men around her fought over her future, and I wondered whether, in relating Ömer's story, I somehow shared in their guilt.

14

The Gate of Plagues

The Ottoman Fortress of the Seven Towers, Yedikule, and its environs had a long association with plagues, epidemics and infectious diseases. The famous seventeenth-century Ottoman traveller Evliya Çelebi claimed that before the Conquest its previous Byzantine version had been used as a quarantine point for those arriving in the city from stricken regions. Later, in Ottoman times, the city's Greek community would set up a small wooden plague hospital at the Yedikule Gate, the city entrance adjacent to the fortress, a position they probably chose due to its proximity to the holy spring at Balıklı, which lay nearby. Later, on the objection of the Armenians who had built their hospital across the road, the Greek plague hospital was moved and enlarged, eventually becoming a regular hospital. In the early twentieth century a tuberculosis ward was built and operated there by an American governmental charity for tubercular Greek, Armenian and Jewish children.

The city would suffer waves of plague, smallpox, cholera and tuberculosis over its long lifetime, with its position as the gateway for trade from Asia making it the launching point for many of the epidemics that swept Europe. The first historically recorded bubonic plague pandemic hit the city in AD 542, having probably originated in Central Asia and been brought by ship from Egypt. It would last for two hundred years and claim between 15 and 100 million lives. Due to its association with Constantinople it would come to be known as the Plague of Justinian, the Byzantine emperor who ruled during its emergence and who himself was struck down by it but recovered. The Byzantine historian Procopius, who was in the city during the first wave, described it as 'a pestilence by which the whole human race came near to being annihilated' and claimed that at its peak more than 10,000 people were dying daily. The corpses were so numerous, he said, that when there was no more space to bury them the bodies were dumped inside the walls of the defensive towers at Galata. The economic life of the city ground to a halt and the lack of production caused famine. '[W]ork of every description ceased,' he continued, 'and all the trades were abandoned by the artisans, and all other work as well, such as each had in hand.' According to a conservative estimate 20 per cent of the city's population died. Some historians have linked the plague to the ultimate failure of Justinian's effort to reconsolidate the western half of the Roman Empire, which during the preceding years he had made great strides towards achieving with the reconquest of Italy, much of the coast of North Africa, and southern Iberia. It has even been argued that it facilitated the rise of Islam, since while the Persian and Byzantine Empires were badly hit, Arabia remained relatively unscathed.

In March 2020 another pandemic hit the city. Kader – the AK Party activist from Topkapı who had been inspired to join the party by the suffering of his mother at the hands of an inadequate health system – was to find himself in a modern-day plague ward in the hospital about a ten-minute drive from the Yedikule Gate. Covid-19 was far less deadly than the medieval plagues, but in a more complex and connected world that had become less inured to death, its economic and social impacts would prove far-reaching.

The doctors and nurses in Kader's hospital had little idea of what they were dealing with. The nurses who came to take his blood twice a day were swathed in protective wear, gloves, masks and visors that fogged up with their breath. When a doctor needed to talk to him, he would call him by phone from outside the room and a nurse would hold it to his ear. Even cleaners didn't enter. Outside the open window, it was quiet for the first few days, but over time more and more often he heard the sound of ambulance sirens, and the following week people were wailing and howling outside the hospital doors as they received news of the dead, until police set up a cordon to stop them gathering there.

Since I had last spoken to him, Kader had got married and when the pandemic struck his wife was seven months pregnant, and initially it was she who he feared for most, because no one knew what the virus did to pregnant women or unborn babies; then when she didn't become ill he thought about the possibility of his own death, and worried how she would cope without him. During the first week of his illness, he couldn't breathe and was on a ventilator; he couldn't eat either and lost a total of eleven kilos over his period of treatment. The doctors pumped him with a cocktail of drugs – his discharge sheet would run to five pages. One must have worked because within two weeks the virus had cleared his system, but the treatment itself had caused serious liver damage. He spent a total of forty days in hospital before being sent home to continue his convalescence. It would take him a further month to recover.

Kader was no longer involved with the AK Party. When it had held its fifth district congress in 2018, a new president of the Fatih youth arm was elected, and he brought his own team with him, which meant Kader was out. By that time his passion had ebbed and he didn't want to stay involved anyway. He had begun to feel the party had lost its way.

'I still support the AK Party, but I was supporting it fanatically back then and I was a part of their work. Right now all I would do is to vote for them,' he said. 'I started to find their work wrong lately.'

He believed the party had lost its cause and ceased to be animated by social or political ideals that served the public, and had become focused on its own narrow and self-serving objectives. He had witnessed it in the changes in the party's grassroots outreach work. In the past, while volunteering for the youth arm, he and other party members would go around Fatih, knocking on doors. 'Every week after our meetings, we used to go to people's houses and ask them about their well-being, if they had any problems and so on, and we noted these down. You knock every door and ask how people are, if they are OK. We used to have a party that embraced the public.'

But then the structure and management of the party on a local level changed. It had become, he said, 'directly liable to the presidency' – in other words, to Erdoğan. 'Now the party members go to a house and just make it seem like they are chatting and share the photo as if they have been chatting . . . I think they are detached from the public now.'

It therefore came as no surprise to him when the AK Party lost the March 2019 municipal elections in Istanbul. He blamed the defeat on the party's lack of vision and its increasing reliance on the figure of Erdoğan.

'İmamoğlu took to the stage to say, "I'll do this, I'll do that, I'll embrace the public", and what did Binali Yıldırım do? He said, "We did this and that in the past" . . . You couldn't even find one image of Binali Yıldırım, it was only Recep Tayyip Erdoğan's images all over Istanbul, like the competition was between Recep Tayyip Erdoğan and İmamoğlu. On CHP's side it was only İmamoğlu . . . That was a major mistake. [The AK Party] said: "You are not choosing Binali Yıldırım, you are choosing Recep Tayyip Erdoğan" and the people said, "No . . . we are choosing a mayor and if the mayoral candidate is not in front of us, why would we choose him?"'

The change in the municipality leadership was felt by Kader personally, since he was an employee of IGDAŞ, Istanbul's household gas distribution company, a subsidiary of the municipality, where he now worked as a construction engineer. The change in leadership didn't affect him personally, but some of the higher-ups in his company were fired and replaced with İmamoğlu's people. This was, he said, only normal for an incoming administration of a different party.

'I can guarantee you that if you do a public poll right now, 90 per cent of the people would not vote for the AK Party if not for Recep Tayyip Erdoğan. People are not about parties any more, they are about people. We are in a situation where they say if Recep Tayyip Erdoğan is in, we are in.'

———

Fırat – the Communist activist from Paşa who had set up the association to prevent the bulldozing of homes along the walls – had been doing his military service at the start of the pandemic, cooped up in a barracks with scores of other young men. He was sick for about seventeen days, but he didn't think it was Covid. The conditions were generally unhygienic and it was not unusual to get ill there.

'There was an air of fear; it was too crowded, an all-male environment, everybody was dirty,' he recalled. To him the pandemic had seemed at first 'like a dystopian movie'. 'I was talking with my mother the other day and she said something about her father: that the more crowded your funeral is, the more clear it is that you were valued. And I keep thinking about all those people who died because of Covid and their loved ones could not be with them.'

It was also clear to him that the government was manipulating the pandemic to advance its ideological agenda. While religious gatherings and the AK Party's own political rallies seemed to be exempt from lockdown restrictions, venues associated with a more secular lifestyle – restaurants, cafés, nightclubs and so on – remained subject to strict bans that seemed to linger even when the threat of the virus had receded.

'The assault goes on in every area of life and now something like this pandemic has happened, and it's really tough,' he told me. 'It made it easier for them to interfere with things. They wouldn't allow opening the art galleries but the shopping malls are open. You are free to do everything you want in the daytime, you can go to the shopping malls but you are not able to go to a café in your neighbourhood and have a cup of tea.'

I spoke to Fırat while the pandemic was still in full swing. He said it also had some upsides: it brought relief from the grind of work. 'A lot of people are complaining about it because of the financial strains but at the same time, we are also happy to be staying at home. That part of it makes us content. People in Turkey work for long hours and it's always intense . . . I want to say things are bad but our life was already the worst so all I can say is that it's an advantage to be able to spend time with your family. Other than that, I really hope it goes away soon.'

I'd met with Fırat several times in person since my first encounter with him in 2015. His life had changed a lot in the interim. He'd broken up with Deniz, met a new girlfriend, got married, and now had a baby on the way. The Walled Neighbourhoods Living and Support Association had failed: shut down by a combination of official pressure and internal division.

Their troubles had begun during the atmosphere of heightened oppression that had followed the coup attempt, during which the left-wing enclave of Kocamustafapaşa felt like it was under assault. Hayat TV, a popular left-wing television station which had its studio in the neighbourhood, was raided by the police then shut down by emergency decree three months after the coup attempt. The government had introduced a nationwide system of 'night guards' – young people either close to the AKP or ultranationalist youth groups would patrol neighbourhoods in groups of three or four after 11 p.m., ostensibly to keep public order. They were basically state-employed *kabadayıs*, enforcing a national moral code which was received poorly in areas that were more secular or left-leaning.

'They stroll around in groups, three or four people. They are supposed to apply something, some rule or law, but instead of doing that, they just bully people for anything they don't like.'

The association itself closed a few months after the coup, but its ending was more complicated. It was served with an official notice of legal proceedings on the basis of not having filed proper accounts. This was true: the organisation's treasurer had only kept an incomplete paper ledger that fell far short of what the authorities required, and when they worked out what needed to be done and the potential fines involved the committee threw in the towel and closed it down.

They believed it was political – all around them there were

other associations operating in obviously illegal ways, but since these were mainly Islamic-oriented they faced no obvious pressure. But by that point things had begun to fall apart for them in other ways. The meeting with the municipality had yielded nothing and many of the residents who had initially supported the association had now cut deals to sell their homes. They'd never really succeeded in uniting the community in the way they had intended, and there was also tension between the Turkish Communist Party leadership and the Mevlanakapı-based activists like Fırat over the direction of the association. The party had decided to prioritise women's rights issues and was less interested in educational assistance, which had become one of their main operations. In the wake of this row Fırat quit the party, and as a result the various teachers who had been volunteering began to leave.

He was angry with the Communist Party, which he felt had abandoned the association just as it had begun to have success in collectively confronting the urban renewal project. 'The municipality requested a meeting with us. It was so important for us. We went door to door, we spoke with everyone, we became a legal entity and the municipality saw us as an equal to be corresponding with. They said, "Let them come and let's speak." We gained something of value there, it was precious . . . But my party's own agenda was about women's rights. I am not saying it's not valuable, it's very precious too – but people are also losing their houses. We wanted a completely different agenda. This caused a lot of arguments.'

After that he'd faced financial difficulties. He'd been made redundant from his job at a market. The boss there was a member of a religious sect. Every Friday he'd be asked if he would be going to prayers with the other employees, and every Friday he declined. He believed this was the reason he had been laid off. He had other friends in similar situations – a law graduate who wanted to be a prosecutor but whose political views effectively made him unemployable, a medical graduate who was blacklisted from getting work because of his leftist leanings. Everything about the current situation was designed to pressure people to acquiesce. When I met with him around that time, his mood was one of defiant fatalism.

'How does it feel to know nothing's going to work out in the end? It feels like this: I don't really care. I am like this and it's not working out but does it work out for the rest of the 81 million people in this country? No, it doesn't. The country isn't working for AKP supporters either. Almost everyone is suffering . . . But I do care about my siblings. One is eighteen years old, another sixteen and another one is ten years old. One of these days I might have a child too. What will they do? We are going through a brutal time compared to the past. People are abused more, both financially and spiritually. This will increase in the next generations. I can manage it now, but I wonder what they will do.'

The last time I spoke to Fırat he, like Kader, had stepped back from political activism. His last foray had taken place just before the pandemic, when he had run to be *muhtar* of Paşa. In theory the position was non-political: candidates did not run under any party's banner. But this was something of a fiction and the political allegiances of candidates were well known. Although supporters of the left-leaning opposition parties formed a majority of more than 60 per cent in the neighbourhood, the current *muhtar* was known to be pro-AKP, mainly because the opposition could never unite around a single candidate. Fırat decided to run for the office, but the Kurdish-aligned party never accepted him and ran their own candidate, once again splitting the anti-AKP vote and ensuring that the incumbent retained his post. Fırat and the Kurdish party both blamed each other for dividing the vote.

But his disappointment was tempered by the wider success of the opposition. Fırat had been part of the local campaigning for Ekrem İmamoğlu. It was a special point of pride for him that Fatih was among the districts that had backed İmamoğlu – Fatih, the old city, that was widely perceived as a bastion of conservatism. But the sense of hope it brought was fleeting. The economy had continued to decline and he saw signs of growing acquiescence to the regime; as people got poorer the 'charity'-based model of Erdoğan's populism tightened its grip. Cleaving to the party offered the only means of advancement in a system that didn't work for outsiders.

'I am their opponent and I know that if I am not one of them, I can make nothing of myself. It makes one hopeless. People who can stomach it, become one of them – a lot of people change sides.' Now when he considered the prospect of becoming a father, he felt more sympathetic to the generation of parents who had witnessed the 1980 coup and tried to inculcate an apolitical mindset into their children.

'On one hand I am angry with these parents because whatever else, they shouldn't have done that, they should have taught us about the struggle, but on the other hand, it's your child. You don't want to see them harmed and they saw what happened in the 1980 coup. It's not your partner or friend or brother, it's your child. The person you have to protect and defend the most. But while they were trying to protect them, they ruined them. This pressure is even worse now. It's getting harder and harder because now they make people poorer and they make them subject to charity. Those support packages, bonuses, charities, they give all of that to their supporters . . . It's harder every day now because AKP's basis is built on this charity culture. You get to live if you are on their side, and if you are not on their side, you go to hell.'

In the end Fırat decided to leave Istanbul because it became too expensive to live there. He and his wife took the opportunity to move to Antalya when a job offer came up. 'We partly went there for the job, but it was more that living in Istanbul became impossible. The cost of living, the rent was too expensive. The job opportunities in Istanbul are better, but if you get a good offer somewhere else, you take it . . . But I miss my neighbourhood a lot though, I miss it all the time.'

He liked his new job, and he'd learned to keep his political views private. 'I am careful to not bring these things up at work any more. So in a way, they intimidated me, and I am not alone any more, I can't just think of myself and leave. I am at home, I have some responsibilities. That scares me. I learned to stay silent.'

———

Yurdanur – the Alevi mother who lived on Foot-of-the-Tower Street – and her family lost their home to the municipality's redevelopment plan. In the end all their neighbours had caved in apart from them and their friend and next-door neighbour Ayten and her family. They shared ownership of their home with her husband's brother, who lived downstairs.

'The municipality seduced him, he said he would give in, Hasan and Ayten would not give in, they were fighting,' she told me when I went to have tea with her in her new apartment. 'There was quite a sibling fight. It became a huge problem between them. Finally, Hasan had to give in so that there would be no more problems, so that the argument would not get bigger, but they experienced great sadness.'

The two houses had a party wall, and so the municipality

could not demolish Ayten's house without also damaging Yurdanur's. 'Since there was only one wall, they started to pressure us, saying things like "If yours is damaged when we demolish this house, the responsibility isn't ours", etc.' The municipality later claimed to have found a crack in the wall of their house that made it uninhabitable, and ordered them to vacate it within ten days. This was during a Covid lockdown, when it was almost impossible to find a rental property.

Her daughter's boyfriend, who was studying law, helped them draft a legal challenge and they took the municipality to court. The judge examining the case ordered the municipality to draw up a report showing on what basis they found the house unsafe.

'That put a fire under them,' Yurdanur said. 'After that they were constantly trying to come to terms with us.' The municipality had valued their house at 280,000 lira, which would be put as equity into one of the new apartments out in Kayabaşı, the distant development on the fringe of the city where the rest of the residents had been given property. Yurdanur and Sadık refused to take one of the apartments, and said they would accept no less than 400,000 lira for their old house.

The municipality claimed that their hands were legally tied in the matter because they couldn't sell the apartments to anyone else, they had been purpose-built for people in this area. Eventually, the representative of the municipality came up with a compromise: he himself would line up a buyer for the Kayabaşı apartment, and transfer it to Yurdanur and Sadık, so they could immediately sell it to the new buyer on the same day, leaving them with the equity from their old home as cash.

They reluctantly agreed to consider it, and a meeting was arranged at a local café. After a long bout of haggling, they made a deal for 340,000 lira. A short while later they bought a new apartment as near to Foot-of-the-Tower Street as they could find for 400,000. The shortfall they made up by using up a small pot

of savings they had kept to one side as a rainy-day fund. That
was their victory after a bitter struggle: a smaller home than their
old one, and with their savings gone, but at least they were still
in their old neighbourhood and had no debts.

The whole thing could have gone in a smoother way, she
said, if the municipality had behaved in a way 'without abusing
people'. 'They have the audacity to choose a living space for
us . . . You do not have the right to choose my living space.
I get to choose my living space. You give back the real worth
of my house. This is the historical peninsula and the land is
really precious here. They put a price of 2,000 to 3,000 lira
per square metre here, but the real value is between 16,000
and 25,000 lira per square metre at worst . . . If you want to
destroy it, it is yours to do so, but pay me the value of my
property first.'

Their new home, where Yurdanur was recounting all this to
me, was on the second floor of a four-storey building a hundred
metres or so away from Foot-of-the-Tower Street. It was a
pleasant, clean place with none of the character of their old
home. 'It looks like a hospital to us,' she said as we drank tea
in the living room. They'd had to send a lot of their furniture
to their village as there was no space for it, and there were certain
other inconveniences: 'A tiny kitchen,' she said, 'so it's impossible
for me to fit in. We are used to living with stores, buying
everything family size, three or five kilos, etc., and it is a habit
we can't give up.'

She liked the new street, however. In fact, it was lovely. 'I
had fears, I was paranoid about what kind of people there would
be in this street. But the neighbours in the building are great.
We see them, they come for coffee and so on, and most people
in the street know each other and say hello to each other. There
is a good community feeling.'

There was not the same ease as there had been before, the

deep knowledge and familiarity of living side-by-side for decades. For example, Yurdanur's new neighbours did not know she was an Alevi. 'As Ramadan was approaching we came together in my house for coffee and everyone, without knowing my religious community, was automatically proposing plans for Ramadan: "Let's fast together, let's go to the mosque together to pray on this night, let's do this and that" – and I didn't really make a comment about it. It would be better if I could openly say this; my conversation is much more fun when I am with people who know who I am or with like-minded people around me, but it's not such a big deal for me.'

Another thing that made her happy was that in the end Foot-of-the-Tower Street really did become a park. We went to look at it together – it wasn't finished yet, but there was already a children's play area, benches, rows of saplings, a cobbled path and a bright blue cycle lane. The trees from the gardens of the houses had been preserved, including the mulberry tree that had grown in Yurdanur's garden – a square hole had been cut out of the edge of the cycle lane to accommodate it.

'I'm glad the mulberry tree is still there, because it means we can see exactly where our front door was, we can work out where the windows were and the walls were.' In a way, she said, being so close to their old home also made it more painful. 'It was so much more than a house to me. I've had my troubles but my relationship with the place I lived, even in my most troubled times, was something very special. I get emotional still, I look at photos and sometimes I say I must forget about it but it's hard . . . We keep being reminded of the house. It's the time when the storks are migrating now. My husband asked me if I'd seen them passing over, and I said do I even have a chance to see the sky?'

I met Cem on the first-floor terrace of an empty diner on a sliproad overlooking the highway heading out towards Esenyurt, a kind of nowhere place anchored only to the noisy torrent of traffic that passed ceaselessly beyond it. Cem chose to meet there because his mother was sick – she had diabetes – and it was near to the hospital where he was attending to her.

He looked unchanged from when I had last seen him. At first he said he'd been lucky during the pandemic because he'd been able to carry on working, but as we talked it seemed like this had hardly been the case. He had broken up with his fiancée. The stress of the pandemic had driven them apart; they started to argue, and eventually spent less and less time together until the relationship ended.

'Recently I haven't been able to pull myself together after this break-up. And right now, frankly, I feel incomplete because knowing that you have someone with you that knows you are an addict is something that makes you feel very comfortable. You can speak the same language with them, but now . . . I'm going out with girls for a night or two sometimes, but it goes nowhere because we don't have a chance to communicate. And this bothers me a lot.'

Now, he said, he was focusing on his relationship with his daughter and his work. This had also changed though. During the pandemic the inpatient centre at Esenyurt municipality had closed down and it had never reopened. The municipality still operated an outpatient counselling facility, but the work he had been so proud of last time I'd seen him was over. During the various lockdown restrictions he had carried on doing counselling sessions online, and then in person again when he was able to, and he still met regularly with the eight heroin addicts he had succeeded in getting clean. He was still doing consulting work for the police and various addiction recovery organisations. As a way of making money on the side, he was also chauffeuring several private schoolchildren to and from school.

'The pandemic has also affected the therapy groups a lot; they also started meeting only on Zoom, so I started to feel unwell for the last year and a half, too. I started to feel lonely. I felt out of sorts, I still feel that way. I'm only focusing on work at the moment to get me through. I get up at six o'clock, I drive a school car. I have four kids, they're all rich kids. I take them to Avcılar, I drop them off by car, then I go to work. I take them home in the evening, then I come home, and I finish the day like this.'

The end of the inpatient centre was a particularly hard blow. 'I absolutely think it's less effective now. With an inpatient you can actually heal a person, have a chance to tell this person what you have learned from scratch, and if that person does something wrong, you have a chance to say this is wrong and correct them. But now it is not like that, when something goes wrong, reusing happens. They come back to us using again. Frankly, this makes me sad. It is very difficult for these people to stay clean now.'

The centre's closure was about more than just Covid. During the municipal elections that brought İmamoğlu to power, Esenyurt was among the district municipalities that also passed from the AK Party to the opposition CHP. The transfer meant certain unofficial funding streams which the municipality once had access to were now cut off. 'They had been creating money,' he said simply. 'The costs, the number of staff, the number of meals for the patients, etc. began to stand out. The pandemic is 50 per cent of it, plus the interruption of the services provided by the municipality is 50 per cent, but if you ask anyone, they'd say it was the pandemic in the end.'

His plan now was to work for another four years and then try to get the funding or a loan to start his own rehabilitation centre. He saw his work now as primarily about keeping himself in line, giving his own life meaning, and wasn't hopeful of the prospects of broader societal change or action by government to combat the burgeoning problem of addiction. Part of the problem, he said, was that whatever individuals and some branches of government were doing to combat addiction, there seemed to be almost nothing happening to combat the supply side.

———

Turkish organised crime had long been the dominant player in the trafficking of heroin from Afghanistan to Europe, due mainly to the country's geographical location. Heroin passing into Turkey was sent onwards through criminal networks in the Balkans, the former Soviet nations, or by ship directly to western Europe. This trade inevitably had a corrupting influence that extended into the nation's murky politics; in the 1990s, elements of the state and intelligence services, who had a long relationship with organised crime, became directly involved in the heroin trade ostensibly as part of the struggle against the Kurdish separatist PKK, which also played a major role in it.

More recently, Turkey had acquired global importance as a distribution hub for South American cocaine. An investigation by the think tank Insight Crime in 2022 suggested that increased seizures in Europe and North America were leading to an increase in cocaine trafficking through Turkey, whose organised crime networks already had a well-developed shipping network and longstanding ties to Central and South American cartels. The volume of cocaine seizures in Turkey has hit new records every year since 2017. 'There wasn't a lot of cocaine in Istanbul the last time you came here. Now there is an incredible amount of cocaine, it's unbelievable,' said Cem.

As we were discussing this, Cem mentioned an old acquaintance of his who was now very much in the news: a well-known mafia boss and ultranationalist named Sedat Peker, who had himself been a key part of the nexus where organised crime mingled with far right politics and state security. Cem said he and Peker had been part of the same Fenerbahçe youth supporters' group when they were teenagers. They would act as touts, buying tickets from the club and then selling them on outside the football ground. Later, while Cem was spiralling into addiction after his fateful military service, Peker progressed into the world of organised crime. One of the people Cem remembered meeting with Peker was a man named Veli Küçük, a general in the Turkish army and an infamous figure in the so-called 'Deep State', who had known Peker's father and was later alleged to have recruited him to carry out contract killings.

The last time Cem had seen him had been as he was sliding into addiction, when Peker helped a friend of his to force someone to pay a debt they were refusing to pay. 'After I came from the military service, I saw him two or three times; we went to him. In fact, a friend of ours had a job back then, so we went to see him to take care of it. He wasn't getting paid, he couldn't get what he was owed, they knew it too, so we went to see Sedat. I couldn't find his phone, then I found it, and I gave him a call and told him about the situation. We went to see him, thank goodness, he received us, and he got the job done.'

Peker's career had been a colourful one. Over the past three decades he has been tried and acquitted on murder charges, tried and convicted for drug-trafficking, protection racketeering and coercion, and then in 2005, he was tried and sentenced to fourteen years in prison for leading a criminal organisation, robbery, forgery and false imprisonment. During this time he had not shied from the public eye, vocally engaging in politics and trumpeting various charitable endeavours. When he was released from prison in 2014, he became an outspoken supporter of Erdoğan, holding his own pro-government rallies during election campaigns, sometimes attended by thousands of people, and denouncing his foes, sometimes in strikingly violent terms. Most notoriously, when a group of liberal and left-wing academics released a petition calling for a renewal of peace talks with the PKK after their collapse in 2005, he publicly threatened to 'shed their blood in streams and then shower in their blood'. His warmth towards the AK Party appeared to be reciprocal, with pro-government media describing him as a 'businessman' in its favourable coverage of him.

But things took a dramatic turn in 2021, when Peker, who had apparently fled Turkey after another criminal probe, began releasing a series of YouTube videos from the United Arab Emirates in which he launched a barrage of criminal allegations relating to members of Erdoğan's government. The videos, released over a period of weeks in May and June, transfixed the country and were viewed millions of times. Peker appeared like a teacher, addressing the camera while sitting behind a desk stacked with neatly arranged papers in what appeared to be a hotel room. Wearing a shirt unbuttoned to reveal a hefty silver medallion, he issued veiled threats to members of the government regarding dirt he claimed to have on them. 'You all know what I have,' he said in his first video. 'You can hide like cockroaches no longer.' Over the following weeks he went on to detail a plethora of crimes by prominent politicians and members of the government, including his own dealings with them. The most shocking was his claim that the apparent death by suicide of a Kazakh journalist in 2019 was in fact a cover-up for her rape and murder by the son of a former government minister in whose apartment her body was found.

Another of his allegations was that the son of Binali Yıldırım – the failed AK Party mayoral candidate and former prime minister – was personally involved in cocaine trafficking and had visited Venezuela in January 2021 to set up a new route. Yıldırım denied this, saying the trip had been to distribute Covid supplies. Peker's claims were never seriously investigated or their validity determined, but they added to the growing miasma of corruption that surrounded the AK Party.

———

The last time I had met Zehra – the young master's student who was joining her cousin Nagihan in a career in academia at the restored dervish lodge at Merkezefendi – she had finished her MA and was trying in vain to find a job. For the time being she was working as an instructor at the Alliance of Civilizations Institute where Nagihan was still a professor. But the job didn't pay her a living wage, and she could barely afford to remain in the city. Having spent years in education, she felt there was no market for her skills and was disillusioned by the corruption she saw around her, especially in education.

'Academia is very corrupted, this is the place where the most corruption happens,' she said. 'Let's say a university is opening a position as a researcher, a very simple position, and you apply: they won't give it to you. They don't assess the quality of applications, they already know who they're going to hire.' At that time the media was abuzz with a scandal concerning an academic who had been hired as a professor at a university in Anatolia, even though it had been discovered that his PhD thesis was eighteen pages long and consisted mainly of a table of contents. 'There are many people like this,' she said.

She had recently applied for a PhD in English Literature at Cambridge in the UK. Amid the deteriorating economic situation, nepotism and lack of prospects, friends of hers were increasingly talking about leaving Turkey. 'They are all telling me, "Oh, we should leave this country, we're not able to live here any more." And many of them are leaving . . . All from different backgrounds. But for me, I want to come back because if we all leave what's going to happen? You need to come back and improve the country. Because we have potential and we can't leave it to all these corrupted bigheads.'

She said she was concerned about the arrests taking place in the country in the wake of the coup. 'There are many innocent people being jailed for this,' she said. She mentioned a cousin of her mother's who was very pro the AK Party – 'he might even be violent about defending the AK Party' – who had been arrested and jailed for nine months because he had an extension on his phone associated with the ByLock app which was being used as criminal evidence of Gülenist links. 'He didn't have any hearing or anything, he had no way of showing he was innocent, and at the end of nine months they said, "Oh, we're sorry that extension can be downloaded without you realising, someone else might have put it on your phone", and they released him.' Even after he cleared his name, he found it impossible to get work and started being the target of suspicion in his community. 'It's happening to him and happening to many, many other people as well, they're just putting them in prison without thinking.'

She also knew an academic at Boğaziçi, a Kurdish woman who had once been a classmate of hers, who had been jailed on terrorism charges. 'I know that academic in person from Boğaziçi, she was my classmate, and she was involved in the PKK . . . Even in the class she was saying that revolution and violence were justified: she was a pro-violence person. So I knew this about her. And when she was jailed I thought she must have been involved in something. And then we heard that she was hiding two PKK terrorists and they were going to bomb one of the neighbourhoods in Istanbul, so then I thought, "Right, it's good she was jailed then" . . .'

'I'm sure that not all these people are terrorists,' she added. 'I'm sure the government is trying to put different voices in prison under the name of terrorism. But I know some of them are really terrorists, and some of the arrests are really justified . . . You really don't know who to believe or what to believe, and to understand you have to be inside different circles, you have to go and explore different circles of people around the country . . . This is all going on in the country I'm living in, and my life is as normal as at any time.'

———

It wasn't until after the Covid pandemic that I spoke to Zehra or her cousin Nagihan again. Zehra had been in China when Covid struck. She had won her PhD place at Cambridge, but had been unable to take it up because she couldn't get the financial funding she needed. In the end she had gone to do an MA at the Shanghai Theatre Academy, writing about multiculturalism in 'Karagöz', a traditional Ottoman shadow play not dissimilar to the English puppet show 'Punch and Judy'. Now she was in Berlin, doing her PhD in English Literature at Humboldt University, and also teaching full time at an online US Islamic high school and middle school, teaching world history, cultural geography – 'and even, believe it or not, US history!' The time difference meant she could study in the mornings and do her teaching in the evenings.

In Turkey, the economy was in an increasingly parlous state. Over the previous year Turkey's official inflation rate had at one point hit 85 per cent, although this was widely believed in the country to be an underestimate of its true extent. She felt more than ever that no immediate future lay open to her in Turkey, but she was confident it would be some day.

'I'm a patriot, I love my country, I would love to serve my

country. The reason I want to get good qualifications is because I want to go back and contribute to it and be part of its development, but in a way that I feel I can use my potential in a happy way. I do want to go back but not right now. I can say I am optimistic. I think this is temporary. I feel like it's a circle. I remember my childhood when my social group was suppressed financially, religiously, in terms of identity but then things changed, things got better, now they have got worse again, and they will change again.'

Nagihan had recently been out to visit her and the two had toured the Berlinale film festival together. She was still teaching at the Alliance of Civilizations Institute, which was now operating under the aegis of a different university, one set up and funded by TURGEV, an educational charity linked to Erdoğan's son. As a result, the institute had left the old dervish lodge and now occupied part of the former *medrese* of the Süleymaniye Mosque, the huge edifice that crowned one of the city's seven hills built for Süleyman the Magnificent by Sinan, the prolific and pre-eminent genius of Ottoman architecture. It had graduated from the heretical fringe of the city to its orthodox heart.

For a long time all her teaching had been online, and she found that in the process her view on public space and the university had changed. 'During the pandemic we went to collect what we needed from the university offices. We entered the university and it was empty. And I thought for years we fought to be in this space and now it barely exists any more. Universities are losing their power for all kinds of reasons.'

Like Zehra, over time she had become more angry about the cronyism she saw in the government. 'It's the nepotism that is going to bring their votes down,' she said. 'It's the most unpalatable of all the things . . . There seems to be a total collapse of human resources allocation. There are so many people in positions of power who are not able to do the job.'

On the question of the looming presidential elections, she felt conflicted. 'The way the currency dropped and all kinds of things, I was very angry with the government, and every time I say I'm not going to vote for them. But people who say they won't vote for them, they will not switch sides and vote for CHP. I could never do that. The most I could do would be to leave the ballot without crossing anything. Nagihan described her typical experience voting at the local primary school on election days in Etiler, the well-to-do, secular suburb where she had grown up and still lived.

'When I go to vote in the local primary school, by the time I reach the school gates, I stand in line and it's time for the ballot, I've been exposed to so many Etiler people looking at me in their Etiler way, that I'm thinking, "I have to vote AKP." There's no way I can survive otherwise . . . So I don't know what's going to happen this time. If they look at me nicely, they may get a void vote.'

I asked her how she felt about teaching at a university linked to the charity run by Erdoğan's son. It had been linked to allegations that it had been used to siphon money out of the country, and in 2019, after winning control of the Istanbul municipality, the new opposition CHP mayor İmamoğlu raised questions over generous sums given to it from the municipality budget when it was previously under AK Party control. When he raised the issue on live television his feed was cut off.

'Yeah,' she laughed, 'maybe I'm a product of nepotism myself and I should stay at home – I'd be very happy to stay at home if someone more qualified was teaching my course.'

'I didn't mean it in that way at all,' I said.

'Well, we joke about it all the time,' she continued, before switching to a serious tone: 'To be perfectly honest, the thing

that I value about Ibn Haldun is that there are so many international students from the Middle East and Africa, and I see
Ibn Haldun's importance through that lens. We probably have
the highest number of MENA region students, and when we
read applications it's so interesting to see that they still see Turkey
as their window onto the world, and they can come here and
get a good education. And that's quite moving, to be honest,
and it's wonderful that that university's there.'

Sometimes, she added, they would get Turkish students
applying who would ask in their interviews what would happen
to the university if the AK Party were to lose power. 'And we
say, "Well, we don't know, you'll have to take that risk."'

⸺

When the big earthquake finally hit, it was not the one Turkey
had expected. The pair of powerful tremors that rocked the
country in the early hours of 6 February 2023 did not strike on
the North Anatolian Fault that ran through Istanbul, but on
the East Anatolian Fault parallel to the border with Syria. Like
the Marmara quake twenty-four years earlier, the first tremor
occurred at the worst possible time: just after four in the morning
when people were asleep in their beds. At magnitude 7.8, it was
the second most powerful quake ever recorded in Turkey. It
caused a surface rupture 200 miles long, with the ground slipping as much as 8 metres in some places, devastating a vast area
of southern Turkey and northern Syria. The second quake hit
in the afternoon and was almost as powerful at 7.7.

At first it was impossible to get news from the worst-affected
zones; phone networks were down and electricity was cut. As
aerial footage began to emerge, cities like Antakya and
Gaziantep looked more like their war-devastated counterparts
across the border in Syria. In places whole street blocks had

collapsed into heaps of shattered masonry, apartment blocks lay toppled against each other like dominos, and individual buildings stood askew like foundering ships on a sea of rubble. As reports of the toll of death and devastation began to flood in, there were elements of the disaster that were reminiscent of the Marmara quake which had helped propel Erdoğan to power. As in 1999, the state appeared to be startlingly absent in the early days, with residents clawing through the rubble on their own to rescue trapped loved ones. Unlike in 1999, however, Turkey had theoretically been preparing for such a calamity. The dedicated AFAD disaster agency had been created to address such crises, and an earthquake tax instituted after the Marmara earthquake had raised an estimated total of $37bn. Among the thousands of buildings that collapsed, many were recently built, supposedly in line with stringent construction codes. Among the most notorious examples was a luxury apartment complex in Antakya that had advertised itself as earthquake proof. The Rönesans ('Renaissance') Residence was an oblong twelve-storey building with 249 apartments that simply toppled onto its side. As many as 700 people died in the building.

Once again, the government seemed as anxious about censorship and message control as it did about addressing the disaster. At a time when quake victims and their relatives, friends and neighbours were using social media to try to coordinate rescue efforts, the government banned Twitter for twelve hours. Erdoğan said the move had been to stop disinformation. 'In such a period, I cannot tolerate the viciously negative campaigns for the sake of simple political interests,' he explained.

Kader was on the bus to work when he first heard about the earthquake. He had been feeling sick – it was so bad, he wondered if he had Covid again – and he'd planned to ask the workplace doctor to let him go home for the day. His brother, who also lived in Istanbul, called him and asked if he'd heard any news of an earthquake. Kahramanmaraş, Kader's home province where his parents and most of his large extended family lived, was about twenty miles north of the epicentre.

'I don't remember anything from that moment until the second earthquake,' he told me when I spoke to him a few months later. 'I remember in that panic, I was just trying to save my parents.' It was impossible to get through to the area, and it was the next day when his sister called him from the house to tell him she was trapped inside with their parents.

'My sister in the village called and said, "The stove collapsed on us, the doors won't open, there are cracks in the walls, and the ground is shaking."' The line cut out. Many of his cousins outside of the quake got in their cars to head straight there, but since he was sick they decided he should stay behind and he tried to organise help over the phone.

'I couldn't get over the feeling of panic inside me,' Kader recalled. 'I couldn't even regulate my breathing. Only the status of Hatay and Adana [provinces] were broadcast on television; Kahramanmaraş was not. We did not receive any news. We did not receive any news from social media either.'

His parents and sister were eventually released by neighbours and suffered only minor injuries. The number of deaths in the village was relatively low because the houses were all single-storey. It was mainly the older generations who lived there, but his younger relatives who were living in the city centre of Kahramanmaraş were not so lucky. It was there that the destruction took its worst toll.

In the coming days he would learn that twenty of his first cousins and their children had perished. When he included the descendants of his great uncles and aunts, many of whom the family were still close to, the figure rose to a hundred. Among his wider relatives in the region the figure was more like three hundred.

He learned their stories over the coming days. There was his cousin Murat, a geography teacher killed along with his wife, leaving four young children behind them; there were his cousins, Orhan and Meral, who also died, while their two teenage children were pulled alive from the rubble. 'When [they] took them out, they didn't even remember their parents due to the shock,' said Kader.

Then there was Kader's second cousin İbrahim, who he had gone to school with. One of İbrahim's cousins had been a soldier who had been killed three years earlier, martyred in Syria. The anniversary of his death was approaching and the entire family had gathered in his parents' home to plan a commemoration. Ten people died in the house, including four children and a woman pregnant with twins: their bodies were discovered on the anniversary of the martyr's death. Only the dead soldier's father survived, who had been in the village at the time. When Kader called his cousin who was at the ruined house, he told him he could no longer feel his fingers from having clawed through the wreckage for so long.

'By the third or fourth day, I could no longer look at the TV or Twitter either. Every time you look at it, it is not healthy to hear that another relative has died, to see a person you know lying in blood. When my mother and father came here, I felt slightly relieved, at least because my mother and father were with me.'

His parents stayed with him for a month. They were so traumatised that the sound of Kader's three-year-old son running around the apartment made them jump, reminding them of the constant aftershocks that followed the earthquakes. In the end they returned to the village because they didn't want to abandon the people who had stayed behind.

Kader went back with them. He planned to use his skills as an engineer to assess the state of the family's house and if it was uninhabitable, find a safe building for his parents to stay in.

When he visited the city centre, it was impossible to recognise it as the same place where he had grown up and gone to school. 'It was so alien,' he said. The urban space seemed to have shrunk; landmarks that had seemed distant from one another before seemed closer together now because many of the streets and buildings between them were devastated. 'None of the buildings I knew existed. I only found a flat land. In that flat land, I felt as if I had just arrived at the workplace and was working at the construction site: flat land, rubble, trucks and shovels, like some excavations being done. I could not understand that it was the city, bazaar or market where I lived.'

According to a government report two weeks after the quakes, in Kahramanmaraş 3,752 buildings had collapsed, and a further 19,194 were severely damaged and in need of demolition. This represented more than 20 per cent of all the buildings in the province. The official death toll for the earthquake given four months afterwards was 50,783, with another 8,500 dead in Syria. Watching Turkish news channels, which had back-to-back coverage detailing the lives and deaths of some of the thousands of victims, there was the sense of a vast scythe having swept through the nation. Among the public figures who were killed were top footballers and football managers, well known social media influencers, reality TV stars, artists, actors, musicians and singers, dying either alone or with members of their families.

In the aftermath of the earthquakes, Kader's disillusionment with Erdoğan and the AK Party crystallised into anger. The promises made by the government and its account of the rescue efforts were dramatically at odds with what he saw on the ground.

'I have no confidence in them. There is a reality that I saw with my eyes, an event that I lived,' he said. 'Two container cities and tent cities were established in Kahramanmaraş. They were still being installed when I got there. It had been a month since the earthquake. But when I was in Istanbul, and I hadn't left yet, there was news like this: our president said we had no problem, tents have been distributed to everyone. Everyone is taken to the containers. He said food is being served. When I went there, we stayed in a tent made of makeshift rags for a week.'

Some promises made in the wake of the disaster were either rolled back or forgotten. In coordination with the government, mobile phone companies had told people in the affected regions they would receive free phone calls for at least a month afterwards – Kader said it was even sent as a text message from the local governor's office. 'I paid my brother's bill of over a thousand lira last month,' he said. 'They billed people with interest because they were not able to pay it at the time.'

He believed that the government was deliberately underestimating the severity of the damage to buildings in order to avoid compensating victims. Buildings had been divided into four categories, ranking from undamaged up to heavily damaged. Kader estimated that his sister's house, which he examined, was at least moderately damaged, but the official report filed on the government's website classified it as undamaged. 'Consider a two-storey house. My sisters live downstairs; my aunts live upstairs. They said the upper floor was damaged. They said the lower floor was undamaged, the same building with the same column. They make this distinction because when they say heavy damage, they give you aid according to that; if it is medium damage, they give you support according to that. If it's undamaged, they don't.'

Much of his anger focused on the official Turkish aid organisation Kızılay, the Red Crescent. When he went to his village he had been shocked to see that although there were tents from many different foreign countries, there were none at all from Kızılay. 'I am a person who has been donating blood for years. For years, I have been a person who buys mineral water just to help Kızılay. I show such sensibility, and 90 per cent of our citizens show the same sensibility too. A tent is coming from Pakistan . . . I said to myself, but why didn't it come from my own state? When you question this you question everything.'

To make matters worse, Erdoğan, when he first came to Kahramanmaraş, had scolded the public for the widespread complaints that were being made of Kızılay, saying it was 'immoral' to criticise. 'This was terrible,' said Kader.

He believed the AK Party and Erdoğan had become 'poisoned by power', with no possibility of internal criticism or debate and every decision going back to the leader himself. 'Now they say that the slightest thing needs the president's permission even it has nothing to do with the president. I saw this change grow like a snowball effect . . . I left for these reasons. The things you contribute with your opinions don't matter. There is only the order given, and the fulfilment of that order. No criticism.'

It would transpire, however, that he was one of the few among the heavily Erdoğan-supporting province who lost faith in this way. At the presidential elections which took place in May, three months after the quakes, 72 per cent of Kahramanmaraş voters backed Erdoğan in the first round, the highest of any of the regions affected by the earthquake, and only two percentage points lower than at the previous poll in 2018. Erdoğan would go on to win in the second round despite widespread predictions that the ailing economy and poor earthquake response could end his rule, just as the Marmara earthquake had helped propel him to power.

Kader believed his victory, at least in Kahramanmaraş, was due to the promises the government had made in the lead up to the election, which the still-desperate residents there clung to for lack of other hope. 'When I went there, I always heard from the villagers and my uncles: "They came here, they visited. They said they would give us a free house." That's what they promised, so they said let's vote for them. With this belief, people voted because despite how many months have passed since the earthquake people are still on the streets. Someone who lives in a tent doesn't have the luxury of not believing them, when they say I will give you peace and give you a house.'

The new house promised to his uncle would supposedly be built on a piece of private land within sight of his home. Kader kept trying to explain to him that there was no legal mechanism by which the government could just give away private land and built free houses for people. 'I said, Uncle, there is no such thing, they cannot give it even if they wanted to, according to the law. He said no, they would. I said, Uncle, it's someone else's land anyway, how can they give it to you? He said they will. I couldn't break his chain of thought. We saw in the election as well, no one could break this chain of thought.'

I wondered if, after his long tenure in power, with his total dominance of the media space and the public narrative, after all the airports and bridges and opening ceremonies, many people fed on a diet of propaganda could no longer conceive that anyone other than the AK Party was capable of building things in Turkey, that they were inevitable, that there was no possible alternative?

Kader himself voted for the opposition candidate, the CHP leader Kemal Kılıçdaroğlu: the same man who, years earlier when Kader had been a child, had headed the Social Security Administration that oversaw the hospital where his mother languished for years after her accident. 'I gave my vote to the strongest opponent,' he said. 'Sadly, that opponent wasn't as strong as we thought he was.'

The Marble Tower

The Marble Tower had changed little from when I'd first stood there several years ago at the outset of my exploration of the walls, but it seemed once more to have moved inland. The coastal highway that once divided it from the walls now lay to the north and its former route was being turned into a park. A group of young workmen, topless in the summer heat, were in the process of retrieving the packed lunches that they'd stowed in the crevices of the tower. The ground around it had recently been resurfaced with fresh rolls of dark green turf, squidgy from the rain of recent days. Its base was plastered with the grey paint that was used all over the city to cover up graffiti, and nettles had grown up in the old cistern, obscuring the rubbish within.

The wide new coastal highway had been built on land claimed from the sea. All along the coast, the city was creeping into the water. A mile or so down the road a huge bulge of land had been added some years earlier, about a quarter of a square mile: a rallying ground with a capacity for 2.5 million people, purpose-built for the massive showings of popular acclaim Erdoğan's regime seemed to crave and require. It had generated outrage when it was first constructed, transforming the shape of the old peninsula. It distended the seahorse head of the old city like a goitre on the underside of its neck. But perhaps it didn't matter – you could only see it on a map, and most people had long since grown accustomed to it; it was just another new thing.

The Sea of Marmara seemed the same as ever; the ships lay stretched out across the horizon, the distant shore of Anatolia visible through the haze, but beneath its sparkling waters troubling changes were taking place. A couple of hundred metres from the tower, on the other side of the highway, I met İhsan Özçakal, head of a small fishermen's cooperative that operated out of the harbour there. Adjacent to the quayside was the Istanbul Fish Museum, its interior comprising a single room not much bigger than a shipping container. Its walls were covered with shelves of preserved fish representing the dozens of species taken from the seas around the city over the past sixty or seventy years. The fish were lit by glaring strip lights, their bloated and milky-eyed remains suspended in tanks and jars of yellowing formaldehyde. One contained a turtle, another the severed head and tail of an enormous tuna; a desiccated swordfish hung from the ceiling. It was a macabre place.

İhsan scanned the rows of tanks, pointing out the species that had disappeared in recent years. There were a lot.

'Scorpion fish – there used to be many of these, so few now . . . İşkine – we still find them but not many . . . *karaca balığı* – that's extinct . . . *mora* is gone, sturgeon is gone . . .'

In total more than forty species in the Sea of Marmara have

either gone commercially extinct or been wiped out entirely. Now in his sixties, İhsan had been fishing in Istanbul since he was thirteen and had witnessed the precipitous decline first-hand.

———

The Sea of Marmara is dying. That reality became dramatically visible in the summer of 2021 when a tide of viscous grey sludge rose up from the depths, carpeting the surface of the water and swamping beaches and harbours around its coasts. Known as mucilage, or 'sea snot', the substance clogged fishing nets and the rudders of boats, rendering the sea almost unnavigable for small craft, and leading to the mass death of sea life through suffocation. It was the result of a phytoplankton bloom and a warning sign of an ecosystem in crisis.

Early on a summer morning I went out with İhsan on his fishing boat, a small vessel that he piloted alone, catching sardines and bonito from a line. He sold his catch at various markets around the old city. As we headed north along the coast, I saw men going for their morning swim off the coastal embankment – skins tanned to walnut, elbows jutting as they picked their way down the rocks to slough off the last vestiges of sleep in the lapping waves. Behind them I saw the remains of the Byzantine sea wall hanging like a scrap of old parchment strung out to dry in the sun.

İhsan smoked and looked at the water. He had a broad, stubbled face with a rough moustache and eyes narrowed as if from a lifetime of squinting at the sun. He always seemed to be smiling. The mucilage had closed the fishery for three months, he told me; it would destroy the engine of any boat that tried to go out in it. Just as damagingly, people had stopped buying fish even after the prevailing winds had blown the mucilage away. Several news reports suggested the pollution in the sea had made the fish dangerous to eat. Luckily the mucilage had not come back this year to the same degree, but now he was worried about jellyfish.

The story of the mucilage started in the 1980s, connecting back to the other end of the land walls, to Tokludede and the Golden Horn and the great cleaning project enacted there by the former mayor, Bedrettin Dalan, so lauded at the time. Dalan oversaw the rerouting of the city's sewage discharge from the Golden Horn into the Sea of Marmara using a process of deep sea pumping, in which the city's waste was piped deep beneath the surface where, it was claimed, the current would carry it through the Bosphorus into the Black Sea, where it would safely sink. Some experts expressed doubt about this at the time, but the cleaning of the Golden Horn, which for years had been a stinking dead zone in the heart of the city, was widely celebrated and few people worried about where all that pollution was now going. The industry that had once befouled the city's natural harbour had also been removed far from sight at the other end of the Sea of Marmara, around the Gulf of İzmit.

But nothing had really changed, except that the Sea of Marmara was a larger body of water than the Golden Horn, and the scale of the problem had become greater. Notionally, Istanbul's sewage plants were processing the waste before it was pumped, but inspections were lax and this was often not the case, and since they were discharging deep under water, no one noticed anyway. In fact, little of it ended up in the Black Sea, with one study suggesting that 90 per cent of pumped waste remained in the Sea of Marmara. When this system was first instituted, the population of Istanbul was around 6 million. By 2021, it was more like 20 million. Meanwhile, the Gulf of İzmit had become Turkey's largest industrial zone, accounting for 13 per cent of the country's output, and was home to its dirtiest industries: scrap metal smelting, paint and cement factories, many of them run by large multinational companies. The Marmara's once-crystal waters had become turbid, with visibility reducing from 8 metres in the 1960s to under 1.5 metres in 2021. Its murkiness meant it absorbed more heat, amplifying the effects of a warming climate and leading to an average temperature rise of 2.5° Celsius.

It had been a place of extraordinary marine wealth, a migratory corridor and ecological transition zone between the Mediterranean and Black Sea. Vast shoals of pelagic fish, such as bluefin tuna, bonito, bluefish and mackerel, poured through the Marmara and the Bosphorus twice a year on their annual migration. Its waters were rich in lobster, mussels, oysters, shrimp and octopus. As late as the 1960s and 1970s, it was possible to catch fish from the quayside simply by lowering a basket into the water. The advent of industrialised fishing with nylon nets and radar caused a glut in supply that saw excess catches dumped in landfill. For several decades the expansion in the size and effectiveness of Turkey's fishing fleet meant that the total catch increased even as overall fish numbers plummeted. It was only in 1999 that catches began to decline. Among the most dramatic extinctions was the bluefin tuna, which used to migrate through the Bosphorus in vast numbers. In the 1950s, a single stationary trap called a *dalyan* could catch between two and three hundred of them, each weighing 300 to 400kg. Their numbers plummeted until, in 1985, the entire migratory spawning group was captured in a single day and exported to Japan. After that the bluefin migration ceased entirely.

The death of the Sea of Marmara was a result of both pollution and overfishing in a relatively small and constricted body of water. Even after the government tried to put curbs on the fishing industry, illegal trawlers continued to raid spawning grounds, using nets that raked up the sea floor, destroying beds of molluscs and important habitats. Invasive species released from the bilge tanks of ships from across the world wrought further damage. As diversity plummeted, the species able to tolerate the pollution and warming waters proliferated in unstable waves of superabundance: some years jellyfish, others years red algae that washed onto the shores in heaps and coloured the water like blood. In 2021, it was a kind of phytoplankton that multiplied wildly thanks to nitrates and phosphates in the water and a dearth of natural predators. The mucilage was the aggregated fluid from the dead phytoplankton cells after this bloom died off.

For months it floated deep in the water column. The first thing anyone knew about it was in November the previous year, when fishermen casting deeper than 30 metres began to bring up nets so loaded with sludge that they were almost impossible to haul in. Some had to be cut and abandoned. Gradually the mucilage absorbed air bubbles until it became buoyant enough to rise to the surface. Throughout the summer, municipal and state authorities engaged in the futile task of trying to manually clean the sea, pulling the mucilage out with long nets and carting it off in municipal garbage trucks to be incinerated. It was a cosmetic measure, meaningless, but the government also promised to introduce tough new controls monitoring the release of waste water from both industry and households into the Marmara.

'It is not possible to rescue the Marmara,' declared Levent Artüz, a hydrologist who led a project monitoring the Sea of Marmara's health, and for years had been warning of its plight, speaking to a Turkish news website at the height of the crisis. 'The Sea of Marmara will find a new path. If we help pave this path, maybe we can ensure that there is a Sea of Marmara that does not smell, that is not pitch black and has only two kinds of fish. But forget the old Marmara completely, it is gone, it was killed, it will not return.'

İhsan was less pessimistic. He believed that if the authorities clamped down on illegal trawling then the fish would come back. Most of his anger at the state of affairs was directed at the illegal trawlers who were going out at night to fish at prohibited times and places. This was when fish populations were particularly vulnerable during spawning season. Once he'd seen a trawler come back in the morning with a catch of undersize bluefish, and he'd confronted the ship's owner.

'I looked at him and said, "Why did you catch all those baby fish?" He just said, "What do you care?" He said that when there are no fish he will fill his boat with earth and turn it into a garden. In the last twenty-five years people became like this: they cannot have enough.'

He believed the authorities were beginning to do more to protect the waters. As we headed towards the Bosphorus we passed a new coastguard station set up two years earlier that allowed them to respond instantly when they had reports of illegal trawlers. They could no longer act with impunity. 'This year the coastguard are very strict . . . They recognise that the sea is dying.' A few months ago they had done something dramatic. They had taken several offending trawlers, lifted them out of the water and destroyed them with a digger. The message had hit home, and the illegal trawling had almost stopped. In the past year, he said, the fishermen had even begun to catch larger bonito, which had grown over a couple of seasons. These were traditionally called *torik*, whereas the smaller, younger fish that were still caught were *palamut*. He said it had been twenty years since he'd caught *torik*, but they'd just begun to appear again.

As the boat chugged along towards the mouth of the Bosphorus I could see the Princes' Islands as blue-grey shadows lying across the glittering water, and to the right of them rose the forbidding silhouette of Sivriada, like a jagged tooth. Unavoidably, it made me think again of the dogs, for the place was indelibly associated with events that unfolded there more than a century earlier, when almost the entirety of Istanbul's dog population was rounded up and dumped on this waterless, uninhabited rock and left to die.

Official attitudes towards the city's street dogs had changed as a reflection of the shifting relationship between the Ottoman Empire and its European neighbours. Over the course of the seventeenth and eighteenth centuries the empire gradually ceased to command the kind of fear and curious admiration that it had in the time of Suleiman the Magnificent, as it was eclipsed by the technological and economic superiority of its Western adversaries. The advancements of the Enlightenment and the Age of Reason brought new ideas and innovations that tore at the fabric of the Ottoman world. At the beginning of the nine-teenth century the Sultan's territories still sprawled from the Atlantic coast of Algeria to the Persian Gulf and from Yemen to Ukraine, but the empire had become weak, indebted and decrepit. Over the following decades the doctrine of modern nationalism wreaked havoc on its multi-ethnic, multi-confessional polity; as the empire's subject Christian peoples started to organise and agitate for self-rule, they found patrons among the European powers jostling to carve up the territories of the so-called 'Sick Man of Europe'.

Europeans began to write about Turkey in a different way. It became a foil against which the Western imagination defined the contours of its own superiority. The Turkish accommodation of street animals came to be seen as a symptom of a hidebound and benighted culture. To visitors from Western countries in which notions of modern public hygiene and municipal management were taking root, the presence of dogs in such large numbers was an obvious health risk, and while earlier writers might have acknowledged the services they provided, in the eyes of nineteenth-century Europeans the job of cleaning and guarding the city should belong to the authorities. Later European writers were reluctant even to acknowledge the Turks' charity, characterising it instead as a kind of infantile whimsy: 'a childish fondness for amusement' in the words of the rabidly xenophobic French diplomat François de Tott. The accounts began to dwell on the leanness of the dogs, on their dirty, mangy coats, on their scars, and even on their supposed laziness, as if they were proxies for the people who tolerated them.

'They hardly seemed to have strength enough or ambition enough to walk across the street,' wrote Mark Twain in the 1860s. 'They are the sorriest beasts that breathe – the most abject – the most pitiful. In their faces is a settled expression of melancholy, an air of hopeless despondency.'

Inevitably, the pace of innovation in Europe forced the Ottomans to question their own ways of doing things. Mounting military defeats and the seeping disruption of new technologies and ideas created an atmosphere of perpetual crisis, with different sections of society divided over both the diagnosis of the problem and its solutions. The empire's political and intellectual elites advocated the adoption of some European innovations, but differed as to how deep reform should go. Meanwhile, within the lower echelons of Muslim society – the clergy and the now-bloated and truculent Janissary corps – it was generally held that the empire's decline derived not from a lack of innovation but from too much of it: a spiritual malaise brought on by adopting the ways of the infidel.

Reforms themselves had the potential to generate resistance and thus deepen instability, even those of obvious expedience such as the efforts by successive sultans to adopt modern European arms and training. Unpopular army reforms brought about the downfall of more than one sultan at the hands of the angry Janissaries, and it was only after Mahmut II used a small corps of newly trained soldiers to massacre and disband them that the way was opened to further reforms. New military academies operating under the guidance of Germans and French would create a different kind of Ottoman officer: heads brimming with the latest ideas from the continent and chests swollen with patriotic zeal and a modern sense of national consciousness. They were like foreigners in their own country, sharing the European disdain for Turkish backwardness with an eagerness that bordered on self-loathing. Unwittingly, the sultans had created the generation of men who would eventually get rid of them.

Before that, though, these Ottoman reformists sought to emulate Europe in a range of matters, including urban management and sanitation. Many of Istanbul's administrators came to share an unfavourable view of the city's dogs. It was Mahmut II, after successfully purging the Janissaries, who first took them on. Amid great resistance, the dogs were rounded up and put on a boat bound for an island in the Sea of Marmara, but while still close to shore the ship met with a violent storm that led to the dogs escaping and swimming back to land; in the city this was widely interpreted as an act of God, and the Sultan relented and let them be. A few decades later Sultan Abdulaziz made another attempt, and had them rounded up and sent to Sivriada. But soon after a fire broke out in the city which, though a common occurrence, was again interpreted as another sign of God's displeasure, and so under popular pressure the dogs once more received a reprieve. The will of the authorities was not yet equal to the strength of feeling on the streets.

In 1908, the class of Westernised military officers finally had their moment, seizing power in a coup d'état against Sultan Abdulhamit II. The Committee of Union and Progress, or the 'Young Turks' as they were widely known were implacable enemies of the city's dogs, regarding their dominion of the streets as emblematic of the filth, superstition and backwardness from which they planned to deliver their country. Their hatred was lent additional animus by the fact that the dogs were especially beloved in the pious neighbourhoods, and so were unwittingly aligned with the social forces against which the Young Turks had pitted themselves. In a screed titled 'The Dogs of Istanbul', Abdullah Cevdet, one of the Young Turks' founders, described Istanbul's street dogs as a source of national shame, demanding: '[h]ow and with what justification can the inhabitants of such a country face the brotherhood of civilised nations?'

Over the following year calls for action grew, and the city's authorities convened to consider their options. There were some, such as the Frenchman Paul Remlinger of Istanbul's Pasteur Institute, who urged an even more radical and comprehensive solution: the systematic gathering up of the dogs by a private concessionary who would take them to purpose-built butchering facilities around the outskirts of the city in which they would be rendered down into raw products that could then be sold for a sum that he estimated at about 200,000 to 300,000 francs. He had described in detail the proposed 'rendering pens' in which the dogs would be destroyed. Remlinger wrote in an article:

> These would include an airtight chamber communicating with a gas pipeline and a butchering workshop provided with what would be necessary for the treatment of usable animal products. The animals would be apprehended discreetly at night and transported to their destination in European-style carriages. Ten rendering pens could each process a hundred dogs a day.

We do not know why the city's leaders rejected this idea, but it is easy to imagine that rendering down the dogs to raw products would be deemed too offensive and inflammatory to the public sentiment, which by and large still afforded them the dignity of personhood. Their solution of sending them to Sivriada seems to betray a sense of guilt. Perhaps they told themselves that this was exile, not death? Perhaps some would survive? And if they did not, they could claim it was the island, not the city's authorities, that had killed them.

The deportations took place in 1910 at the height of summer, with the dogs rounded up at night in order to minimise resistance from the population. In the Christian and European quarters it proceeded with little difficulty, but in the Muslim neighbourhoods opposition was so fierce that brawls erupted between locals and municipal police charged with overseeing the operation. Near the Hagia Sophia, a crowd of people opened up the cages holding the dogs and released them.

'On the evening the operation took place in our neighbourhood none of the drivers of carts which had been requisitioned took part,' wrote P. Columban, an Augustin missionary living in the city. 'They all replied that this was a sin and they preferred going to jail.' In the end the work was mostly carried out by the city's gypsies, who used large wooden tongs to catch the dogs and were paid on a per-animal basis.

After they were taken to the island, the dogs' plight generated the horrified interest of the international press. 'SUFFERING DOGS: THE CANINE EXILES OF CONSTANTINOPLE' read the headline of one Reuters report from October 1910, in which the correspondent described a harrowing trip to Sivriada. Among those who visited the island was the French caricaturist Sem, who described what he saw in an account published in a Parisian newspaper:

[The dogs] crowded and jostled each other on the beach; they climbed on top of each other to reach the water, seeking to refresh their limbs burned by the sun and fever. Many of them swam, fighting in the sea for the carrion floating on all sides. Some, half dead with thirst, tried to drink the salt water. On the ground, a mix of wild dogs tore at corpses. Groups of them, fleeing the bite of the sun, huddled in the shadows afforded by the smallest of outcrops. Others, suffering from a sort of madness, ran about agitatedly as if possessed.

Bands of them were swimming desperately towards us. The yacht was soon surrounded by them. They were close to touching us, trying to cling to the slippery sides of the ship. Many had half-devoured ears, they were covered with hideous wounds, which were brightened by the salt, and left streaks of blood on the clear water.

An Englishwoman, unable to bear the sight of this spectacle, begged the sailors to finish off the dogs.

One kilometre from the island, we still met with wandering groups of these dreadful mutilated swimmers, waving their paws like arms with convulsions of agony, who persisted in following us and ended up drowning in the swirl of the propeller.

———

As İhsan's fishing boat reached the mouth of the Bosphorus a view of the old city unfolded before us. There among the domes stood the Hagia Sophia, the vast basilica built by Emperor Justinian sixteen centuries earlier: a squat, immovable presence on the skyline. From the outside I always thought it looked ungraceful, almost ugly: a mess of jutting buttresses and arches which seemed to loom over you like an Escher drawing as you approached it. It had little of the harmony of the great Ottoman mosques that were built in echo of it, nor the ornamentation of Europe's Gothic cathedrals. It seemed more like a mould than a building, a prototype engine whose external design was wholly subordinated to its inner function.

It was from the inside that its power became clear. You stepped across a marble threshold worn away by fifteen hundred years of human footsteps into a nave so impossibly cavernous it seemed to be a bubble of masonry sustained by the air itself. It was an edifice turned in on itself, proclaiming its wonder not to the world but to those within, to its congregation, and in this respect I found it more spiritual than most of the cathedrals of the West. I often thought of the travel writer Robert Byron's comment, comparing it with the showiness of St Peter's: 'One is a church to God: the other, a salon for his agents.'

It was a treasure house of mosaics. Among them: the emperors Constantine and Justinian offering the city and church to an enthroned Virgin and Child, Leo VI prostrating himself before the Pantokrator, and the face of Christ, penetrating and solemn, flanked by the suffering figures of the Virgin and John the Baptist in the great Deësis created at the first stirrings of the Renaissance. There were the enormous Ottoman roundels that hung about the dome proclaiming the names of Allah, the Prophet, his descendants, and the first caliphs, sunlight glancing off the gold loops of calligraphy.

All this felt incidental to the structure itself. What always struck me was the combination of enormity, age and fragility. The Hagia Sophia was created during a time of plague and economic crisis after its predecessor was destroyed by rioting. At the time of its construction it was the world's largest enclosed space, and remained the world's largest cathedral for a thousand years. Its dome suffered three major or partial collapses, the first soon after it was first built. It was damaged by generations of earthquakes and each time was restored and renewed, first under the aegis of the Byzantine emperors and then the Ottoman sultans. It was not built to defy death but to be sustained by life: the life of the city, of its people and the foresight and governance of its rulers. It had remained at the core of Istanbul's life through all the upheavals of war and the transformations of culture and religion, violent and gradual; it was the stone heart that pumped the city's lifeblood.

Its function had changed according to those times. For sixty years, during the Latin occupation that followed the capture of the city by the Fourth Crusade – a time of neglect and catastrophic decline for the city – it served as a Roman Catholic cathedral. Then following the Ottoman conquest it became a mosque on Mehmet's decree. In 1934, a few years after the fall of the empire, Atatürk transformed it into a museum as part of his drive to secularise Turkey and build stronger ties with Greece, the Balkans and the West.

In July 2020, it had changed function again, when Erdoğan decreed that the Hagia Sophia should once again serve as a mosque. Its status as a museum had been a source of lasting bitterness to Turkey's Islamists and conservative Muslims. He had often signalled that he intended to transform it back to its old status, but had seemed unwilling to follow through on this promise, dangling it like a carrot at times of political pressure, a wrong yet to be righted, a reason to keep faith. And so it was at a moment of particular crisis, as the country was wracked by the Covid pandemic and a deepening economic slump, that he signed a presidential decree to revert the building to a house of worship. It was a decision that provoked condemnation and criticism from secular Turks, as well as from Orthodox Christian leaders, the Pope, UNESCO and the US government among others, who argued it was a divisive move that might damage its status as a place that represented different cultures that offered the possibility of dialogue between religions.

However, it hit on the core themes with which he appealed to his nation: a righting of wrongs and assertion of sovereignty, the twinning of post-colonial grievance with a yearning to recapture post-imperial grandeur. It cast Atatürk's conversion not as a gesture to bridge cultures but as a concession to foreign domination. Moreover, it tied Erdoğan to Mehmet, imagining him as a latter-day conqueror rescuing the city and its talismanic monument from a century of Western cultural influence.

'The resurrection of the Hagia Sophia takes the chains off its doors and the shackles off the hearts and the feet of those who stand alongside it,' Erdoğan said after announcing his decree. After holding the first prayers there a month later, he went straight to Mehmet's tomb at the Fatih Mosque to pay homage.

I had visited it on the second anniversary of its reconversion, along with my wife and our three young children. A long but fasting-moving queue snaked across the square outside it, the flags of tour guides fluttering in the fitful breeze. Vendors sold roast chestnuts and corn cobs. Once you had to pay entry but now, as a mosque, it was free of charge.

On entering, hanging prominently in the narthex were Erdoğan's signed decrees reverting the building to a house of worship, and alongside them a translation of the original document of endowment written by Mehmet after seizing the city. The most striking change was the muffling acoustic effect of the carpets that now covered its marble floors. The mosaics in the tympana on the ground floor were still visible, but the Virgin and Child above the apse were hidden by white curtains, and the upper galleries closed. Across the ocean of carpet there were almost no exhibits or directions, nowhere to go and little to do other than gaze up at the vast shadowy dome. Families sat there taking selfies; toddlers and small children rolled around, shouted and played. The atmosphere was utterly different from the heavy, contemplative silence of a museum, but nor was it like any

house of worship I had been in. Our children began to play
with some Turkish children from a family sitting near us, my
eldest son speaking in broken Turkish to a little girl. I felt a
burst of pride: how long until he would speak it better than
me? The mood of the place was not irreverent, but innocently
recreational, like in a public park. The building felt no less
wondrous but somehow more human, more alive. I felt a kind
of joy – something like the same kind of shared wonder I previously described feeling on public transport in Istanbul, of
partaking in something wondrous and free.

It was not the feeling I had expected, and I felt a little guilty
about it. My wife, who had been so depressed by the conversion she had been unwilling to visit at all, admitted that she
had a similar feeling. There were significant worries within the
archaeological and architectural heritage community about
what long-term effect the conversion of the Hagia Sophia
would have on the building. The number of people visiting it
a year, which rarely exceeded 3 million before its conversion,
surged to 13.6 million in 2022. Some experts have warned that
the moisture from so many people's breath could damage its
interiors, and that the volume of people could damage the
substructure of the building. In spite of the presence of dozens
of security guards, instances of vandalism have taken place,
with plaster chipped from the walls and damage done to the
door of the main Imperial Gate.

When Mehmet's army had finally burst through the walls, on
29 May 1453, it was to the Hagia Sophia that the multitudes of
the terrified populace looked for refuge. As panic set in they
flocked to the great church, pinning their hopes, Doukas claimed,
on a prophecy well known among the people that the city's
invaders would penetrate as far as the column of Constantine,
where an angel would descend with a sword and drive them
away and out of Anatolia entirely. 'In one hour that famous and

enormous church was filled with men and women. An innu-
merable crowd was everywhere: upstairs, downstairs, in the
courtyards, and in every conceivable place. They closed the gates
and stood there, hoping for salvation.'

The Hagia Sophia lay three miles from the land walls. When
they first entered the city, the Ottoman forces – fresh from
combat, addled by the long siege, and believing enemy troops
still lay in reserve – slaughtered everyone they came across. It
was customary for a city that had been captured without
surrender to be given over to the victorious army for three days
of pillaging, and as it became clear that the prize was truly theirs
they turned their attention to looting, raping and taking captives.

'Their soldiers ran eagerly through [the city], putting to the
sword all who resisted, slaughtering the aged and the feeble-
minded, the lepers and the infirm, while they spared those of
the rest who surrendered to them,' wrote Bishop Leonardo, who
was himself taken prisoner, bound and beaten. Churches and
monasteries were plundered and houses emptied of their riches.
The city's holiest talisman, the icon of the Virgin Hodogetria,
kept at the Chora Monastery close to the walls, was hacked into
four pieces and divided up as loot.

The Venetian surgeon Nicolò Barbaro, who had been fighting
on the land walls but succeeded in escaping to his ship in the
harbour, described how the invaders would tie a banner to each
house to indicate it had been plundered. '[A]nd so they put
their flags everywhere, even on the monasteries and churches.
As far as I can estimate, there would have been two hundred
thousand of these flags flying on the houses all over Constantinople:
some houses had as many as ten, because of the excitement
which the Turks felt at having won such a great victory.'

It was still only seven in the morning when the first Ottoman
troops arrived at the Hagia Sophia to hack down its barred
doors with axes. Inside a service of matins was being held,

the men and women of the congregation taking their appropriate places. That was how Byzantium ended: in a series of contracting circles, from empire to city state, from the circuit of the walls to the bounds of the huge edifice that had formed its spiritual heart, in which the illusion of normality and the hope of deliverance were preserved even as that collapse reached its crescendo.

The congregation were herded off 'like sheep' into captivity, in Doukas's telling. Each soldier claimed his own captive, and there were so many that they came back for a second or a third. 'Within one hour they had bound everyone, the male captives with cords and the women with their own veils. The infinite chains of captives who like herds of kine and flocks of sheep poured out of the temple and the temple sanctuary made an extraordinary spectacle! They wept and wailed and there was none to show them mercy.'

Similar scenes played out across the city, as pockets of resistance were mopped up, and civilians dragged out of their homes and churches. A few fled to the Christian fleet lying in the harbour, desperately swimming out to the boats which became loaded with refugees. These included the Florentine merchant Jacopo Tetaldi, who stripped off his armour and swam out in time to see those following him caught by the Turks on the shoreline. The crews of the Turkish fleet, seeing the city had fallen and not wanting to miss out on the plunder, had abandoned their boats. The Christian fleet waited until midday, as long as they dared for those of their officers and crew still missing, before cutting the boom across the Horn and fleeing.

Kritovoulos gives the total number of defenders and civilians taken prisoner as 50,000, along with 4,000 dead in the final battle and sack, although these numbers must be inflated as they would exceed the population of the city at the time. Captives were either retained by those who captured them or taken and sold to slave dealers who had set up markets in the Ottoman camp. Among those captured was the young scholar Ubertino Posculo, who was later ransomed, and Cardinal Isidore, who was wounded in the face with an arrow close to the Hagia Sophia. As a senior member of the defence forces he was a valuable captive, but succeeded in hiding his identity by swapping his sacred robes with the garb of a dead civilian. His identity unknown, he was able to buy his freedom on the spot and then hid for ten days in Pera, hunted by Mehmet's forces, before escaping – improbably – on a Turkish galley. Bishop Leonardo too managed to escape within a few hours of being captured, probably also by hiding his identity. He even managed to buy a few religious texts he saw being sold on the day of the fall before escaping on a Western ship.

A number of prominent officials on both sides were executed on Mehmet's orders. Among them was Loukas Notaras, a senior Byzantine noble who was beheaded along with his children, and Halil Paşa, Mehmet's father's right-hand man against whose tutelage the young sultan had chafed for most of his life. Halil was arrested just three days after the fall of the city and imprisoned at Edirne, where he was executed a month later. His death marked the end of the power struggle between aristocratic traditionalists and *devşirme* expansionists that had simmered in the Ottoman court over the previous decades, leaving the triumphant Mehmet and his *devşirme* advisors in total control.

The emperor Constantine's close confidant George Sphrantzes was captured along with his wife, son and daughter. He himself was ransomed a few months later, but his wife and children remained slaves 'in the possession of some elderly Turks, who did not treat them badly'. He managed to buy his wife's freedom, but his children's youth and good breeding attracted the attention of Mehmet's court, and they were purchased into the imperial seraglio. His fourteen-year-old son John was executed soon afterwards (by Mehmet personally, he claimed) 'on the grounds that the child had conspired to murder him'. Two years later, 'my beautiful daughter Thamar died of an infectious disease in the sultan's seraglio. Alas for me, her wretched father! She was fourteen years and five months.' These personal tragedies are sparsely noted in Sphrantzes's autobiographical chronicle of the calamitous final years of the Byzantine Empire, a painful, laconic and self-lacerating account that he wrote years later after withdrawing to a monastery on Corfu, where he died at the age of seventy-six. It opens:

> I am George Sphrantzes, the pitiful First Lord of the Imperial Wardrobe, presently known by my monastic name Gregory. I wrote the following account of the events that occurred during my wretched life. It would have been fine for me not to have been born or to have perished in childhood. Since this did not happen, let it be known that I was born on Tuesday, 30 August 1401.

The fate of Constantine remained shrouded in mystery. It is almost certain that he died, but how and where are unknown; most accounts suggest he was killed somewhere near the St Romanos Gate – Topkapı – in the moments after the Ottoman forces broke through and routed the defenders, but the sources diverge on whether he died fighting, fleeing, or was crushed and trampled in the scrum of defenders escaping through the postern left open after Giustiniani's departure. Tetaldi, the Florentine merchant, summarised the situation succinctly: 'The Emperor of Constantinople was killed,' he wrote. 'Some say that his head was cut off, and others that he died in the press at the gate; both stories may very well be true.' He may have removed his imperial insignia, which would have made identifying his body more difficult. After the sack Mehmet tried to confirm his fate and although a head was brought to him that was stuffed with straw and sent round the Islamic courts of the Middle East, some doubt remained as to whether it was actually Constantine's.

In this way a myth was born that would persist for centuries, linking him back to the prophecies in the Apocalypse of Pseudo-Methodius, which foretold that a last Roman emperor would arise to defeat the enemies of Christendom and herald the Apocalypse. Future generations of Greeks clung to the hope that he was sleeping beneath the Golden Gate, turned to stone, waiting for his time to return.

Mehmet entered Constantinople in triumph at around midday. During the course of the long and bloody siege he had dangled the promise of plunder before his men but he was so concerned at the destruction he saw around him that he may even have called an early end to the customary three days of pillaging, although the eyewitness accounts generally contradict this. It may simply have been that the city was so impoverished there was little left to plunder.

Both the chronicle of Nestor-Iskander and the history compiled by Doukas describe the moment he arrived at the Hagia Sophia, and in both accounts it is an encounter that impresses him with awe and reverence. According to Nestor-Iskander, on arriving at the church, '[he] dismounted from his horse, and fell to the ground upon his face; he took earth and sprinkled it over his head, thanking God.' Inside he found some of those who had been sheltering in the church still hiding, and in a spontaneous act of charity ordered his soldiers to allow them to leave unmolested. In Doukas's telling, he enters the church and berates one of his own soldiers who he finds hacking up a marble pavement – a rare moment in which the viscerally anti-Turkish chronicler portrays Mehmet in a positive light. Whatever truth there is behind these accounts, they are consistent in depicting his entrance to the great edifice as a moment in which he ceases to be a despoiler of the city and people and becomes their protector.

According to Tursun Beg, he would later ascend through the galleries of the church up to its dome, from where he looked out across the city that he now ruled and which would become the heart of his empire. Seeing the ruins of the original imperial palace, long since derelict: 'he thought of the impermanence and instability of this world and of its ultimate destruction', and quoted a couplet relating to the destruction of the Persian Empire by the Arabs in the seventh century:

> *The spider is curtain-bearer in the palace of Chosroes*
> *The owl sounds the relief in the castle of Afrasayib.*

In spite of the bitterness and hatred directed at him by the Christian world, Mehmet would pour prodigious energy into reviving Constantinople and re-establishing it as a great imperial city. Schooled in classical history, he saw himself as the inheritor of the Roman emperors as well as the holy warrior of Islam. Under his rule the city would be flooded with artisans and builders, but also injected with new life in the form of Greek and Armenian Christians who were brought in to repopulate the long-ruined metropolis. He styled himself as the protector of Greek Orthodoxy, appointing as a new patriarch the anti-unionist firebrand Gennadios, who had previously harrowed the citizenry with his warnings against union with Rome. He assigned different soldiers and leaders from his army to various districts, tasking them with restoring and maintaining the areas under their purview. And so the city rose once more as a new imperial capital, the great mosques that were built by him and his successors taking as their prototype the basilica built by

Justinian and in which the call to prayer was first declared
on the day of the Conquest.

———

İhsan cut his engine and cast out the lines near the Maiden's
Tower, not far from the junction of the Bosphorus and the
Golden Horn. Sarayburnu, the tip of the old city where the
Topkapı Palace stood, was perhaps the last place in Istanbul that
retained a feeling of a city in harmony with the natural world,
where the predominant colours were still the white marble of
the palace buildings and the green of the trees in its grounds.
I thought of the description of Constantinople attributed to
Osman, the Ottoman progenitor who foresaw his empire's rise
in a dream: 'That city, placed at the junction of two seas and
two continents, seemed like a diamond set between two sapphires
and two emeralds.'

I also thought of Tanpınar's praise for the great Ottoman
architects instructed by Mehmet and his successors to create the
mosques which would come to define the city's skyline. 'The
true success of our old masters lies in their ability to create a
union with nature,' he wrote in *Five Cities*. 'With the exception
of the mosques of Istanbul, there is very little architecture where
the mechanical function of stone and the enduring strength of
form can be ignored; very few buildings surrender so delightfully
as those of Istanbul to the play of light, to be reborn and renewed
at every moment.' The Istanbul of his earliest memory, already
fading in his own time, was a city of fountains of crystal water,
of plane trees and groves of cypresses, of bounteous seas and
wooded hills, adorned with 'monuments that stand simply as
they are, like a naked human body'.

I felt an uncertain longing for that city; I wanted to believe
it had existed, that it was not always an illusion, that there had

not been some hidden cost in it, some imbalance. Was it ever real? Could it be again?

İhsan reeled in his line; now and then a sardine emerged from the water, dancing and flipping on the plastic thread. I watched as he clamped a silver fish between his thumb and finger, unhooked it and cast it into a dark tank of water in the hold, where it darted around for a moment before pausing to take stock of its surroundings. I thought of Meral and her dogs at the animal shelter, of Alev, the burned pitbull, her body skipping and writhing like the fish on the hook; I thought of the *bostans*; of the ailanthus springing from the cracks in the concrete; I thought of Kader, and Cem, and Fırat, and Yurdanur, and the men of the teahouse, and the near-inexhaustible strength that ran through them all: each fighting for their way through the world. Overhead, a gull passed by and glanced down at us with an imperious scowl. It shook its body in mid-flight like a wet dog. Further off, a flock of cormorants seemed to drape a lighthouse in rags, and out at sea more tankers were arriving, engines like pyres, threading smoke into the morning air.

Acknowledgements

To The City has been long in the works, and there are many people to whom I owe thanks: firstly, to the editors and foreign staff at *The Times*, especially the late Richard Beeston, who gave me an opportunity in Istanbul that set me on this road; also, to the team at *The White Review*, who gave me a venue to develop my writing.

My agent Peter Straus agreed to represent me when this book was a barely-formed idea; without him it would not have arrived in the hands of the passionate and dedicated team at William Collins. Commissioning editor Arabella Pike's enthusiasm and insightful feedback helped me pull the manuscript together, and her patience and pressure pushed it over the finish line. I am grateful also to editorial assistant Sam Harding, publicity manager Laura Meyer, editor Alex Gingell, copy editor Martin Bryant and proof-reader Jane Donovan. I was blown away by Jo Thomson's cover design, and the chapter illustrations created by Joe McLaren are a wonderful accompaniment.

I thank those people who read all or part of the manuscript

and offered invaluable feedback: John Angliss, William Armstrong, Nick Danforth, Oya Erez, Dov Friedman, Olivia Heal and Barbara Neil. I was buoyed early on by the enthusiasm of Piotr Zalewsky and Dan Dombey, journalists whose work I have long admired. Writing is a lonely and often demoralising process, and for helping me through it I thank Cathy Nottingham; also Chris Elliot, Steve Jones and everyone at Norwich Last Stand, for providing some much-needed diversion.

Few shared this path more closely with me than the friends, translators, and fixers who helped conduct many of the interviews and were often sounding boards for my ideas. They are Reyhan Baysan, Ece Bulut, Selçuk Erez, Elvan Kıvılcım, Gülten Sarı, Shadi Türk, and Barış Yazıcı. In particular I want to thank Heval Okçuoğlu for her extraordinary passion and dedication to this project over the course of years; and Batu Boran, who accompanied me on so many adventures along the walls, offering his deep insights on our encounters. It is a source of lasting sadness to me that his sudden death in the summer of 2023 meant he never saw the fruits of our labour.

I want to thank my parents-in-law, Selçuk and İrem, on whose hospitality I often relied when visiting Istanbul; both of you have forever made the city a home to me. I must also mention the love and support of my parents; becoming a parent myself has made me understand the depth of what they have given me. The arrival of Haldun, Reyhan and Raif certainly extended the gestation of 'To The City', but they lent me reserves of strength and joy that helped me see it through. Most of all, my wife Oya has lived with and shared the weight of this endeavour more than anyone, believed in me, and been my first and finest editor.

Finally, I would like to thank the people whose stories I have tried to relate. My gratitude to them is not just for the trust and patience they showed in allowing me into their lives, but also for inspiring me and renewing my faith in the future of Turkey.

List of Illustrations

FIRST PLATE SECTION

View of the Theodosian land walls (Deutsches Archäologisches Institut)

Modern view of the land walls (Koç University Sevgi Gönül Center for Byzantine Studies (GABAM), Istanbul City Walls Project)

İsmet Hezer (Alexander Christie- Miller)

Forests of apartment blocks (towfiqu Barbhuiya / Alamy Stock Photo)

Street dogs being fed (Chronicle / Alamy Stock Photo)

Street dogs being sleeping (Joerg Boethling / Alamy Stock Photo)

Medallion (Granger / Bridgeman Images)

Portrait of Mehmet II (CPA Media Pte Ltd / Alamy Stock Photo)

Visitors at Istanbul's Panorama 1453 Historical Museum (Bradley Secker)

Recep Tayyip Erdoğan during his youth (Yusuf)

Erdoğan as prime minister (REUTERS)

Ceyda Süngür (REUTERS)

Demonstrators at the Gezi Park protests (Alexander Christie- Miller)
Celebratory flares over Taksim Square (Alexander Christie- Miller)
The third bridge over the Bosphorus, (Tminaz / Alamy Stock Photo)
A modern view of the land walls near to Edirnekapı (Yusuf Aslan / Alamy Stock Photo)

SECOND PLATE SECTION

The Golden Gate (Koç University Sevgi Gönül Center for Byzantine Studies (GABAM), Istanbul City Walls Project)
Bust of Emperor Theodosius II (Fine Art / Getty images)
A painting of the siege of Constantinople (Science History Images / Alamy Stock Photo)
Erdoğan delivers a speech to the nation (YouTube/Habertürk TV Canlı Yayın)
A demonstrator uses his belt (Getty Images / Stringer)
Rioters destroy Greek businesses (Public domain)
Kurds displaying nationalist symbols (Alexander Christie- Miller)
Newly constructed highways (tekinturkdogan / Getty images)
Land allocated for developmentof Istanbul's new airport (Bloomberg / Getty images)
The airport under construction (Associated Press / Alamy Stock Photo)
Bostan market gardens (OZGUR TOLGA ILDUN / Alamy Stock Photo)
Destroyed buildings in Kahramanmaraş (Xinhua / Alamy Stock Photo)
Municipal vessels attempt to clean (Anadolu / Contributor)
The Hagia Sophia (Anadolu / Getty images)
Erdoğan attends the first official prayers at the Hagia Sophia (Handout / Getty images)

Notes

THE MARBLE TOWER

7 – . . . *Greek* stin polin: *'in/at/to the city'*: Stachowski, M. & Woodhouse, R., 'The Etymology of Istanbul: Making Optimal Use of the Evidence', in *Studia Etymologica Cracoviensia*, vol. 20, pp.221–45.

CHAPTER 1: THE TANNERS' GATE

17 – . . . *new from the foundations*: Van Millingen, A., *Byzantine Constantinople*, p.102.

19 – . . . *off our waste*: Morey, F., *Dogs: Domestication and the Development of a Social Bond*, pp.71–4.

19 – . . . *in response to a poorer diet*: ibid., pp.76–7.

20 – . . . *offered to the loneliness of man as a species*: Berger, J., *About Looking*, p.6.

20 – . . . *to this then-isolated spot*: Ervak, B.(ed.), *The Other Side of the City Walls: Zeytinburnu*, p.71.

21 – . . . *the scent quite upsets them*: Freely, J., and Sumner-Boyd, H., *Strolling Through Istanbul*, p.341.

22 – . . . *such actions as entirely pious*: de Busbecq, O.G., trans. Forster, E.S., *Turkish Letters*, p.114.

22 – . . . *the bounds of their rule*: ibid., p.60.

22 – . . . *the forms of the body, which would be better hidden*: ibid., p.61.

23 – . . . *to rescue him from the furore*: ibid., pp.115–16.

23 – . . . *among them by commons*: Thevénot J., *The Travels of Monsieur Thevénot into the Levant*, p.51.

24 – . . . *uneaten food a sin*: Işın, E., *Everyday Life in Istanbul*, pp.220–21.

24 – . . . *innocent creatures find their subsistence?*: Oliver, G.A., *Travels in the Ottoman Empire*, p.69.

CHAPTER 2: THE BURIED GATE

40 – . . . *church bells of the Balkans*: Crowley, Roger, *Constantinople: The Last Great Siege, 1453*, p.89.

40 – . . . *women to abort*: Doukas, trans. Magoulias, H.J., *The Decline and Fall of Byzantium to the Ottoman Turks*, p.201.

40 – . . . *withstood them at all*: Kritovoulos, M., trans. Riggs, C.T., *History of Mehmed the Conqueror*, p.45.

43 – . . . *crown at the back of his head*: Runciman, S., *1453: The Fall of Constantinople*, Plate IIb.

43 – . . . *went to war at sixteen*: Babinger, F., *Mehmed the Conqueror and his Time*, p.51.

45 – . . . *philosophy and the sciences*: Runciman, p.56.

46 – . . . *who burned him alive*: Runciman, ibid., p.56.

46 – . . . *before Mehmet granted them one*: Babinger, pp.35–6.

46 – . . . *encouraging the boy's dreams of conquest*: İnalcık, H., 'Mehmed the Conqueror (1432–1481) and His Time', *Speculum*, vol. 35, pp.410–11.

47 – . . . *eagerly accepted their terms*: Doukas, p.189.

47 – . . . *I stood speechless*: Sphrantzes, G., trans. Philippides, M., *The Fall of the Byzantine Empire*, p.59.

48 – . . . *prove an important ally*: Doukas, pp.188–9.

48 – . . . *continue to be detained there*: Runciman, pp.60–61.

48 – . . . *its design and construction*: Kritovoulos, pp.19–21.

49 – . . . *whom he hoped to emulate and exceed*: Runciman, p.56.

49 – . . . *the captain impaled and publicly displayed as a warning to others*: Doukas, p.201.

50 – . . . *had not yet attained but had in mind, as if they already had it*: Kritovoulos, p.26.

50 – . . . *also have been honestly held*: Doukas, p.193.

50 – . . . *he both desires and is determined to accomplish*: ibid., p.196.

CHAPTER 3: THE GATE OF SAINTS

55 – . . . *major American and European cities*: Lepeska, D., 'How Istanbul Became one of Europe's Safest Cities', Bloomberg, February 2012.

57 – . . . *Ottoman citizen was shaped*: Mardin, Ş., 'Religion and Secularism in Turkey', in *The Modern Middle East: A Reader*, eds. Hourani, A., Khoury, P. & Wilson, M., p.368.

58 – . . . *impossible in the old neighbourhoods*: Gül, M., *The Emergence of Modern Istanbul*, p.119.

58 – . . . *should be demolished and rebuilt*: ibid., pp.80–1.

58 – . . . *their way to the cities*: ibid., p.114.

60 – . . . *and Republic of Ireland*: Statistica, 'Annual per capita tea consumption worldwide as of 2016'.

61 – . . . *religious or temporal authority*: Işın, p.276.

61 – . . . *the Golden Horn*: ibid., p.273.

61 – . . . *of historian Ekrem Işın*: ibid., p.276.

62 – . . . *impoverished part of the country*: Beller-Hann, I. & Hann, C., *Turkish Region*, pp.48–51.

68 – . . . *metres of fabric*: Gül, M., *Emergence of Modern Istanbul*, pp.36–7.

69 – . . . *rackets or brothels*: Deal, R., *Crimes of Honor, Drunken Brawls and Murder: Violence in Istanbul under Abdülhamid II*, pp.78–9.

69 – . . . *nineteenth-century kabadayıs*: Yeşilgöz, Y. & Bovenkerk, F., 'Urban Knights & Rebels in the Ottoman Empire', in *Organised Crime in Europe*, eds. Fijnaut, C. & Pauli, L, p.214.

71 – . . . *of Turkish citizenship*: Öktem, K., *Angry Nation: Turkey since 1989*, pp.59–60.

74 – . . . *cafés, and beaches*: Gül, M., *Architecture & the Turkish City*, pp.59–62.

78 – . . . *frailties are erased*: Hoş, M., *Big Boss*, p.17.

79 – . . . *the next day*: Yılmaz, T., TAYYİP: Kasımpaşa'dan Siyasetin Ön Saflarına, quoted in Hoş, p.18.

79 – . . . *was banned following the coup*: Sontag, D., 'The Erdoğan Experiment', *New York Times*, May 2003.

CHAPTER 4: THE CANNON GATE

91 – . . . *'remarkable revolution in health'*: the foregoing details of Turkey's health system and AK Party reforms are drawn from Yılmaz, V., *The Politics of Healthcare in Turkey*.

97 – . . . *the Conqueror is reality*: Kemal, Y., Aziz İstanbul, p.83.

98 – . . . *dark, awe-inspiring spirituality*: Tanpınar, A.H., *Five Cities*, trans. Christie, R., p.151.

99 – . . . *gleams like the eye of a frog*: ibid., p.151.

99 – . . . *threshold we had stood hesitating for a hundred years*: ibid., p.121.

100 – . . . *so to speak, in this hovel*: Kemal, Y., *Allah'ın Askerleri*, p.74.

103 – . . . *the constitutional institution in Turkey*: BBC, 'Profile: Fethullah Gülen's Hizmet Movement', December 2013.

103 – . . . *100 charter schools in the United States*: Christie-Miller, A., 'The Gulen movement: a self-exiled imam challenges Turkey's Erdogan', *Christian Science Monitor*, December 2013.

CHAPTER 5: THE GATE OF THE RIVEN TOWER

116 – . . . *quickly so strong a citadel*: Van Millingen, A., *Byzantine Constantinople*, p.47.

117 – . . . *dollars and forty-five cents*: Kinzer, S., 'Turkey's Political Earthquake', *Middle East Quarterly*, Fall 2001.

119 – . . . *Architects and Urban Planners*: Winter, C., 'Istanbul unprepared for next big deadly earthquake: experts', *Deutsche Welle*, August 2019.

120 – . . . *the conquering of hearts*: Singer, S.R., 'Behind Gezi Park', *American Interest*, August 2013.

123 – . . . *joined the demonstrations*: 'Gezi Park protests: Brutal denial of the right to peaceful protest in Turkey', Amnesty International, October 2013.

123 – . . . *to revive history there*: Singer, S.R., 'Behind Gezi Park', *American Interest*, August 2013.

125 – . . . *by 1° Celsius*: Finkel, Andrew, 'The Bridge to Nowhere', *New York Times*, November 2011.

125 – . . . *be 'the murder of the city'*: Letsch, C., 'Plan for new Bosphorus bridge sparks row over future of Istanbul', *Guardian*, June 2012.

125 – . . . *will reject the rejection'*: Vardar, N., 'Başbakan'ın Topçu Kışlası Israrı', Bianet, February 2013.

125 – . . . *he had become the 'master'*: Altüncü, Ö. & Arslan Ö.,
'Başbakan: "2011'de ustalık dönemi başlayacak"', *Hürriyet*, April 2011.
126 – . . . *desire to stay in power*: quoted in Christie-Miller, A.,
'Occupy Gezi: From the fringes to the centre, and back again', *The
White Review*, July 2013.
127 – . . . *reduced women's childbearing capacity*: Christie-Miller, A.,
'Caesareans are plot to stop our nation's growth, claims Erdogan',
The Times, May 2012.
127 – . . . *religious youth in the country*: Butler, D., 'Turkey lifts
headscarf ban in religious schools', Reuters, November 2012.
129 – . . . *look like police and protesters*: Christie-Miller, A., 'Occupy
Gezi', *The White Review*, July 2013
131 – . . . *It is not necessary to make a big deal out of this*: 'Testimony
Project: Roboski Massacre', StateCrime.org.
133 – . . . *six women were dead*: Marcus, A., *Blood and Belief: The PKK
and the Kurdish Fight for Independence*, p.115.
134 – . . . *Kurdish problem is my problem*: Christie-Miller, A., 'The
PKK and the Closure of Turkey's Kurdish Opening', The Middle
East Report, August 2010.
135 – . . . *try to prevent the freedom of the people in the streets*: 'Turkey
Deputy PM apologises to Gezi Park protesters', BBC, June 2013.
135 – . . . *got the well-intended message*: 'President Gül: "The state got
the well-intended messages from the people"', *Daily Sabah*, June
2013.
136 – . . . *we will crush Taksim!*: Christie-Miller, A., 'Occupy Gezi',
The White Review, July 2013.
137 – . . . *being responsible for his death*: 'Erdogan makes crowd boo
Berkin Elvan's family', Al-Monitor, March 2014.

CHAPTER 6: THE GOLDEN GATE
140 – . . . *now-lost inscription had proclaimed*: Van Millingen, A.,
Byzantine Constantinople, p.60.
141 – . . . *vigour of memorable crimes*: Gibbon, E., *The History of the
Decline and Fall of the Roman Empire*, Volume III, p.24.
143 – . . . *art and architecture has vanished*: Ash, J., *A Byzantine
Journey*, p.19.
144 – . . . *walls would soon be necessary*: Bogdanović, J., 'The
Relational Spiritual Geopolitics of Constantinople, the Capital of

the Byzantine Empire', in *Political Landscapes of Capital Cities*, eds. Bogdanović, Christie, & Guzmán, p.106.

145 – . . . *time in four hundred years*: Van Millingen, A., *Byzantine Constantinople*, pp.67–8.

147 – . . . *and marry in the city*: Tafur, P., *Travels and Adventures 1435–1439*, pp.117–25.

147 – . . . *the place where these relics were kept*: de Clavijo, R.G., *Embassy to Samarkand*, pp.31–2.

148 – . . . *empire most sorely needed*: Runciman, S., *1453: The Fall of Constantinople*, p.1.

149 – . . . *weren't required to insert them into their daily creed*: Crowley, R., *Constantinople: The Last Great Siege, 1453*, p.68.

149 – . . . *souls and hastened their downfall*: ibid., p.68.

150 – . . . *Bulgaria, Russia, and the Ottomans*: Nicol, D.M., *The Immortal Emperor*, p.5.

151 – . . . *its inhabitants into slavery*: Babinger, F., *Mehmed the Conqueror and his Time*, pp.49–50.

152 – . . . *vain hope of help from the Franks*: Crowley, R., *Constantinople: The Last Great Siege, 1453*, pp.69–70.

152 – . . . *the words of the historian Doukas*: Doukas, *The Decline and Fall of Byzantium to the Ottoman Turks*, p.210.

152 – . . . *Woe to you when you are judged!*: ibid., p.204.

152 – . . . *700 trained fighting men*: Runciman, S., *1453: The Fall of Constantinople*, pp.83–4.

152 – . . . *supply of excellent military equipment*: ibid., p.211.

153 – . . . *criticised by some of the survivors*: Melville Jones, J.R., *The Siege of Constantinople 1453: Seven Contemporary Accounts*, p.30.

153 – . . . *known only to the emperor and myself*: Sphrantzes, *The Fall of the Byzantine Empire*, p.69.

CHAPTER 7: THE GATE OF THE DERVISH LODGE

158 – . . . *rival factions over the preceding days*: '37 Years After Maraş Massacre', Bianet, December 2015.

159 – . . . *intellectuals, poets, and musicians*: Öktem, K., *Angry Nation: Turkey since 1989*, pp.96–8.

177 – . . . *and science in Turkey's OECD rankings*: 'Turkey's education problems revealed in OECD-wide education test PISA', *Hürriyet Daily News*, December 2016.

178 – . . . *among the least competitive academically*: 'Rise of Islamic schools causes alarm in secular Turkey', Agence France Presse, December 2014.

181 – . . . *the second highest after New York*: Aşıcıoğlu, F., et al., 'Investigation of temporal illicit drugs, alcohol and tobacco trends in Istanbul city: Wastewater analysis of 14 treatment plants', *Water Research Journal*, Volume 190, February 2021.

CHAPTER 8: THE GATE OF THE MARTYRS

187 – . . . *been an insurrection*: 'Başbakan Binali Yıldırım'dan açıklama', NTV, July 2016.

189 – . . . *dismissed from office,' it declared*: '"Yurtta Sulh Konseyi": Yönetime el koyduk', *Evrensel*, July 2016.

189 – . . . *Until today, I have not seen a force greater than the people's will.*: 'Erdoğan: Milletimi meydanlara davet ediyorum', BBC, July 2016.

191 – . . . *'We want executions.'*: 'Erdoğan'ı karşılayan halk idam istiyor!' Yeni Akit, July 2016.

192 – . . . *2,200 were wounded*: Ibrahim, A., 'What was Turkey's failed coup about – and what's happened since?', Al Jazeera, July 2022.

192 – . . . *state once and for all*: 'Cumhurbaşkanı Erdoğan: Vatana ihanet hareketinin bedelini çok ağır ödeyecekler', Anadolu Ajansı, July 2016.

193 – . . . *elements once and for all*: ibid.

205 – . . . *many as 75,000 people*: Bowcott, O., 'Turks detained for using encrypted app "had human rights breached"', *Guardian*, September 2017.

204 – . . . *criminally responsible for his fate*: documents provided to the author by Tülay Açıkkollu.

204 – . . . *leaked to a pro-AKP newspaper*: Karaman, N., 'İşte FETÖ yalanlarının perde arkası! Gökhan Açıkkollu hem mahrem imam hem ByLock'çu çıktı', *Sabah*, March 2018.

205 – . . . *considered as a contributing factor*: report provided to the author by Tülay Açıkkollu.

206 – . . . *initiated by Erdoğan in 2009*: Christie-Miller, A., 'The PKK and the Closure of Turkey's Kurdish Opening', *The Middle East Report*, August 2010.

208–9 – . . . *of the country's public employees*: Solaker, G., Toksabay, E.,

'Turkey's emergency rule expires as Erdogan's powers expand', Reuters, July 2018.

209 – . . . *total value of more than $11bn*: 'Turkey takes control of nearly 1,000 companies since failed coup: deputy PM', Reuters, July 2017.

209 – . . . *were shut down by decree*: Akyol, K., 'Turkey: "Worst country" for media freedom in 2016', Deutsche Welle, December 2016.

218 – . . . *our own homes,' it concluded*: Pamuk, O., 'Orhan Pamuk's manifesto for museums', *Art Newspaper*, July 2016.

CHAPTER 9: THE PROPHESIED GATE

225 – . . . *bristlecone pines show signs of exceptional frost*: NASA Jet Propulsion Laboratory, 'JPL Confirms 15th Century Volcanic Eruption', December 1993.

226 – . . . *but it was actually a red refraction in the hazy atmosphere after sunset*: Olson, D.W., Doescher, R.L & Olson, M.S., 'When the sky ran red: The story behind the "Scream"', *Sky & Telescope*, 107(2), pp.28–35.

226 – . . . *leaving its people to their fate*: Nestor-Iskander, *The Tale of Constantinople*, trans. Hanak, W. & Philippides, M., p.63.

227 – . . . *laying waste to the fields' beyond the city*: Posculo, U., *Constantinopolis*, trans. Whitchurch, B.A., p.93.

228 – . . . *until the [Forum of the] Ox*: Kraft, A., 'Constantinople in Byzantine Apocalyptic Thought', *Annual of Medieval Studies at CEU*, vol. 18, pp.25–36.

228 – . . . *or Tekfürsarayı, which abuts them*: Van Millingen, A., *Byzantine Constantinople*, pp.89–94.

230 – . . . *followers who had come in hope of plunder*: Barbaro, N., *Diary of the Siege of Constantinople*, trans. Melville Jones, J.R., p.27

231 – . . . *to the Pope a few weeks after the siege*: Melville Jones, J.R. *The Siege of Constantinople 1453: Seven Contemporary Accounts*, p.15.

231 – . . . *Oh, the wickedness of denying Christ in this manner!*: ibid., p.16.

232 – . . . *hole falling earthward in a dense mass*: Posculo, U., *Constantinopolis*, p.97.

232 – . . . *thick enough to be able to withstand it*: Kritovoulos, *History of Mehmed the Conqueror*, p.45.

232 – . . . *eleven hands in circumference*: Melville Jones, J.R., *The Siege of Constantinople 1453: Seven Contemporary Accounts*, p.16.

233 – . . . *smoked out or flooded*: ibid., pp.17–18.

233 – . . . *earth and barrels piled together*: ibid., p.17.

234 – . . . *and they patch up the hole*: Posculo, U., *Constantinopolis*, p.99.

234 – . . . *who fought among the defenders*: Melville Jones, *The Siege of Constantinople: Seven Contemporary Accounts*, p.7.

234 – . . . *as 'the guardian of all our fortunes'*: ibid., p.29.

234 – . . . *fustae, low boats crewed by teams of rowers*: Barbaro, N., *Diary of the Siege of Constantinople*, pp.30–31.

235 – . . . *having by day and by night to stand to our arms.'*: ibid., p.31.

235 – . . . *vessels of these evil dogs.'*: ibid., p.33.

236 – . . . *observe the sea far and wide.'*: Posculo, U., *Constantinopolis*, p.107.

236 – . . . *happiness and fear,' wrote Posculo*: ibid., pp.107–9.

236 – . . . *and encouragement to his men*: Doukas, *The Decline and Fall of Byzantium to the Ottoman Turks*, pp.213–14.

237 – . . . *so that this victory is assured.'*: Pertusi, A., *La Caduta di Constantinopoli*, pp.301–3.

239 – . . . *Tetaldi, the Florentine merchant*: Melville Jones, *The Siege of Constantinople: Seven Contemporary Accounts*, p.5.

239 – . . . *a mixture of impiety and cruelty.'*: Melville Jones, *The Siege of Constantinople: Seven Contemporary Accounts*, p.24.

239 – . . . *because it seemed to us that our victory was assured'.*: Melville Jones, *The Siege of Constantinople: Seven Contemporary Accounts*, p.132.

240 – . . . *skies would split apart.'*: Barbaro, N., *Diary of the Siege of Constantinople*, p.58.

240 – . . . *unable to breathe either in or out.'*: Doukas, *The Decline and Fall of Byzantium to the Ottoman Turks*, p.221.

241 – . . . *number, so that to us it seemed to be a very inferno.'*: Barbaro, N., *Diary of the Siege of Constantinople*, p.61.

242 – . . . *dying on one side or the other.'*: ibid., p.62.

242 – . . . *but were met with similar slaughter*: ibid., p.62.

242 – . . . *approach the fosse again and again.'*: Melville Jones, *The Siege of Constantinople: Seven Contemporary Accounts*, p.36.

243 – . . . *twelve miles away from their camp.*': Barbaro, N., *Diary of the Siege of Constantinople*, p.63.

243 – . . . *and Greeks began to tremble with fear.*': Posculo, U., *Constantinopolis*, p.165.

243 – . . . *with the Ottoman standard*: Doukas, *The Decline and Fall of Byzantium to the Ottoman Turks*, pp.221–2.

244 – . . . *His wrath had reached their lips.*': quoted in Philippides, M. & Hanak, W.K., *The Siege and Fall of Constantinople in 1453*, pp.228–9.

CHAPTER 10: THE CANNON GATE

251 – . . . *sites across the country*: Hawramy, F., 'Isis militants kidnap Turkish diplomats after seizing consulate in Mosul', *Guardian*, June 2014.

CHAPTER 11: THE GATE OF THE SPRING

258 – . . . *Istanbul's Rum community*: Öktem, *Angry Nation*, pp.44–5.

261 – . . . *size of 200 football pitches*: Istanbul International Airport website, accessed August 2023.

262 – . . . *the size of London Heathrow*: Christie-Miller, A., 'Erdogan's Grand Construction Projects Are Tearing Istanbul Apart', *Newsweek*, July 2014.

262 – . . . *200 million passengers a year*: Pitel, L., 'Turkey's national carrier completes move to new $11bn Istanbul airport', *Financial Times*, April 2019.

263 – . . . *species in the British Isles*: Tuncay, Tuncay, H.O. & Akalin, E., 'Endemism in Istanbul Plants', *European Journal of Biology*, vol.77 (1) 2018, pp.38–41.

263 – . . . *involve felling 2.5 million trees*: 'They Said "We Will Cut 2.5 Million Trees for 3rd Airport", They Cut 13 Million Instead', Bianet, June 2019.

263 – . . . *was no alternative site*: Christie-Miller, 'Erdogan's Grand Construction Projects Are Tearing Istanbul Apart', *Newsweek*, July 2014.

264 – . . . *grip over Turkish society and politics*, ibid.

264 – . . . *€6.3bn over the first twelve years of operation*: Köker, İ., 'İstanbul Havalimanı: İhale sürecinde neler yaşandı, proje için hangi garantiler verildi?', BBC, October 2018.

264 – . . . *an environmental impact assessment*: Özbilgin, Ö., 'Court delays Istanbul airport project, requires further reports', Reuters, February 2014.

264 – . . . *in the workers' accommodation*: Garner-Purkis, Z., 'Investigation: the human cost of building the world's biggest airport', *Architect's Journal*, October 2019.

264 – . . . *with some five hundred of its participants detained*: Sinclair-Webb, E., 'Construction Workers At Turkey's New Airport Jailed For Protesting Work Conditions', *Human Rights Watch*, September 2018.

265 – . . . *'not just an airport, but a victory monument.'*: 'Sadece havalimanı değil bir zafer anıtı inşa ediyoruz', Anadolu Ajansı, June 2014.

265 – . . . *history, was built in our country.'*: 'Cumhurbaşkanı Erdoğan yeni havalimanının adını açıkladı: İstanbul Havalimanı', NTV, October 2018.

269 – . . . *only led to worse treatment*: 'Following torture and sexual abuse, female prisoner dies by alleged suicide in prison', *Duvar*, December 2021.

270 – . . . *suffering from early onset dementia*: 'Sick prisoner Aysel Tuğluk forced to present defense during hearing', *Duvar*, August 2022.

270 – . . . *news website soon afterwards*: Zaman, A., 'Turkish army accused of throwing Kurdish farmers from helicopter', *Al Monitor*, September 2020.

270 – . . . *logistical aid to the rebels*: 'Thrown from a helicopter, Osman Şiban faces "terror" charges', Bianet, December 2021.

272 – . . . *serving 64 million passengers in 2022*: Dunn, G., 'Istanbul heads European airports in 2022 passenger numbers', *FlightGlobal*, January 2023.

272 – . . . *similar to other European airports*: Walther, B., 'Istanbul Airport (IST) – Flights, Punctuality & Cancellations in 2021', Information Design.

273 – . . . *be as high as 400*: Garner-Purkis, 'Investigation: the human cost of building the world's biggest airport', *Architect's Journal*, October 2019.

273 – . . . *but was in fact closer to 13 million*: 'They Said "We Will Cut

2.5 Million Trees for 3rd Airport", They Cut 13 Million Instead',
Bianet, June 2019.

CHAPTER 12: THE REBUILT GATE

275 – . . . *'maintain our national nobility'*: 'Sur restorasyonuna 4
milyar', *Cumhuriyet*, December 1988.

275 – . . . *it into a 'Universal film set'*: Gökdağ, R., 'Surlarda
restorasyon ikinci turda', *Cumhuriyet*, March 1991.

278 – . . . *with an annual turnover of $4.2bn*: Duran, A.E.,
'Büyükşehirleri kaybetmenin bedeli ne?', *Deutsche Welle*, April 2019.

278 – . . . *the money to build four new metro lines*: Pitel, L. & Güler,
F., 'Istanbul mayor looks to global markets to fund investment',
Financial Times, December 2020.

282 – . . . *derelict, neglected areas gives us.'*: 'Ekrem İmamoğlu:
'İstanbul›da, 30 milyon turisti hep birlikte göreceğiz ve yaşayacağız›',
Cumhuriyet, September 2022.

CHAPTER 13: THE CROOKED GATE

291 – . . . *the bitter winter cold*: Mango, A., *Atatürk*, p.141.

CHAPTER 14: THE GATE OF PLAGUES

300 – . . . *in the city from stricken regions*: Yıldırım, N., *A History of
Healthcare in Istanbul*, p.57.

300 – . . . *at Balıklı, which lay nearby*: ibid., pp.63–4.

300 – . . . *Armenian, and Jewish children*: ibid., p.110.

301 – . . . *between 15 and 100 million lives*: Mordechai, L., et al.,
'The Justinianic Plague: An inconsequential pandemic?',
Proceedings of the National Academy of Science of the USA,
Volume 116 (51).

301 – . . . *well, such as each had in hand.'*: Procopius, *History of the
Wars*, Volume I, trans. Dewing, H.B., pp.451–73.

301 – . . . *Arabia remained relatively unscathed*: Sabbatini, S., 'The
Justinian plague (part two). Influence of the epidemic on the rise of
the Islamic Empire', *Le Infezioni in Medicina*, Volume 20(3),
pp.217–32.

306 – . . . *months after the coup attempt*: '12 TV, 11 radyo kanalı
kapatıldı', *Cumhuriyet*, September 2019.

316 – . . . *in Turkey has hit new records every year since 2017*: Ford, A.,

'Turkey: Cocaine Hub Between Europe and the Middle East', *Insight Crime*, June 2022.

318 – . . . *and then shower in their blood'.*: 'Probe launched into mafia leader's "bloodbath" threats against academics', *Hürriyet Daily News*, January 2016.

318 – . . . *can hide like cockroaches no longer.*: Peker, S., '(1.BÖLÜM) Şahsıma Yapılan Kanunsuzlukların Taşeronu mehmet ağar ve pelikancılardır', YouTube, May 2021.

318 – . . . *whose apartment her body was found*: Keddie, P. & Uras, U., 'Sedat Peker's case: Videos grip Turkey, rattle government', Al Jazeera, May 2021.

319 – . . . *been to distribute Covid supplies*: Kuşçuoğlu, V., 'Sedat Peker claims to reveal new cocaine route between Colombia-Venezuela-Turkey', Bianet, May 2021.

321 – . . . *underestimate of its true extent*: 'Yearly inflation in Turkey rises to new 24-year high of 85%', Associated Press, November 2022.

325 – . . . *earthquake had raised an estimated total of $37bn*: Sönmez, M., 'Turks question "quake taxes" after deadly tremor', Al Monitor, January 2020.

325 – . . . *700 people died in the building*: Yackley, A.J., et al., 'From "paradise" to hell', *Financial Times*, February 2023.

325 – . . . *interests,' he explained*: Said-Moorhouse, L., 'Emotions run high in Turkey amid questions over state response to deadly quake', CNN, February 2023.

328 – . . . *all the buildings in the province*: Uludağ, A., 'Depremde hangi ilde kaç bina yıkıldı?', *Deutsche Welle*, February 2023.

CHAPTER 15. THE MARBLE TOWER

334 – . . . *the precipitous decline first-hand*: Ulman, A., et al., 'The Lost Fish of Turkey: A Recent History of Disappeared Species and Commercial Fishery Extinctions for the Turkish Marmara and Black Seas', *Frontiers in Marine Science*, August 2020.

335 – . . . *Black Sea, where it would safely sink*: Gül, M., *Architecture and the Turkish City*, p.163.

336 – . . . *large multinational companies*: Şentek, Z. & Shaw, C., 'The Toxic Valley', TheBlackSea.eu, September 2019.

336 – . . . *1.5 metres in 2021*: Olcan, A. & İdemen, S., 'Cesedin çürümesidir bu', Bir Artı Bir, May 2021.

336 – . . . *temperature rise of 2.5° Celsius*: ibid.

336 – . . . *excess catches dumped in landfill*: Ulman, et al., 'The Lost Fish of Turkey', *Frontiers in Marine Science*, August 2020.

336 – . . . *that the bluefin migration ceased entirely*: ibid.

338 – . . . *was killed, it will not return.'*: Olcan & İdemen, 'Cesedin çürümesidir bu', Bir Artı Bir.

340 – . . . *French diplomat François de Tott*: quoted in Thornton, T., 'The present state of Turkey; or, a description of the political, civil, and religious, constitution, government, and laws of the Ottoman Empire', p.160.

340 – . . . *an air of hopeless despondency.'*: Twain, M., *The Innocents Abroad*, p.163.

341 – . . . *once more received a reprieve*: Pinguet, C., 'Istanbul's street dogs at the end of the Ottoman Empire', *Animals and People in the Ottoman Empire*, ed. Faroqhi, S., pp.355–6.

342 – . . . *the brotherhood of civilised nations?'*: ibid., p.364.

342 – . . . *process a hundred dogs a day.'*: ibid., p.20.

343 – . . . *dogs and were paid on a per-animal basis*: ibid., p.17.

344 – . . . *in the swirl of the propeller.'*: ibid., pp.17–18.

345 – . . . *to God: the other a salon for his agents.'*: Byron, R., *The Byzantine Achievement*, p.200.

346 – . . . *dialogue between religions*: 'World reacts to Turkey reconverting Hagia Sophia into a mosque', Al Jazeera, July 2020.

347 – . . . *Fatih Mosque to pay homage*: Pitel, L., 'Erdogan orders Istanbul's Hagia Sophia to revert to being a mosque', *Financial Times*, July 2020.

349 – . . . *stood there, hoping for salvation.'*: quoted in Philippides & Hanak, *The Siege and Fall of Constantinople in 1453*, p.230.

349 – . . . *himself taken prisoner, bound and beaten*: Melville Jones, *The Siege of Constantinople 1453: Seven Contemporary Accounts*, p.13.

349 – . . . *four pieces and divided up as loot*: Doukas, *The Decline and Fall of Byzantium to the Ottoman Turks*, p.225.

349 – . . . *at having won such a great victory.'*: Barbaro, N., *Diary of the Siege of Constantinople*, p.200.

350 – . . . *none to show them mercy.*': Doukas, *The Decline and Fall of Byzantium*, p.227.

350 – . . . *of the city at the time*: Kritovoulos, *History of Mehmed the Conqueror*, p.76.

351 – . . . *close to the Hagia Sophia*: Philippides & Hanak, *The Siege and Fall of Constantinople in 1453*, p.16.

351 – . . . *improbably – on a Turkish galley*: ibid., p.16.

351 – . . . *before escaping on a Western ship*: ibid., p.16.

351 – . . . *did not treat them badly.*': Sphrantzes, *The Fall of the Byzantine Empire*, p.70.

352 – . . . *She was fourteen years and five months.*': ibid., pp.74–5.

352 – . . . *I was born on Tuesday, August 30th, 1401.*': ibid., p.21.

352 – . . . *stories may very well be true.*': Melville Jones, *The Siege of Constantinople 1453: Seven Contemporary Accounts*, p.8.

353 – . . . *to allow them to leave unmolested*: Nestor-Iskander, *The Tale of Constantinople*, p.91.

354 – . . . *portrays Mehmet in a positive light*: Doukas, *The Decline and Fall of Byzantium*, p.231.

354 – . . . *relief in the castle of Afrasayib.*': Quoted in Crowley, *Constantinople: The Last Great Siege*, p.233.

355 – . . . *sapphires and two emeralds*.': quoted in Hughes, B., *Istanbul: A Tale of Three Cities*, Epigraph.

355 – . . . *they are, like a naked human body*.': Tanpınar, *Five Cities*, pp.133–4.

Note on the Use of Historical Sources

I am not a trained historian, and although I have read the first-hand sources available in English, my telling of these events involved no original research and has relied entirely on the work of historians. While I have acknowledged these where appropriate in the notes and bibliography, I wanted to mention three writers whose work was particularly useful to me. Steven Runciman's *The Fall of Constantinople, 1453*, the classic account of the siege, was immensely helpful in terms of familiarising myself with the overall structure of events and the origins of our knowledge of them. Marios Philippides' and Walter K. Hanak's *The Siege and the Fall of Constantinople in 1453: Historiography, Topography, and Military Studies*, forensic in its overview of the historical sources and crammed with fascinating details and insights, was also an invaluable resource. Finally, Roger Crowley's gripping and elegantly-written *Constantinople: The Last Great Siege, 1453*, was both an inspiration and a burden, since after reading it I often felt myself to be labouring in its shadow. I can't see how a better popular account of the siege will ever be written, and many of the themes that drew me to those events, such as the intimations of apocalypse and the battle between new and old technologies, are explored in greater depth in his book. I would recommend anyone further interested in this subject to read it.

Bibliography

COLLECTED HISTORICAL SOURCES

Melville Jones, J.R., *The Siege of Constantinople 1453: Seven Contemporary Accounts* (Amsterdam, 1972)

Pertusi, Agostino, *La Caduta di Constantinopoli* (Milan, 1976)

INDIVIDUAL HISTORICAL SOURCES

Barbaro, Nicolo, *Diary of the Siege of Constantinople, 1453*, trans. J.R. Melville Jones (New York, 1969)

Çelebi, Evliya, *An Ottoman Traveller: Selections from the Book of Travels of Evliya Çelebi*, trans. & ed. Robert Dankoff & Sooyong Kim (London, 2010)

Doukas, *Decline and Fall of Byzantium to the Ottoman Turks*, trans. Harry J. Magoulias (Detroit, 1975)

de Busbecq, Ogier Ghiselen – *The Turkish Letters of Ogier Ghiselen de Busbecq*, trans. Edward Seymour Forster (Oxford, 1927)

de Clavijo, Ruy Gonzales – *Narrative of the Embassy of Ruy*

Gonzales de Clavijo to the Court of Timour, at Samarcand, trans. Clements R. Markham (Cambridge, 2010)

Gautier, Theophile, *The Works of Theophile Gautier Vol. 10: Constantinople*, trans. F. C. de Sumichrast (Harvard, 1901)

Gilles, Pierre, *Constantinople*, trans. Kimberly Byrd (New York, 2008)

Komnene, Anna, *The Alexiad*, trans. E.R.A. Sewter & ed. Peter Frankopan, (London, 2003)

Kritovoulos, *History of Mehmed the Conqueror*, trans. Charles T Riggs, (Westport, 1970)

Liudprand, *The Complete Works of Liudprand of Cremona*, trans, Paolo Squatriti (Washington DC, 2007)

Nestor-Iskander, *The Tale of Constantinople*, trans. & ed. Walter K. Hanak, & Marios Philippides (New York, 1998)

Oliver, Guillaume Antoine, *Travels in the Ottoman Empire, Egypt, and Persia, undertaken by order of the Government of France* (London, 1801)

Posculo, Ubertino, *Constantinopolis*, trans. Bryan Alan Whitchurch (New York, 2019)

Procopius, *History of the Wars: Books I and II*, trans. H.B. Dewing, (London, 1919)

Sphrantzes, George – *The Fall of the Byzantine Empire: A Chronicle by George Sphrantzes 1401–1477*, trans. Marios Philippides (Amherst, 1980)

Tafur, Pero, *Travels and Adventures, 1435–1439*, trans. Malcolm Letts (London, 1926)

de Thevénot, Jean, *The Travels of Monsieur Thevénot into the Levant*, (London, 1750)

Thornton, Thomas, *The present state of Turkey* (London, 1807)

de Tournefort, Joseph Pitton, *A Voyage into the Levant by the King's Express Command* (London, 1741)

ESSAYS

Aşıcıoğlu, Faruk, et al, 'Investigation of temporal illicit drugs, alcohol and tobacco trends in Istanbul city: Wastewater analysis of 14 treatment plants', *Water Research Journal*, vol. 190 (February 2021)

İnalcık, 'Halil, Mehmed The Conqueror (1432-1481) and His Time', *Speculum*, vol. 35 (1960)

Kraft, András, 'Constantinople in Byzantine Apocalyptic Thought', *Annual of Medieval Studies at CEU*, vol. 18 (2012)

Mordechai, Lee, et al, 'The Justinianic Plague: An inconsequential pandemic?' *Proceedings of the National Academy of Science of the USA*, vol. 116 (51) (December 2019)

Olson, Donald W., Doescher, Russell L., & Olson, Marilynn S., 'When the sky ran red: The Story Behind the "Scream"', *Sky & Telescope*, vol. 107(2) (February 2004)

Sabbatini, Sergio, Manfredi, Roberto & Fiorino, Sirio, 'The Justinian plague (part two). Influence of the epidemic on the rise of the Islamic Empire', *Le Infezioni in Medicina*, vol. 20 (3) (September 2012)

Stachowski, Marek & Woodhouse, Robert, 'The Etymology of Istanbul: Making optimal use of the evidence', *Studia Etymologica Cracoviensia*, vol. 20 (2015)

Tuncay, Hüseyin Onur & Akalin, Emine, 'Endemism in Istanbul Plants', *European Journal of Biology*, vol.77 (1) (2018)

Ulman, Aylin, et al, 'The Lost Fish of Turkey: A Recent History of Disappeared Species and Commercial Fishery Extinctions for the Turkish Marmara and Black Seas', *Frontiers in Marine Science*, vol. 7 (August 2020)

OTHER WORKS

Ahunbay, Zeynep, Dinçer, İclal & Şahin, Çiğdem, *Neoliberal Kent Politikaları ve Fener–Balat–Ayvansaray* (Istanbul, 2015)

Akça, İsmet, Bekman, Ahmet & Özden, Barış Alp (eds), *Turkey Reframed: Constituting Neoliberal Hegemony* (London, 2014)

Akçam, Taner, *The Young Turks' Crime against Humanity: The Armenian Genocide and Ethnic Cleansing in the Ottoman Empire* (Princeton, 2012)

Andrić, Ivo, *The Bridge over the Drina*, trans. Lovett F. Edwards (London, 1959)

Andrić, Ivo, *The Damned Yard and other Stories*, trans. Celia Hawkesworth (London, 1992)

Ash, John, *A Byzantine Journey* (London, 2006)

Atasoy, Yıldız, *Islam's Marriage with Neoliberalism: State Transformation in Turkey* (London, 2009)

Atayman, Veysel, *Samatya Dinmeyen Tını* (Istanbul, 2010)

Babinger, Franz, *Mehmet the Conqueror and his Time,* trans. Ralph Manheim (Princeton, 1978)

Baker, Bernard Granville, *The Walls of Constantinople* (London, 1910)

Baldick, Julian, *Mystical Islam: An Introduction to Sufism* (London, 1989)

de Bellaigue, Christopher, *Rebel Land: Among Turkey's Forgotten Peoples* (London, 2009)

de Bellaigue, Christopher, *The Islamic Enlightenment: the modern struggle between faith and reason* (London, 2017)

Bellér-Hann, Ildikó & Hann, Chris, *Turkish Region* (Oxford, 2000)

Berger, John, *About Looking* (London, 1980)

Bertram, Carel, *Imagining the Turkish House: Collective Visions of Home* (Austin, 2008)

Boyar, Ebru & Fleet, Kate, *A Social History of Ottoman Istanbul* (Cambridge, 2010)

Buğra, Ayşe & Savaşkan, Osman, *New Capitalism in Turkey, The Relationship between Politics, Religion, and Business* (Cheltenham, 2014)

Byron, Robert, *The Byzantine Achievement: An Historical Perspective* (London, 1929)

Christie, Jessica Joyce, Bogdanović, Jelena & Guzmán, Eulogio, *Political Landscapes of Capital Cities* (Denver, 2016)

Crowley, Roger, *Constantinople: The Last Great Siege, 1453* (London, 2005)

Clark, Bruce, *Twice a Stranger: How Mass Expulsion Forged Modern Greece and Turkey* (London, 2006)

Danforth, Nick, *The Remaking of Republican Turkey: Memory and Modernity since the Fall of the Ottoman Empire* (Cambridge, 2021)

Deal, Roger, *Crimes of Honor, Drunken Brawls and Murder: Violence in Istanbul under Abdülhamid II* (Istanbul, 2010)

Delibas, Kayhan, *The Rise of Political Islam in Turkey: Urban Poverty, Grassroots Activism, and Islamic Fundamentalism* (London, 2015)

Dayan, Colin, *With Dogs at the Edge of Life* (New York, 2018)

Ervak, Burçak, *The Other Side of the City Walls: Zeytinburnu*, trans. Ahmet Arkan (Istanbul, 2006)

Faroqhi, Suraiya (ed.), *Animals and People in the Ottoman Empire* (Istanbul, 2010)

Finkel, Andrew, *Turkey: What Everyone Needs to Know* (Oxford, 2012)

Finkel, Caroline, *Osman's Dream: The Story of the Ottoman Empire 1300-1923* (London, 2005)

Fijnaut, Cyrille & Pauli, Letizia (eds.), *Organised Crime in Europe: Concepts, Patterns and Control Policies in the European Union and Beyond* (New York, 2004)

Frankopan, Peter, *The First Crusade: The Call from the East* (London, 2012)

Freely, John, *Istanbul: Imperial City* (London, 1996)

Freely, John & Sumner-Boyd, Hilary, *Strolling through Istanbul* (London, 2001)

Genç, Kaya, *The Lion and the Nightingale: A Journey through Modern Turkey* (London, 2019)

Genç, Kaya, *Under the Shadow: Rage and Revolution in Modern Turkey* (London, 2016)

Gibbon, Edward, *The History of the Decline and Fall of the Roman Empire Volume III* (London, 1788, Penguins Classics edition, 1994)

Gingeras, Ryan, *Heroin, Organized Crime, and the Making of Modern Turkey* (Oxford, 2014)

Goodwin, Jason, *Lords of the Horizons* (London, 1998)

Grissman, Carla, *Dinner of Herbs* (London, 2001)

Gül, Murat, *The Emergence of Modern Istanbul: Transformation and Modernisation of a City* (London, 2009)

Gül, Murat, *Architecture and the Turkish City: An Urban History Istanbul since the Ottomans* (London, 2017)

Gürakar, Esra Çeviker, *Politics of Favouritism in Public Procurement in Turkey* (New York, 2016)

Hanioğlu, M. Şükrü, *Atatürk: An Intellectual Biography* (Princeton, 2011)

Hansen, Suzy, *Notes on a Foreign Country: An American Abroad in a Post-American World* (New York, 2017)

Harvey, David, *A Brief History of Neoliberalism* (Oxford, 2005)

Hikmet, Nazım, *Beyond the Walls*, trans. Ruth Christie, Richard McKane, Talât Sait Halman (London, 2002)

Hikmet, Nazım, *Human Landscapes from my Country*, trans. Randy Blasing, Mutlu Konuk (New York, 2002)

Hoş, Mustafa, *Big Boss: Neo Türkiye'nin Panzehiri Hafızadır* (Istanbul, 2014)

Hourani, Albert, Khoury, Philip S. & Wilson, Mary C., (eds.), *The Modern Middle East: A Reader* (London, 1993)

Hughes, Bettany, *Istanbul: A Tale of Three Cities* (London, 2017)

Işın, Ekrem, *Everyday Life in Istanbul*, trans. Virginia Taylor Saçlıoğlu (Istanbul, 2001)

Kaplan, Sefa, *Recep Tayyip Erdoğan* (Istanbul, 2007)

Karpat, Kemal H. *The Gecekondu: rural migration and urbanization* (Cambridge, 1976)

Kemal, Yahya, *Aziz İstanbul* (Istanbul, 1964)

Kemal, Yaşar, Allah'ın Askerleri (Istanbul, 1978)

King, Charles, *Midnight at the Pera Palace: The Birth of Modern Istanbul* (New York, 2014)

Kinross, Patrick, *Atatürk: The Rebirth of a Nation*, (London, 1964)

Kinross, Patrick, *The Ottoman Centuries* (New York, 1977)

Maalouf, Amin, *The Crusades through Arab Eyes*, trans. John Rothschild (London, 1984)

Macauley, Rose, *Pleasure of Ruins* (London, 1953)

Mango, Andrew, *Atatürk* (London, 1999)

Mansfield, Peter, *A History of the Middle East* (London, 1991)

Marcus, Aliza, *Blood and Belief: The PKK and the Kurdish Fight for Independence* (New York, 2007)

Mazower, Mark, *The Balkans* (London, 2000)

McManus, John, *Welcome to Hell? In Search of the Real Turkish Football* (London, 2018)

Mills, Amy, *Streets of Memory: Landscape, Tolerance, and National Identity in Istanbul* (Athens, 2011)

Morey, Darcy, *Dogs: Domestication and the Development of a Social Bond* (Cambridge, 2010)

Morris, Chris, *The New Turkey: The Quiet Revolution on the Edge of Europe* (London, 2005)

Nicol, Donald M., *The Immortal Emperor: The Life and Legend of Constantine Palaiologos, Last Emperor of the Romans* (Cambridge, 1992)

Norwich, John Julius, *A Short History of Byzantium* (New York, 1999)

Ortaç, Sevgi, *The Monument Upside Down* (Arnhem, 2010)

Orwell, George, *The Road to Wigan Pier* (London, 1937)

Öktem, Kerem, *Angry Nation: Turkey since 1989* (London, 2011)

Özkan, Behlül, *From the Abode of Islam to the Turkish Vatan: The Making of a National Homeland in Turkey* (New Haven, 2012)

Özyalçıner, Adnan, *Karagümrüklü Yıllar* (Istanbul, 2009)

Pamuk, Orhan, *A Strangeness in My Mind*, trans. Ekin Oklap (New York, 2015)

Pamuk, Orhan, *Istanbul, Memories and the City*, trans. Maureen Freely (London, 2005)

Pamuk, Orhan, *Other Colours*, trans. Maureen Freely (New York, 2007)

Philippides, Marios & Hanak, Walter K, *The Siege and the Fall of Constantinople in 1453: Historiography, Topography, and Military Studies* (London, 2011)

Pinguet, Catherine, *Les chiens d'Istanbul: Des Rapports entre l'Homme et l'Animal de l'Antiquité à nos Jours* (Clamecy, 2008)

Pope, Hugh, *Sons of the Conquerors: The Rise of the Turkic World* (New York, 2006)

Pope, Nicole & Pope, Hugh, *Turkey Unveiled: A History of Modern Turkey* (New York, 2004)

Runciman, Steven, *The Fall of Constantinople, 1453* (Cambridge, 1965)

Scott, Alev, *Ottoman Odyssey* (London, 2018)

Scott, Alev, *Turkish Awakening: A Personal Discovery of Modern Turkey* (London, 2014)

Sherrard, Philip, *Constantinople: Iconography of a Sacred City* (Oxford, 1965)

Smith, Hannah Lucinda, *Erdoğan Rising: The Battle for the Soul of Turkey* (London, 2019)

Sophocles, *The Complete Greek Tragedies: Sophocles II*, eds. David Grene & Richard Lattimore (Chicago, 1957)

Tanpınar, Ahmet Hamdi, *Five Cities*, trans. Ruth Christie (London, 2018)

Tanpınar, Ahmet Hamdi, *The Time Regulation Institute*, trans. Maureen Freely & Alexander Dawe (London, 2013)

Temelkuran, Ece, *Turkey: The Insane and the Melancholy*, trans. Zeynep Beller (London, 2015)

Tuğal, Cihan, *Passive Revolution: Absorbing the Islamic Challenge to Capitalism* (Stanford, 2009)

Tunay, İnci, *İstanbul Sur Kapıları* (Istanbul, 2014)

Turnbull, Stephen, *The Walls of Constantinople, AD 324–1453* (Oxford, 2004)

Türker, Orhan, *Pili Adrianupoleos'tan Edirnekapı'ya* (Istanbul, 2013)

Twain, Mark, *The Innocents Abroad* (Hartford, 1869)

Uçman, Abdullah, *Fatih'te Geçen Kırk Yılın Hikâyesi* (Istanbul, 2009)

Üngör, Uğur Ümit, *The Making of Modern Turkey: Nation and State in Eastern Anatolia, 1913–1950* (Oxford, 2011)

Van Millingen, Alexander, *Byzantine Constantinople: The Walls of the City and Adjoining Historical Sites* (London, 1899)

Waldman, Simon A., & Çalışkan, Emre, *The New Turkey and its Discontents* (London, 2016)

White, Jenny, *Muslim Nationalism and the New Turks* (Princeton, 2013)

Wood, Michael, *In Search of the Trojan War* (London, 1985)

Yıldırım, Nuran, *A History of Healthcare in Istanbul*, trans. M. İnanç Özmekçi (Istanbul, 2010)

Yılmaz, Volkan, *The Politics of Healthcare in Turkey* (London, 2017)

Index